Jackrabbits in the Outfield

*A Journey Inside the Winnipeg Goldeyes and
the Northern League of Professional Baseball*

By

John Hindle

To Jody,

Thanks so much. Keep
your eye on the ball!

John Hindle

Canadian Cataloguing in Publication Data

Hindle, John, 1952 –

Jackrabbits in the Outfield

ISBN - 0-9739827-1-3

Published in 2006 by John Hindle
in Winnipeg, Manitoba, Canada

Cover design by Carla Neiles

Edited by Richard Johnson

Some pictures provided by the Winnipeg Goldeyes

Some pictures provided by Barb McTavish

Printed and bound by Hignell Book Printing

Winnipeg, Manitoba, Canada

2006

Acknowledgements

This book is dedicated to my mom and dad who taught me love, compassion, and a sense of family. And to my entire family and my friends who offered unwavering support throughout my baseball career and during the writing of this book. In particular, I would like to acknowledge my wife, Bev, who edited and re-edited the book and who kept pushing me to make it the best it could be. And to my two children, Allyson and D'Alton, who gave me unwavering support and help where needed.

To my good friends Paul Edmonds, Kim Robinson, Lorraine Maciboric, Jonathan Green, Sandra Barsy, Winston Smith, Carla and Scott Neiles, Kevin Moore, and all those who gave me direction and guidance when I was struggling with the rigors of writing and then finishing the book. Thank you for your candor and honesty when I needed a push and for your words of support when I questioned myself.

Finally, I would like to thank all those who took the time to talk to me and answer my multitude of questions. Many of the stories that are found sprinkled throughout the following pages are fuller because of your input.

Foreword

By Paul Edmonds

It was under the west grandstand at Winnipeg Stadium back in 1995 that I first met John Hindle. He and some of the other Goldeyes' staff were struggling to assemble a batting cage that was to be used at the club's local tryout camp.

The audition, involving amateurs from surrounding areas in Manitoba and abroad, was one of the many original initiatives that Hindle would bring to the baseball club during his eight years as its first general manager.

His expression that day was one of frustration, but with his characteristic determination, the cage was completed within hours and was ready to be rolled out onto the field for use, as it is today during every Northern League home game in Winnipeg.

That's just the way it was for the former City of Winnipeg employee during his tenure with the local nine. At points during the early years, he was criticized for micro-managing the staff and team operations. But he knew no other way to make sure every detail about the Winnipeg Goldeyes Baseball Club was taken care of properly, professionally, and on time, than to roll up his sleeves, get out the spade, and climb into the trenches.

From rudimentary tasks that could have been deferred to interns to major corporate deals in the boardroom, Hindle involved himself as the patriarch of the Goldeyes with passion, heart, mental awareness, empathy and compassion for one common goal – the success of the local club.

And looking back, that's the way it had to be in order to build and grow a successful minor league sports franchise in a city that hadn't had a professional baseball team in nearly a quarter century.

John Hindle's management skills were exactly what were required to accomplish the many tasks that a full-time operation needed, including the administration of young, impressionable and combustible employees like me. His mantra was simple and one that is still prevalent in the day-to-day theatre of operations of the Goldeyes. "That's not what we do here," Hindle was fond of saying. "That's not what the Goldeyes are about."

We all lived by that hymn and under Hindle we all learned that the Goldeyes were more than just a baseball team and the Northern League was more than just the Goldeyes. You could not have one without the other, he would preach.

Looking back on it now, I can't imagine anyone else successfully guiding the Goldeyes onto the path of prosperity that the club has experienced over its 13 years of existence.

From bringing in 22,000 fans to a single game, to saving the league from complete embarrassment during a wildcat umpire's boycott of Winnipeg, to guiding the club into a new downtown facility, Hindle was our leader.

His time at the helm of the Goldeyes was the epitome of a labour of love. The combination of his experience as a player in amateur baseball in Manitoba and as the former proprietor of a very successful sporting goods business allowed him to know the game of baseball and the business of sports at the same time. That background made him the perfect fit to pilot the Goldeyes from startup to a championship in their first year, and on to becoming one of the most successful independent minor league baseball teams in North America.

Now, after years of talking about writing his memories and sharing the experiences and knowledge he gained over nearly a decade in the Northern League, he has finally put pen to paper and released this publication.

John has attacked this project with the same zest and emotion as he had for every other endeavour he has involved himself in over his career and his life, although from 1994 to 2004, they were one and the same.

From backroom to backstop, this account of the Goldeyes – past and present, of the Northern League, and of other vignettes from his life – takes us behind the scenes into the construction of a minor league baseball club, its difficulties and rewards. Hindle details the humble beginnings of the organization and of the league to the exodus of four teams in the fall of 2005.

This publication is no Ball Four, but a strike over the heart of the plate that will resonate with fans of the Goldeyes, the Northern League and baseball in general.

Enjoy!

My mom is an accomplished author and poet. I am proud to include a poem she wrote from a Goldeyes' fan perspective. JDH

A Great Day at the Ball Park

Have you ever seen the Goldeyes?
What a way to spend the day!
It is great to sit and watch them
They sure know how to play

Baseball is summer's greatest game
What a lot of fun to see
There is colour and excitement
And it's where we like to be

So let's all go to the ball game
Enjoy fresh air and the sun
Goldie keeps us mesmerized
Another part of the fun

Anthems are sung and action begins
"Play ball" the umpire yells
And up to home base struts the batter
While the pitcher holds the ball

Will he hit? Will he miss? We wonder
Is the umpire calling it right?
Oh boy! He sure got hold of that one
It's going to go out of sight

The fielder races over
"Oh no!" We all say aloud
"He can't catch that one can he?"
It's heading right for a cloud

Our batters are trying to do their best
Their pitcher is good we sigh
But we know our team can do it
Just watch those Goldeyes fly

We know our team can win the game
It will only take some time
But as the innings whiz on by
They're tied on number nine

Our hearts beat fast and furious
We hold our breath and wait
Sometimes we'll win, sometimes we won't
But the game has been just great

Doris Hindle – 1997

Table of Contents

Introduction

This book was written by a baseball guy from Winnipeg who was given the chance of a lifetime to be a part of something very special in his community – to take on the job as general manager of the local professional baseball team. It is not a book about statistics or wins and losses. It is written from the heart and is more about personal feelings and perspectives than about numbers. You can look the numbers up if you wish.

In writing Jackrabbits in the Outfield, I hoped to share some insight into what went on behind the scenes of the amazing success story of the Winnipeg Goldeyes and the Northern League of Professional Baseball. This is my real life story and it is about real people.

Baseball has been a driving force in my life for as long as I can remember. I knew at a very young age that it was my game. I played baseball my entire life, coached my children, was involved in the administration of various leagues, and started a business selling baseball equipment across Canada. The chance to work in professional baseball was a true gift.

No one knew that the Northern League, and the Winnipeg Goldeyes in particular, could become so wildly successful. In Jackrabbits in the Outfield, I set out to tell why I believe it happened. The book follows a path from the day I unknowingly found myself in a job interview, through the Goldeyes' chaotic 1994 inaugural season, to my final unforgettable and successful season in Winnipeg in 2001, which included the Northern League all-star game, and finally to my time in Sioux Falls, South Dakota, and an analysis of why the Northern League split apart at the seams after the 2005 season.

To tell my story, I relate anecdotes about the people I met along the way. My personal relationships with an amazing collection of characters are the heart and soul of the book. These relationships with the players, managers, owners, umpires, colleagues, and with now Winnipeg Mayor Sam Katz are all highlighted. You will read about the incredible true story of Jeff Zimmerman, who was thrown a lifeline for his baseball career in Winnipeg and climbed it all the way to the Major League all-star game in Fenway Park in Boston;

about my personal insight into Paul Edmonds, who has broadcast Goldeyes' games since 1995; about my relationships with Hal Lanier, Doug Simunic, Miles Wolff, Mike Veeck, Chris Kokinda, and many more colleagues, players, and characters. They are but a few of the special people who touched my life during my tenure in the Northern League.

Parts of the book show some insight into the workings of a professional baseball team. I try to paint a picture of the life of a general manager and the intense nature of the job. Many of the team's promotions are highlighted, including where they came from, what worked, and what didn't. Also included are stories about life in the office on game days and the work done by professional teams in a community.

But Jackrabbits in the Outfield goes far beyond a story about baseball. It has something for everyone. It will appeal to fans of all sports, anyone interested in how a professional sports team functions, people who can relate to a challenging and diverse job, and to all of those romantics who can picture living one of their dreams.

I hope you enjoy it!

John Hindle

Jackrabbits in the Outfield

Chapter 1: Baseball is in My Soul

Right-hander Tim Cain threw the pitch and the crowd of over 14,000 erupted in a massive roar. Both teams were wearing uniforms – the field looked good – the umpires and both teams had arrived and were in their proper places – the happy throng of fans had found their way into the seats – we had a good supply of baseballs! It looked like, sounded like, and felt like a professional baseball game.

What an incredible feeling of euphoria swept over me! I felt as fulfilled as at any other time in my life as I recognized what we had accomplished. The date was June 7th, 1994. The place was Winnipeg Stadium in Winnipeg, Manitoba, Canada. The Goldeyes of the Northern League of Professional Baseball had just thrown out their first pitch and a new era of professional baseball had begun. Opening Day had arrived and we had somehow survived. Sure, it was just the beginning, but what a great beginning! I was there for the birth of the new Winnipeg Goldeyes.

As I looked out onto the field, gripped with such strong emotion, my mind flashed back over the events of the past several months. It all started in the fall of 1993, when I was sitting at the kitchen table reading the newspaper. I was 41 years old and I had just opened Home Run Sports, a baseball store in Winnipeg, Canada of all places, and I loved the game of baseball. But until I acted upon the story I was reading in the newspaper, I had never done a crazy thing in my life. For those who have seen my favourite movie, "Field of Dreams," you might notice the parallel. As I read the article with interest, I did not realize the profound implications it was going to have on my life. Baseball was about to become an even greater force around me.

The headlines in the newspapers announced great news for baseball fans, "Professional Baseball Coming Back to Winnipeg." For a baseball enthusiast, this was exciting news. No professional baseball had been in the city since the Winnipeg Whips, a AAA club for the Montreal Expos, played in 1970 and 1971.

This new team was to play in the Northern League, an independent baseball league which was a throwback to a league from the nineteen fifties and sixties when the

Northern League was affiliated with Major League Baseball. The original Winnipeg Goldeyes brought the likes of Dal Maxvill and Steve Carlton to Winnipeg on their way to the St. Louis Cardinals.

As a player, coach, and administrator in amateur baseball in Manitoba, I was convinced that professional baseball would be successful. I believed that the strength of grass roots baseball would be very valuable to the new team and it would be supported by the baseball community. Everyone I talked to was excited about the prospect of baseball coming to town.

I was also convinced that amateur baseball would benefit from the exciting news, since the pro team, hopefully, would increase local interest and youth participation in the sport. That would be good for my fledgling business.

A Job Interview?

After reading the announcement of the new franchise, my first reaction was to send a letter to Sam Katz, the president of the team, to inform him of my small business. I requested in the letter that the pro team allow me to quote on its equipment needs. I wanted him to know that there was no longer a need to go to the United States to buy quality baseball products. Selling to the local pro team would be great for the credibility of the business. To my surprise, Katz called me back within a couple of days to tell me he liked my letter and would certainly give a local company every opportunity to get his business.

I did not know Sam Katz personally but I was aware that he was a concert promoter. I had heard him speak at a luncheon once and realized he was a very confident man. I now knew he read his mail and acted quickly when he had something to say.

Over a month passed and I assumed he had forgotten about our discussion. Then, I received the phone call that would change my life. Katz called and asked if I would come over to his house on Sunday afternoon. I thought this was a strange time and place to sell baseball equipment but I accepted his offer. When you own a small business, every lead is critical and this one was especially important to me.

I arrived at his beautiful home in Tuxedo, which is an affluent neighbourhood in Winnipeg, and was ushered into his living room and onto a luxurious leather couch. Katz was totally casual in his approach while I was somewhat apprehensive. He began our conversation by asking me if I knew what kind of bats professional players used. My response was that they used wood bats and the most popular was Louisville Slugger. He seemed satisfied with my answer and followed-up by asking what helmets pro players used. I knew my baseball equipment so I was aware that American Baseball Cap batting helmets were used in the Major Leagues and I assumed by other professional leagues. This answer also seemed to be "correct" and I was beginning to wonder what was going on. My apprehension was growing. Then came his tough question.

Katz told me he had recently hired a field manager from West Virginia named Doug Simunic. Simunic had asked him some questions about Winnipeg, including what type of field the team would be playing on. Since the team was playing at Winnipeg Stadium, Katz informed him that the playing surface was artificial turf. Katz then exclaimed to me, "When I told him what type of field we played on, Simunic told me we would have to get some jackrabbits and put them in the outfield." Katz continued, "John, I've promoted anything you could imagine from Pink Floyd to the Rolling Stones. Why would I need jackrabbits at a baseball game?"

I didn't know what to think. Was this a trick question or some kind of test? Was Katz teasing me or did he really want to know? When in doubt, I decided to play it straight. I informed Katz that "jackrabbit" was a slang expression in baseball that referred to a speedy runner. Simunic was thinking that a ball hit on artificial turf would skip and with over-spin would maintain speed, so quick outfielders rather than slower power hitters would be more appropriate for his new team. Many clubs playing on artificial turf have had success with this philosophy, including the St. Louis Cardinals under the guidance of Whitey Herzog, and the Houston Astros when Hal Lanier was managing. You will soon see why those two names are significant.

Katz seemed satisfied with my answers. We talked about the challenges facing the new team and the likelihood that the organization would be successful. I felt it was a positive meeting. I guess I was right. A couple of days later, I received a call at home. It was Katz. He told me he enjoyed our meeting.

Then he dropped the bombshell which will stick with me for the rest of my life. He said, "You certainly know baseball and I need help with my new team. I have marketing people but I need a baseball guy. I have a list of people who may fill that need and the name at the top of the list is John Hindle. How would you like to be my general manager?"

You could have knocked me over with a feather. In a confused state I blurted out, "Never mind that, how many bats do you want to buy?" Katz laughed and I suddenly realized that he was serious. I asked him why he wanted me for the job – still stunned by his question and wondering if this was some kind of publicity stunt. Katz knew a fair bit about me and it became obvious he did want to hire me and my time spent at his home had been a job interview.

Seldom in my life have I been speechless, but this moment was close. I asked if I could think about the offer and he said, "Sure, take your time." I waited for a few seconds, took a deep breath, and said, "Okay, I accept!" Katz laughed again and that was the end of our discussion.

I'm sure there were other people out there who could have become the general manager of the Goldeyes. I know there would have been many applications from Americans. There were not many Canadians, however, who were as connected in the baseball community as I was. I was both a baseball man and a business man. I guess that was a good fit for Katz.

It was decided that I would start on February 1st, 1994. He believed the job would only be a half-time position. Half-time! It seems comical now but that is the way things started. Neither Katz nor I realized how much work was going to be required to operate the Goldeyes as a first class organization. Neither of us even knew what a minor league general manager did. Learning on the job was going to be my reality during the next several months.

To say this was an amazing experience in my life would be such an understatement. Many times I have thought back to the day in Katz's living room and smiled. There I had been in a job interview and did not even know it!

When I was offered the job, my life changed forever. It was the start of a wild eight years and I recognized that moment as a defining one in my life! Everyone should cherish such crossroads in their lives. I have and always will cherish that moment when Sam Katz asked me, "How would you like to be my general manager?"

My Baseball Background

I have asked myself many times, "How did this happen?" "Why did Sam Katz call me?" It couldn't have been simply because he liked the letter I sent to him. I wondered what in my baseball background may have factored into his decision.

Rumor has it in my family that my grandfather snuck a baseball into my crib when I was a baby. He loved baseball and who knows, maybe some magic rubbed off that ball because baseball surely has been a large part of my life. We played baseball from age five, during recess at school, and at any opportunity we could find on weekends. There were no computers or video games and not nearly the choices that children have today to occupy their time. We didn't even have a colour television until I was in high school. In the summer, baseball was king when I was growing up.

I played most of my baseball in Winnipeg, from Little League in the Optimists system up to senior baseball for the St. Boniface Native Sons. I was also fortunate to have played for Grandview, Manitoba, in the Manitoba Senior Baseball League and for Giroux, Manitoba, in Twilight baseball (over 35 years of age). Those experiences gave me a unique perspective on the state of baseball throughout the province.

As I was growing up, like many boys, I was an avid sports enthusiast. I was small for my age and not very confident. When I was in Grade 9 at Norberry School, I looked at a program for a Christmas basketball tournament. It listed all the players from the eight participating schools and I was the only one who weighed less than 100 pounds. I was five feet, two inches tall and weighed 88 pounds!

But being small may have been a factor in my success in baseball. If you were to make a list of sports in which the smaller athletes have the best chance for success, baseball would be near the top. I don't believe that had any bearing on why I first played baseball because I tried all sports, but it might partly explain why I had such success compared to other sports, especially at an early age. Of course, there are many days now when I would love to be accused of being too skinny instead of carrying around 20 more pounds than I should.

Further proof of the fact that small players can succeed in baseball can be found with the Goldeyes. As of 2006, Brian Duva was the only Winnipeg player to have his number retired by the club. He had tremendous success on the field and when he retired, he held a number of Winnipeg and Northern League records. He was one of the smallest players to ever wear a Goldeyes' uniform, standing a proud five feet, eight inches tall.

At a very young age, I could throw accurately. And it seemed like I was constantly looking for an opportunity to throw at something. Sometimes it would be a rock and sometimes it would be a ball, which I would throw for hours against the front steps of our house, much to my mother's chagrin. On summer vacations, my family would camp near some body of water and my dad would amaze me with his ability to skip stones on the water. It was a real art form to me and I would try hard to emulate him. Even if I was aimlessly throwing a stone in the middle of nowhere, my dad would ask me what I was aiming at. This encouraged me to focus on accuracy.

Hitting was also one of my passions. Many players feel that hitting is the most exciting part of baseball and I am no exception. Hitting a baseball is recognized as one of the toughest things to do in any sport. Even Michael Jordan, one of the greatest athletes of all time, did not succeed at a high level in professional baseball.

Hitting well helped me build self-confidence when I was younger, knowing that I could do something better than some of my friends. As I grew older, I loved coming to the plate with runners on base. Seeing a teammate standing on second base and encouraging me to bring him in was great motivation for me.

It still feels good to have a bat in my hand. I have been known to pace back and forth in my office carrying or swinging a bat to help me think. It's possible, however, that watching me deep in concentration, pacing or swinging a bat, scared some of the people who worked for me over the years. I have wondered how many times someone may have walked towards my office, saw me swinging my bat, and then decided to turn around and see me later.

No other sport has held my interest in the same way as baseball. It is a team sport but individual performance is critical. No one can help you when you are at the plate. It's you against the pitcher. No one can help you catch the ball when it's hit or thrown to you either. At the same time, all of your teammates are supporting you and offering encouragement. Your performance affects them. A base hit might score a runner, or a great catch might save a run or offset a poor throw.

In the summer of 1975, I played baseball in Grandview, which is a lovely small town in the Parklands Region of Manitoba. According to league rules, most teams brought in two American players but Grandview also brought in an American to coach the team. At the time, Jim Clayton was the head baseball coach at Palomar College in Escondido, California. He packed up his motor home and his family and made the long trek to Grandview for the summers of 1975 and 1976.

Coach Clayton taught me a great deal about the game. He coached an aggressive style of play and we would spend time practising bunt plays, special base-running plays, and situational hitting – skills that are often neglected. I was 22 years old when I first played in Grandview and I realized there was so much more to learn about the game. Lack of quality coaching was a reality for many Canadian ball players.

Another reality for Canadian players at that time was the lack of opportunities to play college baseball. There was no college baseball in Canada and almost no Canadians were playing in the United States. Mainly, we played against other Canadians in junior and then senior baseball. During my career, I represented my province in many Canadian play-downs, even winning once in Nanaimo, British Columbia, in 1978. My career culminated in June of 2004 when I was inducted into the Manitoba Baseball Hall of Fame in Morden. Baseball had provided me with great experiences and a lot of good friends but the sight of my picture hanging on a wall in Morden was a little hard to believe.

I watched baseball on television, read books about the game, and I went to watch the original Goldeyes play at Winnipeg Stadium. I loved playing but I also had a strong desire to learn as much as possible about the game. It was my grandpa's favourite game and he talked to me about it constantly. I would listen with undivided attention.

He pointed out, for example, that baseball is one of the few games where the defence has the ball. It is that uniqueness of baseball that draws me to it. He also told me that he believed baseball was the purest of all games. There was no holding the ball in baseball or running down the clock. You had to pitch to the last batter to record the last out! His words would come flooding back to me during the last inning of countless games I played as I found out first hand that the last out in the last inning was frequently the hardest to get.

As I watched Game 5 of the National League Championship Series in 2005, I couldn't help thinking about grandpa. The Houston Astros were winning the series three games to one and leading the fifth game 4-2 in the ninth inning. Brad Lidge, the Astros' dominant closer, came on to finish out the game and struck out the first two hitters he faced. Then he recorded two strikes on St. Louis lead-off man David Eckstein. The game appeared to be over. The next pitch seemed like a mere formality. But not so! A two-strike base hit, a walk to Jim Edmonds, and a monstrous home run off the bat of Albert Pujols and St. Louis suddenly turned a sure defeat into a victory. That was one of the wildest examples of failing to record the last out that I had ever seen.

Other subtle nuances of baseball fascinate me. I admire athletic middle infielders who seem to dance at second base while they turn a double play. I am amazed at the outfielder who can race far to the side to backhand a ball in the gap and then athletically turn and throw a perfect strike to the cut-off man. I am intrigued by defensive players who move as the ball is being pitched because they know the pitch location and can anticipate in which direction it will be hit. With a quick jump, they catch balls that might otherwise be base hits. I smile when I see a pitcher who is so confident he throws a 3-1 breaking ball and paints the black of the plate for a strike. I feel like I am in the batter's box with the hitter who battles every pitch and fights back from a no ball two-strike count – only to walk or beat out a hit and then later come in and score the winning run.

Sure I like to see home runs, but the hundreds of small things that happen during a game are what really capture my attention. Watching a three-hour baseball game unfold is like reading a story. So many things happen during a nine-inning contest that you can easily talk about them for another three hours after the game is over.

Yet, baseball is simple in some ways. People with limited knowledge of the game can easily enjoy watching. You hit the ball and then run; you catch the ball and then throw. On the other hand, it is also a very complicated game, with many different philosophies on how to manage or play it. Some managers play for the big inning or the three-run home run. Others will sacrifice, steal, play hit-and-run, and stress an aggressive style of base running. They take great pleasure in scoring a run without having a base hit. A team can focus on speed or power. They can win games with hitting, pitching, or defence. It sure helps if your team has all three.

My love for the game encouraged me to give something back. I coached and was an administrator in baseball for most of my life. Both of my children played baseball. I coached both my daughter, Allyson, and my son, D'Alton, and I took great pleasure in watching them play and in teaching them the game. As a coach, I recognized that playing baseball was a great way to keep kids occupied. If they played on a baseball team, they were far less likely to get into trouble with their idle time, which really applies to all organized activities.

A Baseball Business in Canada!

Many years ago, I was frustrated with the quality of baseball equipment we could purchase in Canada. Everyone was frustrated with the balls on the market, which sometimes were not even round when they came out of the box. In 1977, I played in a tournament in Edmonton, Alberta. Diamond baseballs – a new brand of balls I had never seen before – were being used. The quality of the ball was far superior to those we were using in Manitoba. I contacted all of the junior and senior league teams in Winnipeg and they were interested in buying Diamond balls.

As luck would have it, shortly after the Edmonton tournament, I went to California to visit Coach Clayton, who lived mere minutes from the Diamond Baseball warehouse. He knew the baseball coaches who had started the company so one night we went to visit the warehouse. I was impressed with their enthusiasm and their desire to create the best baseball in the world. They had no knowledge of baseball in Canada, except that someone had ordered a few dozen balls in Edmonton. I asked if I could buy some balls for my league back home. When I told them I would start with an order of 100 dozen, they were stunned and offered me the rights to sell Diamond all across Canada. That night was the beginning of my sporting goods business.

At the beginning, I only sold Diamond baseballs and ATEC pitching machines. The business seemed to have a life of its own. With very little advertising, the demand for the baseballs and pitching machines continued to grow. They were the best products of their kind on the market. Every night I would come home from work and check the fax machine for orders and, usually, found some. Very early the next morning, I would drive to UPS and ship them out before I went to work.

Each year the business grew, so every spring I needed to order more and more balls to get me through the season. I could repeat orders during the summer but it was far more expensive so I tried to estimate my total sales every spring. After several years of this, I realized I couldn't keep up the pace. Once the baseballs had filled the garage and spilled into various other rooms in my house, I knew it was time to find a retail establishment.

In 1992, as the business was expanding into a retail location, I knew I would have to hire staff. I interviewed a couple of baseball guys who knew the sport and who could do some shipping and receiving.

While I was conducting those interviews, a friend of mine asked me if I would interview an additional person who had recently become unemployed. I agreed and an attractive but nervous young lady arrived at my house for an interview. She did not fit the profile I had in mind for the position, but something about her was special. My primary rule when I interviewed people for any job was to hire the best quality person possible. I believed that smart, positive people could learn what you needed them to know quickly. This philosophy might not work if you're hiring a nuclear scientist or a medical doctor, but it worked well for me in baseball over the years.

I decided to hire two people – one of my better business decisions. Carla Eisner, the young woman I interviewed, was one of them. She is a person with an outstanding character – honest, hard-working, eager to learn, a pleasant and friendly personality. She became a valued friend and employee. The only time she ever broke company rules was when she dated another staff member – Scott Neiles – and wound up marrying him!

The business transformed itself over the years into Home Run Sports, now a sporting goods leader in Canada. No longer did players from Manitoba have to go to the United States to buy top-of-the-line baseball equipment.

As a baseball enthusiast, I took advantage of my new business to promote baseball throughout Manitoba and eventually across Canada. I recognized that baseball participation was declining, so when I found an initiative that I believed would encourage more children to play the game, I took every opportunity to introduce it to all parts of the country.

One such initiative was a concept called "Rookie Ball", in which pitching machines were used in games with players aged seven to 10. Rookie Ball leveled the playing field for all kids. Since the machine almost always threw a good hittable pitch, there was much more action during the game. Players didn't stand around with the bat on their shoulders waiting for a walk but were encouraged to swing. Because there was more hitting there was also more fielding, running, and throwing. The action kept the kids enthusiastic. The only difficulty with Rookie Ball was that some parents believed their child was going to be a great pitcher and needed to develop at a young age. I found no factual basis to that argument. All young players should be taught to throw properly. Pitching can be taught at a later age when youngsters' arms are more developed.

There is a host of very successful Major League pitchers who didn't pitch until they were teenagers. Raphael Gross, who won more games than any other Goldeyes' pitcher, was originally signed by the Los Angeles Dodgers as an infielder. After four seasons in the minor leagues, he began pitching after the 1998 season. He came to the Goldeyes in 2001, never having previously been a starting pitcher. He won a team record 36 games.

Another key entry-level game that I helped introduce in Canada is BlastBall. This unique concept features the

BlastBase, which makes a funny loud noise when it is stepped on. I was sitting in a lounge in a Toronto hotel when Jim Lefebvre walked in carrying a BlastBase. Lefebvre had been a Major League player and manager and was coaching with the Milwaukee Brewers. He was dressed in a suit and was quite a sight as he threw the base on the floor and jumped on it. A loud noise blasted out of the base, startling everyone in the lounge. Along with me, however, many patrons also laughed.

I knew immediately that this was the best innovation I had seen in years. We were always looking for some way to make the game more fun at the introductory level. This was it! The original BlastBall game concept used only one base on the field instead of the traditional three. The young player hit the ball off of a tee and then ran and jumped on the BlastBase. Eventually, the BlastBase was incorporated into more complex games as the kids got older. Just watch a BlastBall game and see the enjoyment on the faces of the youngsters when they jump on the base and make it "honk." It is easy to see that the concept works.

I am proud of my involvement in bringing both Rookie Ball and BlastBall to youth baseball and softball programs across the country. Because of the efforts of Home Run Sports and, much to the amazement of the distributor, more BlastBall kits were sold in Canada in the years following its introduction in 2000 than in the United States. BlastBall is currently part of Baseball Canada's "Winter Ball" program and Softball Canada's "Learn to Play" program. My hope is that these initiatives will keep the sports vibrant and flourishing.

Yes, baseball had been a constant throughout my life. However, the most exciting part of the journey was about to begin. I may never know for sure just what in my background led to the moment I was offered my new job. Perhaps it was the combination of my baseball acumen and my business background. All I knew at the time was that I was about to become a baseball general manager – and I liked the sound of that!

Outfield sign at Winnipeg Stadium

Home Run Sports staff - 2001

L- Allyson & D'Alton with Rookie pitching machine
R- June 5, 2004 Manitoba Baseball Hall of Fame induction
Below – Home Run Sports 2002

Chapter 2: A Rare Opportunity for a Canadian

After Katz offered me the job, it was hurry up and wait. I had been hired in early January but was not to officially start until February 1st. I was never sure why there was a delay, but I'm sure now it was a mistake. Every extra day I could have been in the office in 1994 would have made that first year better. I guess Katz was trying to save a few dollars and he probably did not anticipate the amount of work that was required. Remember, he thought it was just a half-time job.

I phoned him a couple of times in January to see if there was anything I should be doing to prepare for the upcoming challenge. He was abrupt on the phone and wanted to know why I called him. I really didn't have a good reason and he seemed to have no time for that sort of nonsense. Sam Katz was not the type of person to reassure you at every turn. He had made his decision and already moved on to many other projects.

I, however, was still very apprehensive. There was no agreement in writing. I guess I wanted confirmation that the job was really mine. I kept wondering what I was getting myself into. Did I really have the job? What would it be like? Why was I not starting right away? What kind of learning curve would I be on? The questions were racing through my mind.

After getting to know Katz, I realized that he lived with the phone in his ear and another call on hold. He was in a hurry whenever we talked and wanted to keep it short so he could get to his next call. Once I understood that was the way he lived, I realized he was not just rushing when he spoke with me but that he was that way with virtually everyone. Little did I know my life was going to become somewhat like his. The cellular phone companies called us power users.

Later, whenever life became too crazy, I would try to remember how I felt during those first phone calls, and take a deep breath. I would also try to visualize how the person on the other end of the phone perceived me and my tone of voice. I have sometimes been accused of being straight forward and blunt. Some people appreciated that approach while others thought it was too harsh. At the pace we operated at, and with the pressure we were under at the Goldeyes' office, some days it was pretty easy to come across sounding too hurried. I would have to consciously tell myself to slow down. At times, that was easier said than done.

First Day on the Job

Finally, the day came for the press conference to announce the hiring of field manager Doug Simunic and me. Simunic was flying up from Charleston, West Virginia. The date was January 31st, 1994 and the press conference was held at the Blue and Gold Room at Winnipeg Stadium. There were so many media representatives in the room, it was overwhelming. While the day remains a whirlwind in my mind, I can remember a representative from a television station interviewing me and as I looked over the interviewer's shoulder I saw about 10 more people lined up behind him. That was a little out of the league of a baseball guy from south Winnipeg. It was really quite intimidating. Growing up, I had thought many times about how great it would be to play professional baseball but I had never thought about what it would be like to be a general manager.

When Katz stood up to introduce me, he stated that Miles Wolff, the president of the Northern League, had told him that he was required to hire a general manager. Wolff had suggested that the new Winnipeg club should hire an American, presumably because baseball was the American pastime and an American would have more experience and knowledge. Katz informed the media he didn't like being told what to do and that he had found a Canadian who would be perfect for the job. Every media outlet asked me how it felt that I was supposed to be an American. It was really no concern of mine, but nevertheless, I had to answer that question many times.

During that first media scrum, I received a quick education. "Trial by fire" I guess you could say. After I had answered the same question a number of times, the answers didn't sound humorous or interesting even to me, no matter how good they sounded at the beginning. I started adding new material to my answers, which was likely a mistake. The first answers were probably the best and it would have been wise to stick with them. Take television for example. Since each television interview is on a different channel, it might well be the only footage the viewers of that channel would see. They might as well get my best answer. I realized that as I watched the interviews later that night. My first interviews were my best.

While those interviews are now a bit of a blur, I do remember saying I was proud. I said I was a baseball man and Americans had no exclusive club in that regard. I stated that I believed the new Winnipeg team would be successful because baseball was very strong in the community at the grassroots level, and that Winnipeg had a great baseball heritage. When I looked at tapes of those interviews years later, I felt that I did okay for a beginner, but my interviews in later years had more depth to them as I became more comfortable around cameras and microphones.

That first day will always be special in my heart. My life changed the day of that press conference. The public nature of a professional sports team is somewhat unique and I was thrown into it in a big way on my first day. This was a major press conference and it is hard to explain, but it was like stepping into another world. It was so surreal. At times, I would seem to be looking back at myself from a distance, as if this was happening to someone else. I was filled with a sense of awe and excitement at the same time.

A lot of people were proud of me that day. My Mom and Dad had supported me throughout my baseball career, including planning summer vacations around my baseball schedule. My wife, Bev, and my two children, Allyson and D'Alton, were also caught up in the excitement. They saw the sparkle in my eyes and shared my exhilaration.

It is pretty important in these special times in your life to have such support and to be able to share your feelings with people you love and trust. My entire family, my life-time friends, scores of baseball colleagues, and customers of my business from across Manitoba all shared their support for me as I entered my new career.

Finally, the new job had begun. I couldn't wait to go into the office and get started. I wasn't sure what getting started really meant but I knew I was anxious to find out. After the press conference was over and the throngs of people had left, there was an eerie calm in the room. Katz, Simunic and I went out for supper that night and it was easy to see Simunic was a real character. Later, I will explain just how much of a character he was.

I began my new career the next day. There were only 200 people, or thereabouts, in North America who were general managers of professional baseball teams. Now I was one of them. Those first few days were eye-opening and like any new job, the days were filled with wonder. I could not wait to arrive at the office each morning to see what would happen. People who love their jobs know this feeling of exhilaration. It stuck with me all the years I was a general manager.

For the first couple of weeks, we were located in Katz's offices downtown on McDermot Avenue. The place was a zoo! An intercom system interrupted you constantly as it blared through the phone if you were not already on a call. Katz was always on two calls at once and trying to have a meeting with him was next to impossible. I felt like we were in a race. Even if you talked to him quickly and got right to the point, several phone calls would interrupt a meeting. Keeping up with what was going on around the office was a real challenge.

It seems kind of amusing now to think of the chaos that existed. Five years later, in 1999, we would find ourselves back in those offices for a few months while we waited for the completion of our new ball park. I relived the chaos all over again – this time for several months.

Our staff at the beginning included Kevin Moore and Val Overwater. Moore was the director of marketing and was the first employee hired to work for the Goldeyes. He had worked with Katz for years and had been responsible for marketing and promotions for the Winnipeg Thunder basketball team and many other projects for Nite Out Entertainment, Katz's promotions company. He was funny and talented, a joy to work with, and he had an incredible passion for the job.

Moore was primarily responsible for the creation of the Goldeyes' beloved mascot, Goldie. He could sell and was very organized, which worked well for me because I was flying in all directions at once. He was very supportive and respectful to me even though he had more experience in

17

event management. We became good friends and he was the person I hugged the hardest after we won the Northern League Championship in 1994.

Val Overwater was the director of sales and came from the Winnipeg Jets' organization. She was aggressive and could sell herself and her ideas. She also had a huge heart. Many of the office processes we used at the beginning came from Overwater's suggestions. She created the game sponsorship packages, for example, which still separate the Goldeyes from many other teams throughout North America.

Game sponsorships have been a big success for the organization. Every game had a sponsor, who got to throw out an opening pitch and received the use of a suite, a block of tickets, and PA announcements. To provide value for the entire season, the sponsorship also included radio spots and a program ad. Game sponsorships allowed companies to have significant exposure with the Goldeyes without breaking their advertising budgets.

Overwater had grandiose vision, which was very positive for a new organization. The best example was in 1995 when she came into my office and asked me to put my bat down. She thought we could sell enough tickets to one game to set an all-time Northern League attendance record. I was skeptical at the beginning but her unwavering belief that we could accomplish this feat persuaded me. We sold 20,749 tickets to the game on August 29th, 1995. This may be the best example in my career where thinking big created enormous results.

Moore, Overwater and Katz were very interesting people to work with. At our first staff meeting, ideas were thrown around regarding entertainment to bring in during games. They were all into promotions and action. The ideas were bouncing off the wall so fast I was hoping none of them would hit me too hard. What a trip! I soon realized this was the speed at which we would operate for the next several years – a speed many people would have trouble imagining. Moore, Overwater and I were a good team right off the bat. It seemed like I was the sense of reason and tradition while they were the crazy and uninhibited. I loved it and had a lot of fun with them!

One of the ideas thrown out at that first meeting was to put a band behind second base between innings and have it do a choreographed set. I was something of a baseball traditionalist and a 12-piece band playing jazz music during intermission just wasn't going to happen. For one thing, there was no intermission! There were 17 short breaks between every half-inning.

At some point, Katz told me to make sure the promotions were in sync with the flow of a professional baseball game. I was a rookie general manager while Moore and Overwater were talented individuals who had experience in sales and marketing. I, however, did know baseball. We pushed the limits some days, but the Goldeyes always tried to keep a balance. My goal was to not affect the game between the lines.

After a couple of weeks, we moved into the new offices in the Winnipeg Arena across from the stadium. They had been planned before I was hired and, at the last minute, we had to add a new office for the general manager. I presume at one point the Goldeyes were going to operate without a general manager.

My first phone call was something special. I was looking into my vacant office as we waited for the furniture to arrive, when the phone rang. It was sitting on the carpeted floor so I sat on the floor and answered it. The call was from Bill Fanning, the general manager of the wildly successful St. Paul Saints. He was phoning to welcome me aboard. He offered help anytime I needed it because in his words, "I have no idea how you can have a pro team up and running in four months." I thought, "Thanks a lot, Bill. I didn't know this task was supposed to be impossible." As time would show, Bill Fanning was a great colleague and a real help to the Goldeyes and myself over the years. I respected his opinions.

All of our energy that first spring was focused on getting ready for Opening Day. But how were we to do it? Where should I start? Years afterwards, when I was asked to speak in schools, I would describe the feelings I had at the time to the children.

"How do you get a large project done when it just seems too big?" I would ask. "You simply start at the beginning," I would answer. "You do one little piece at a time, then the next piece, and the next, until one day you turn around and are amazed at how much has been accomplished."

That was how I got ready for Opening Day in 1994. One moment I would be ordering baseball equipment, the next looking at merchandise we would sell, the next arranging bus travel, then selling some tickets, completing paper work on a player contract, meeting with our landlords, Winnipeg Enterprises Corporation, and so on. I realized immediately that this was not a half-time job as Katz had suggested. I called him after two weeks and informed him that I knew of no part-time job that required 10 hours per day, seven days a week. He agreed to give me a raise.

Since Katz could not tell me what a general manager was at the beginning, I created the job myself. One thing was for sure. There was no shortage of work to do. I was often asked by people, "Is it a full-time job?" or "Where do you work in the winter?" I would laugh and explain that while I worked 14 hour days in the summer, I only worked 8-10 hour days in the winter.

At the beginning of 1994, we had five full-time employees. There was very little managing to be done in the office. We were all worker bees with more to do than we could handle. The staff grew steadily over the years and after we settled in our beautiful new ball park in 1999, we employed over 20 full-time people. That required a lot more managing.

I readily admit that sometimes I was too busy working to be able to manage adequately. I think many managers feel that frustration. The days were just too short and everyone wanted a piece of me but there were not enough pieces to go around. I tried to keep an open door policy, which I believe in, but once in a while a staff member would put a cartoon on my door with a punch line something like, "Not Today. Tomorrow Doesn't Look Good Either!" I guess my office door wasn't open quite as wide on those days.

Andrew Collier, my successor as the Goldeyes' general manager, commented to me after he had been on the job for a few months, "If I had known what a pain it was to have everyone coming into your office when you were working on something, I would never have bothered you with all my little problems." I guess it is all in the perspective you have. From my perspective, Collier had never been a bother when he worked for me. He had had a few special moments and, like most people, he wanted to be heard. Mostly, I think of him as a great worker and a joy to have had as a colleague.

Actually, the entire staff was key to my enjoyment of the job. We had so much fun together as we built something from the ground up. We shared special moments almost every day. There was so much to learn, not the least of which was how everyone fit into the decision-making process. Sam Katz was an owner and the president and he worked in his downtown office. Jeff Thompson was also an owner and was involved primarily with merchandise. Winnipeg Enterprises owned 50 percent of the club and was also located in the Winnipeg Arena. WEC was responsible for accounting and much of game day and stadium operations. Then there was the full-time staff members who were actively running the organization. It took us a while to figure out the logistics of working together.

I learned a lot during that first year. The job was complex and I dealt with many different issues daily. I believe the diversity was a big reason why I loved the job so much. Since I am a "people person," the job of a general manager was a good fit for me. It gave me the opportunity to interact on a daily basis with a variety of interesting people and share ideas and experiences with them. Those first steps into my new position were taken with wild abandon. There was no time to walk gingerly.

Chapter 3: Jackrabbits in the Outfield

Opening Day – June 7, 1994

The stadium was completely sold out. The opening speeches were great. Everyone was smiling, laughing and enjoying themselves. I joined thousands in singing Oh Canada, and it was the most emotional rendition of the national anthem I could remember. As the players ran on to the field to start the game, the public address announcer screamed into the microphone for the fans to welcome the 1994 Winnipeg Goldeyes.

Everyone was waiting with anticipation for that first pitch for the new organization when the umpire put his hands in the air and called time. He slowly looked around the stadium until he saw me standing behind the backstop. He beckoned me onto the field and with complete disdain, he pointed out that there were no baseballs. I had forgotten to order the balls! The crowd started to boo and there was no place for me to hide. Then, suddenly, I also realized I was not wearing any clothes.

Trust me that was one of the worst nightmares I have ever had. I woke up completely soaked with perspiration.

Do you think that I was worried about Opening Day? Maybe, just a little bit! I could not get back to sleep and ended up going into the office very early in the morning. I immediately went to the storage area to check on the supply of baseballs and breathed a sigh of relief when I confirmed we were well stocked for the season.

The first game for the re-born Winnipeg Goldeyes was going to be at home. Remember, Bill Fanning, one of the most respected general managers in the league, had told me he didn't think it was possible to be ready for Opening Day because we had started too late. His comments were always in the back of my mind.

Can you imagine the excitement and/or the apprehension of staging your first ever public event? Not unless you've been there you can't. The number of details that go into a professional baseball game is mind boggling. The facility must be ready, all staff must be prepared, both teams and the umpires need to be accommodated, and the production of the game must be primed and ready to go. You might be worried that no one will show up, which would render all of your work wasted. Or possibly, too many will show up and you won't be able to accommodate them which would be a much better problem to have. That was my state of mind leading up to June 7, 1994.

I had no idea what to expect. We were so busy working that the days just flew by. Being ready for the magical date of June 7th was the objective. I am a baseball traditionalist and Opening Day in baseball is sacred. A lot of pomp and ceremony is associated with that first game of the season. The beginning of baseball in the Northern League marked the beginning of summer in the minds of many.

In 2004, I met some wonderful baseball fans in Sioux Falls, South Dakota, who gathered from far and wide to share in the magic of Opening Day of the Major League Baseball season. They congregated at one house and watched Opening Day games on television. It is a spring rite of passage for them. A wooden bleacher instead of a sofa and chair adorned the living room of the house. Some might consider that a little eccentric but it certainly set the mood.

At the ball park for Opening Day, I believed you had to have a Dixieland band, dress up the stadium with bunting, announce all the players to the crowd, and throw out a ceremonial first pitch. In 1994, the Goldeyes also needed to open a new era of professional baseball in Winnipeg with speeches.

The Goldeyes' organization was good at details. Scripts written for game days were thorough and precise. Details were never taken for granted in all the years I was there, but on June 7, 1994, they were crucial. This was the Goldeyes' first game and that only happens once for every franchise.

Now, allow me to jump ahead to the first inning of the actual game. We had a great crowd with over 14,000 cheering fans in Winnipeg Stadium. Everyone was smiling and filled with excitement, the speeches were fine, and the game commenced as planned.

Tim Cain took the mound for the Goldeyes. He was a right-handed pitcher who had pitched for Doug Simunic in Rochester, Minnesota, in the Northern League in 1993. He had compiled a stellar ERA of 2.37 during the 1993 campaign, so I was confident with our ace on the mound.

We had arrived at Opening Day much too fast but I was so glad to have baseball being played on the field. It reminded me what my job was all about. June 7th, 1994, is a day I will always remember. We took that first giant step as an organization. It was a great feeling to know that we could put on a professional baseball game and look good doing it.

1994 Season

The Goldeyes won the opening contest 9-1 with Tim Cain getting the victory. The excitement of the evening carried me through the game and beyond. Even though I was tired, sleep was next to impossible that night. The next morning, one of the realities of professional baseball hit hard. We had to put on another game (show) the next day, and the next. The baseball season in the Northern League lasted only three months (three and one-half months as of 2006), but when the team was at home we played several nights in a row. Many times our staff wished we had a football schedule with only eight to 10 games the entire season. Northern League teams currently play 96 games per season in about 110 days. Half, or 48 of those games, are at home.

The Goldeyes swept their opening series with the Duluth-Superior Dukes. In fact, they started the season 5-1. It seemed easy! Tim Cain also started the season 5-1 with a 2.10 ERA and was clearly one of the best pitchers in the league. Then, in early July, his contract was purchased by the Boston Red Sox. The team sputtered to a first half record of 16-24. I guess it wasn't so easy after all!

In 1994, the Goldeyes had ex-Major Leaguers Dann Bilardello, Rich Thompson, Jeff Bittiger, Pete Coachman and Ted Williams. Well, all right, it wasn't the famous Hall of Famer Ted Williams. In fact, this Ted Williams had never played in the Major Leagues so he doesn't actually belong in this list, but his name sure made for a great press release.

One of the reasons why the Goldeyes changed from a 16-24 team in the first half into a 27-13 team in the second half was that they got on a "roll". A "roll" is one of those hard to explain occurrences that happen in baseball, and other sports. During the first half of the season, they seemed to find ways to lose games. The reasons ran the gamut from poor defence, to failure to get a hit when needed, to wild pitches at the wrong time, some bad breaks, and on and on. Every game, a new reason seemed to appear that spelled defeat. They weren't trying to lose. It just happened.

In the second half, things unfolded in the reverse. The Goldeyes won games that would make you scratch your head. There would be two outs in the ninth inning and a routine ground ball would be hit to the opposing second baseman, which looked like it would be the final out of the game. The ball would take a bad bounce and trickle into right field and the Goldeyes would score the tying and winning runs. An apparent defeat would turn into an unexpected victory.

The Goldeyes also had a better team in the second half. Jim Wilson, Pete Coachman, Tim Bruce, Steve Dailey and Jamie Evans were some of the players who didn't start the season in Winnipeg but who all made significant contributions in the second half. Doug Simunic never stood pat with a losing team and was constantly in motion to "right the ship" as he called it. The result was a team that really clicked. The last inning heroics and come-from-behind victories made the Goldeyes a fun team to watch in the latter half of the 1994 season. They won the second half championship and a berth in the playoffs against the first half champion Sioux City Explorers.

While all this excitement was taking place on the field, we were learning how to operate a successful franchise off the field. That first season was an ongoing learning curve. I felt like I could have written a book about every day during the 1994 season because every day was so different. My main objective was to simply hang on for the ride. Planning was difficult – reacting was the reality.

Each day also seemed to bring a new first for me and the organization, which was exhilarating. Some days I would find myself dealing with player issues, other days it could be sales or marketing issues, while still others might be filled with public relations or problems with stadium operations.

Patrick Cairns, a staff member at Woody's Sports, is attributed with the creation of the Goldeyes' logo, which is a snarling fish. It's a great logo and has been widely accepted in the community. Merchandise sales have been strong since the very beginning and Goldeyes' merchandise can be readily seen on the streets of Winnipeg and beyond.

I was actively participating in everything. On occasion, I would try to take a deep breath, sit back, and take stock of what was happening. The job had become all consuming. I felt like I had to be involved in every decision in every department. I didn't have the skills to prioritize very well in those days and found myself responding to every request or phone call. Frequently, several jobs would get half-done and then be interrupted. It felt like I was living in organized chaos. It was fun but a little frustrating some days.

As the staff grew over the years, I learned to back off and allow people to accept responsibility and be accountable for their job functions. In that first season, however, everything was so new I was not even sure what tasks should be assigned to someone else. I, therefore, ended up doing a lot of things myself or in conjunction with another staff member. Somehow, we managed to accomplish a great deal in a short time. Hard work can take you a long way on most jobs.

Throughout this book, I have tried to give insight into why the Goldeyes have been so successful. Many reasons can be found but none are more important than the quality of the staff personnel who have worked for the organization. Right from the beginning in 1994, the staff was the backbone of the franchise. Many minor league baseball teams have come and gone throughout North America in cities as large as Winnipeg without having the same level of success as the Goldeyes. I believe the quality of the people who have worked for the club has made the difference.

The Goldeyes' staff, including owner Sam Katz, was more accessible to the fans and sponsors than their counterparts in other organizations in the community. I want to emphasize this point because it was a chosen philosophy that served the Goldeyes well. Countless numbers of people commented to me that we seemed to care more about their support than they were accustomed to.

That first summer, we only had six full-time employees, which was a very small staff compared to the current contingent. I discussed Kevin Moore and Val Overwater in the previous chapter. Other key people in the organization that first year included Barb McTavish, who started working on February 1st, 1994, the day after I did. Come to think of it, we may have started the same day, since I wasn't actually getting paid on January 31st, the day of the press conference, when I was introduced to the media.

McTavish first got a job with Katz's company by offering to work a number of weeks for free as part of her school program. This was a wise investment on her part. She initially worked for Nite Out Entertainment and Katz must have liked what he saw because he offered her a full-time job when the Goldeyes' organization was being created.

During the first season, McTavish answered the phone and performed office work. She was invaluable because she was very talented and could do almost anything asked of her. She was not too comfortable selling, but when given any other project, you could just watch her go. I never had to worry about the quality of her work. It was exceptional. She became our in-house computer expert, created print pieces, and did so much behind the scenes work it made everyone else's job much easier. Barb's job changed dramatically and quickly and within a couple of years she became the promotions director. Barb McTavish is a real trooper and going into the 2006 season, she is the only staff member left in the organization who was there at the very beginning.

Andrew Collier arrived during the first year also, just not quite at the very beginning. Rumor has it Collier beat Katz in a golf game and the prize was a job with the Goldeyes. One day he arrived in the office and when asked how we could help him, he wanted to know where he was supposed to sit because he had just been hired. I asked him to wait a moment while I phoned Katz to see if this was true. "Did I forget to tell you?" Katz exclaimed. This lack of communication was part of the way we lived, particularly at the beginning.

We did need help, however, and Collier turned out to be just what the doctor ordered. He administered tickets, which were quite a mess when he arrived. Andrew was a welcome addition to the staff.

The Goldeyes won their first Northern League Championship on September 9th, 1994. I remember that date partly because it was also Collier's 25th birthday. He did enough celebrating to last him for an entire year – until his 26th

birthday, which, coincidentally, was the day the Goldeyes lost to St. Paul in the Championship series in 1995.

Collier was my protégé. He committed himself fully to the Goldeyes from the day he was hired. He had skills with computers that I didn't have. If we were trying to create spread sheets to help us track sales, he was the guy I turned to. In 1999, we sent him to Brookings, South Dakota, where he took a training program in the operation of the new Daktronics scoreboard at CanWest Global Park. That allowed him to gain knowledge that no one else in the organization possessed. Andrew put his knowledge to good use and was primarily responsible for making the scoreboard at CanWest Global Park one of the highlights of a game experience.

Over the years, I needed to push Collier into getting involved with all aspects of the company. He wanted to be a general manager some day and I knew the only way that could happen was if he became knowledgeable in sales, public relations, and the baseball side of the business. He was always eager to learn. It was fun to watch him grow and mature. I am proud of Andrew and he is now a great general manager In the Northern League.

We hired a number of seasonal workers that first year, one of whom was Dan Chase. Chase was hired to sell tickets and he did a professional job. I mention this because years later when a position became available as the director of marketing, Chase was one of the people I contacted to see if he would be interested. He was the successful candidate and has been with the club ever since. His career with the Goldeyes all started with cold-calling businesses and selling them tickets.

Katz liked to hold meetings with the staff at night or on Sunday mornings. He had little free time during his regular working day, so that was his solution. This made for some long weeks for Goldeyes' staff. Katz was not involved with the day-to-day operation of the team but was not shy about providing input on any topic he fancied. He was the boss. There was never any doubt about that. Katz, Simunic and I were the public face of the Goldeyes. I did more public speaking engagements and interviews in 1994 than in the rest of my life combined.

I was trying to grasp all of my responsibilities, including how to operate within our agreement with Winnipeg Enterprises Corporation (WEC). WEC was a City of Winnipeg corporation created to oversee the operations of city-owned facilities such as the Winnipeg Arena and Winnipeg Stadium. WEC was our landlord and wielded a great deal of power over the organization. Many members of its staff were involved in the operation of a Goldeyes' game.

I was not a kid when I took this job. I had been in a lot of boardrooms and attended hundreds of meetings. However, I had never experienced anything quite like the meetings between the Goldeyes and WEC, especially when Sam Katz and Larry Neufeld, the chief executive officer of WEC, would attend. We would quickly come to an impasse in the meeting and they would start screaming at each other. Having such beet-red faces and bulging veins in their necks could not have been good for their health. This was something new for me. It all might have seemed funny if I could have viewed those meetings and watched them on video later, but at the time, they were pretty intense.

The biggest problem was the difference in attitude. The cornerstone of the Goldeyes' philosophy was, "The answer is yes; now what is the question!" I could only sum up the WEC philosophy as, "The answer is no; why are you bothering us!" I'm not sure where that attitude came from. Some great people worked for WEC and I enjoyed working with many of them. They simply had too many rules. There was always some reason why something couldn't be done. We often seemed to be stick-handling around the road blocks they put in our way.

Maybe it was just the nature of the relationship. We were using a WEC facility and they were making money from the Goldeyes. They would tell me they weren't making money but that was hard to believe. I had a philosophical problem with WEC making money off the Winnipeg Blue Bombers Football Club, the Goldeyes, or the Winnipeg Jets Hockey Club (now the Moose). These sports teams were good for Winnipeg and they needed to be supported by the city. As far as I was concerned, WEC should have been making its money from concerts or other touring events. We were, after all, paying rent. WEC also received revenue from parking and concessions, and another city entity, Select-A-Seat, was making a commission from the sale of tickets.

No wonder, when the Goldeyes landed in CanWest Global Park in 1999, the club's revenues sky-rocketed. Not only did attendance increase but the Goldeyes' organization was able to keep all revenue generated at its games.

Now back to baseball. In that first season, the Goldeyes captured the second half pennant, which advanced them to the league championship. Playoff time is a thrilling time of year. After Labour Day, there is usually a noticeable nip in the air in Winnipeg. You can feel the cool autumn air coming, which brings an added sense of excitement to the ball park just in time for the Northern League playoffs.

The first two games of the 1994 best-of-five championship series were held at Sioux City by virtue of their winning the first half. I entered the Explorers' ball park for the first playoff game in Goldeyes' history to the music of a Dixieland band. Near the entrance hung a large plaque, which quoted the famous "If you build it they will come" speech from the Universal Studios movie, Field of Dreams. Although this plaque has since been removed, that night I thought it created a great ambience when entering the park.

In fact, the Sioux City Explorers used the theme from the movie as the backdrop to much of the pre-game ceremonies. "Field of Dreams" had brought a lot of attention to the state of Iowa. Prior to the start of the game, as it was in the movie, a section of the centre field fence had been removed and the Explorers' players were introduced as they ran through stalks of corn onto the field. It was very symbolic and brought the fans to their feet. It was a great playoff atmosphere. I could feel the magic. Was I in heaven? No – I was in Iowa, but the stage was set for some real excitement!

Game 1 was a terrific playoff baseball game. Good pitching, good defence, and some timely hitting — what more could you ask for? The Goldeyes triumphed 5-3 behind the pitching of player-coach Jeff Bittiger. Game 2, however, was not a close game as the Goldeyes routed the Explorers by an embarrassing score of 16-1. Next, it was home to Winnipeg for game three of the series. The Goldeyes were up two games to none in a best-of-five series. We were only one victory away from a Northern League Championship.

Goldeyes fans were excited and 8,414 attended the first-ever, at-home playoff baseball game for the new franchise.

There was a tremendous atmosphere in the park but the Goldeyes lost Game 3 by a score of 6-3. Unbelievably, the media speculated the following morning that they had lost intentionally so they could get another playoff gate. No one who knew Doug Simunic would have imagined such a strategy. Simunic wanted to win and he knew baseball well enough to realize that winning was very elusive. He would never intentionally lose a playoff game.

In Game 4, the Goldeyes were not to be denied. Right hander Tim Bruce, a mid-season acquisition from the Thunder Bay Whiskey Jacks, pitched a beautiful game and the Goldeyes triumphed 8-1. We were champions and that night there was a celebration fit for champions!

The entire situation was a bit overwhelming. So much had happened during that first season. The community was excited just to have professional baseball back in Winnipeg. Winning was the icing on the cake. I often wondered if winning the championship in subsequent years would have been sweeter. I'm still wondering. As of the 2005 season, the Goldeyes have never again won the league championship.

I partied alongside the players and staff until very late. At 7 a.m. the next morning, the first player phoned me, looking for his travel arrangements home. I was not ready for reality at that time of day. The day after the season ended turned out to be one of the most demanding. It didn't seem fair, especially when you had just won a championship, but that was the job. In later years, I became very organized at this time of year. Never again did I receive an early morning phone call the day after the season ended because all of the players knew their transportation plans home well in advance.

Once the season was over there was always an emotional let down. The first couple of days were insane as the players left town but once the manager was dropped off at the airport, which usually took a couple of extra days, the season would be in wind-up mode. There were reports to prepare, inventory to take, and a fair bit of clean-up to accomplish.

After a week or two of that, I had to go fishing. As of the writing of this book, I have gone on a fishing trip for 29 straight years with some life-time buddies. What a wonderful release from the pressure of the job, and 1994 was a particularly special trip. I had so many experiences to share and I was still very wound-up from the season. By the time the fishing trip was over, I had one foot back on the ground. Long-time friends have a knack of doing that for you.

Press conference-January 31, 1994-Sam, John, Doug

1994 Goldeyes' staff - Andrew Collier, Val Overwater, Barb McTavish, John Hindle, Kevin East, Arthur O'Bright, Kevin Moore

1994 championship team

Chapter 4: My Dream Job

I have been fortunate throughout my life to have had good jobs that I enjoyed. The job as a general manager of a professional baseball team, however, seemed to be a perfect match. It was not always easy and at times it was very intense, but day after day, I loved going to work. But my dream job was not for the faint of heart. Making 100 decisions a day is not for everybody, and leading up to the first season, that's exactly what it felt like I was doing.

First of all, I had to come to grips with the hours. I was often in the office by 8 a.m. and would not leave until after 6 p.m. – and that was during the off-season! When the team played games at home, we worked from 8 a.m. until long after the game was over, which could be approaching midnight. Six or seven days in a row working those hours can create some stress on the body and the mind. Not too many people would do that if they didn't love the job. Fortunately, I did.

One night at Winnipeg Stadium in 1998, around 11 p.m., I was wearily walking to my car after a long night game. As I approached the car, a vehicle came rolling along the parking lot headed right for me. I was too tired to get excited or even move out of the way, but I was startled when it came to an abrupt stop right in front of me. The driver's window came down and a smiling Sam Katz appeared. He asked me what I was still doing at the stadium. I told him I was checking for cracks in the parking lot. I was trying to be funny but was so tired, Katz probably thought I was losing it.

One significant aspect of the job was that I could never predict what might happen. The next phone call could take my day in a totally different direction than the one I had planned. Player moves, as an example, frequently required immediate attention. No matter what I was working on, it had to be put on hold because a raft of paper work, including contracts, travel arrangements and immigration documents had to be completed. Many times, travel arrangements had to be made so the player would arrive in time to play in a game that same day.

On more than one occasion, our field manager would find me late at night after a game and ask if I could arrange travel for a player for the following day. He would hand me his cellular phone and ask me to welcome a new player to our organization. Many of those transactions were handled initially without a signed contract, so it was important to ensure the player was committed and comfortable with the travel arrangements. We needed to be confident that he was going to get on the plane the next day and arrive in time to complete the paper work and play in our next game.

During the first few years with the Goldeyes, it was impossible to establish a job description for my position because things were changing dramatically in the Goldeyes' organization. Katz would ask me on occasion what I did to earn my pay cheque. I would tell him it was hard to explain but he was welcome to follow me around for a couple of days to get an accurate picture of my work load. He never had the time to do that and I was too busy putting out fires to worry about a job description. After a few years, the job began to stabilize somewhat. By the time I left after the 2001 season, I felt I really knew what the job should entail.

Managing the staff was one of my priorities. In Winnipeg, with 20 full-time people and hundreds of game-day employees, there were a fair number of staff management and personnel issues to handle. During the 2004 season in Sioux Falls, there were fewer personnel issues but also fewer people to share the work load. Job descriptions in the two organizations were very different.

However, the goal of a professional baseball organization remained the same: to fill the seats by providing a quality product, on and off the field, in order to entertain the fans so they would want to return to the ball park. Every function performed by each staff member was directed toward these objectives.

My understanding of being a good manager evolved over the years. Much of my approach, I had learned from a boss from my time spent working for the City of Winnipeg. Bill Davis was a psychologist for the city and was also the manager of the Employee Occupational Safety and Health branch, where I was a Safety and Health Officer. Davis was a hard-working man who wanted everyone to perform to the best of their abilities. As one of his employees, I was frequently impressed with his ability to take a short time-out and talk one-on-one to staff members about how they were doing. I know his personal interest in my problems motivated me to do the best job I could. He was a very good boss. I had been a psychology major at university and I recognized good people skills when I saw them.

I tried to bring this approach to my management style. I wanted to know generally what everyone was doing but I expected the staff to do their jobs with some level of independence. I trusted that they would come to me if there was a problem, if they needed help, or if something was preventing them from meeting their objectives. Weekly meetings helped keep the lines of communication open.

I did not like screw-ups, however, and when something went wrong, I felt a strong temptation to start micro-managing people. I learned to fight those impulses. I would like to think that once my trust was earned, I gave everyone enough latitude to take ownership of their jobs, and the responsibility and authority to carry them out.

Staff members were not machines and during a long home stand, they pushed themselves very hard. It was important for me to keep everyone motivated. Since I truly cared about the people, it was not hard to be concerned for their well-being. I may not have been perfect, but it was not from lack of trying. I'm sure people knew that I cared about them, though, and that genuine concern went a long way.

Over a number of years, the Goldeyes' organization became a well-oiled machine that operated with precision. Andrew Collier, who became the general manager when I left, told me as he started his new job that he felt like Joe Torre, the manager of the New York Yankees who had been quoted as saying he just needed to write down the same line-up every day and watch his team win. Likewise, the Goldeyes' staff was a smooth operating unit that needed little tinkering. Of course, that was a bit simplistic. Both Torre and Collier have put their own ideas and talents into their jobs and added oil to the machines whenever necessary.

A professional sports franchise is a complicated company with various departments: sales, marketing, public relations, facility, and baseball operations just to name a few.

Sales

Sales of tickets, corporate advertising, promotions, souvenirs, and concessions were all a part of paying the bills. The Goldeyes' philosophy was to keep prices low but not to discount them. Only in 1994 was there a discounted ticket available in the Winnipeg market. In the beginning, Katz was unsure how successful the team would be. He was presented with an offer to buy 1000 tickets for all 40 home games in the outfield bleachers at the football stadium. These seats were not otherwise sold to the public. The price was one dollar per ticket. The club cashed a cheque for $40,000 before the initial pitch was thrown; but how do you calculate the impact that had on the perceived value of other tickets? Many of the people who purchased or were given a one-dollar ticket did not even show up. They may not have seen a value in the product.

Except for special circumstances, programs, or promotions, I believed there was little benefit to the team to allow free or discounted tickets into the marketplace. The short-term possible benefit of somewhat increased concession sales is heavily outweighed by the long-term damage to paid ticket sales. Besides, if you wanted to reward a ticket buyer for a larger purchase of tickets (groups, season tickets, or mini-packs), instead of discounting, I believed you should add value to their purchase. That could be done with personalized service, gifts, exclusive functions, or special offers of merchandise.

After the 1994 season, we were able to agree that it was not wise to have a one-dollar ticket. After that, the value of a Goldeyes' ticket was not compromised, which proved to be invaluable to the club because the demand for tickets rose dramatically at CanWest Global Park. The same philosophy has also been shown to be very effective for many other sports franchises across North America.

When I went to Sioux Falls to be the general manager for the 2004 season, I found that free tickets had been abundant in the marketplace. Given how I feel about this issue, it was incumbent upon me to reduce or eliminate them. At a meeting with the owners in the spring of 2004, I was asked if it wasn't better for the franchise to have more people in the stands even if they had received a free ticket, than to have fewer people who paid. The answer for me was simple. In the long term, a professional baseball franchise can only survive if people pay to watch the baseball game. My philosophy remains: keep ticket prices reasonable and affordable and then provide greater value once fans arrive at the game.

The Goldeyes had a lot of corporate inventory to sell at Winnipeg Stadium but it increased exponentially in 1999 when we moved into CanWest Global Park because the entire facility was under our control. I found sales to be rewarding and it kept me in touch with a lot of people.

During the first few years, a number of companies were not interested in participating with the Goldeyes for a variety of reasons. Sometimes, it was a case of "Let's wait and see how you do," and sometimes the company was just not interested in sports marketing. Anyone in sales knows the hardest part of the job is dealing with "no" for an answer. We certainly had our share of "no" at the beginning. Those road blocks were overcome as the Goldeyes grew in stature in the community. Sales jobs are a lot more fun when people are buying!

But no matter what sales were being recorded back in those early years, Sam Katz wanted more. I guess it was easy to get caught up in that attitude because the inventory of signs, radio, promotions, tickets, and game sponsorships seemed endless.

I really tried to share in a salesperson's excitement about a good sale. It was important for their motivation and enjoyment of their jobs. A good sale to me was any sale that was maximized. A $10,000-sale might not be all that good if $20,000 was available with the right approach or promotion. On the other hand, a $2,500-sale was fabulous if that was the most a company was ever going to spend. Not all sales people dealt with large companies, so total amount of sales was not always the determining factor in whether they were doing a good job.

A bad sale, if there was such a thing, was one that devalued the inventory, whether that was tickets, signage, or something else. In Winnipeg, we mostly valued and sold the inventory at the prescribed price on our rate card. There was always some minor give-and-take for larger clients but there was a conscious effort to maintain the prices. That was not the case in many other venues including what I found when I worked in Sioux Falls.

One contract was signed prior to my arrival that confirmed my belief in the approach we had with the Goldeyes. Anyone who went to a local tattoo parlor and had a canary tattooed on their body was granted free tickets for life to see the Canaries play. The tattoo parlor paid a modest rights fee for the promotion. I presume the sale was designed to garner media exposure for the club, but the response I witnessed was luke-warm at best.

Another sale in Sioux Falls allowed customers to receive two free tickets to a game if they had a receipt from a local grocery store. Even though I am opposed to free tickets in the marketplace, I could have begrudgingly accepted this promotion if the store had paid something for the right to provide this perk to its customers, but such was not the case. It appeared the only reason the sale was completed was to get more people to attend the games. I could stand on the corner of the street and hand out free tickets to accomplish that goal. I have seldom been speechless in front of a client during a meeting when I was trying to sell something but it happened to me a couple of times in Sioux Falls.

One unique sale that I was involved in for the Goldeyes occurred in the Toronto airport. Sam Katz and I were changing planes on the way to the Baseball Winter Meetings in Boston. We had a few minutes to kill and I ran into a Toronto-based sporting goods supplier I knew from my baseball business. After a little idle chat, I asked him if he would like to purchase an ad in the Goldeyes' program to promote his products. He agreed to a half-page ad. When I told Katz what had transpired, he said, "You're amazing Hindle." The size of the agreement was obviously not large but the fact that I was always primed for a sale impressed him. As I have mentioned, this was not a job — it was a way of life.

Selling baseball was easy for me. I could bring a lot of passion to my sales calls because I loved the game, the team, and the league. I miss those lively conversations with many of my corporate clients because I was having fun talking baseball. I was convinced that a professional baseball team touched a greater number of individual people than other sports organizations with similar attendance numbers. A Northern League team played 40 home games in 1994 and 48 home games as of the 2006 season. Their games are squeezed into a three-month-plus season. Home stands are frequently six games on consecutive days and sometimes more. It only makes sense that people share their ticket packages more often in this scenario than, for example, when they have only nine football games to attend for the entire season.

Not many people who bought season tickets attended all of those games. There were a few to be sure, but baseball tickets, more than those of any other sport, were shared among families and friends, or were purchased by businesses that distributed them to staff or customers. Therefore, during a season, a larger number of different people attended games. That information appealed to some advertisers.

Other duties

Selling was not the only part of the job that took up a lot of time. Another critical task was to ensure that fans were adequately entertained. It was tough for the organization to be new and exciting every game while maintaining the same overall level of quality service and professional production. If we thought fans would enjoy something, we would try it. If we weren't sure, we would probably try it anyway. We were not into shock value that would offend people; we were interested in good clean family fun.

Dealing with the consequences of crossing the Canadian/American border was another "fun" part of my job. Immigration officials on both sides became people with whom I was very well acquainted. From the beginning, I made it a point to show the inspectors that we were above-board. One inspector initially told me that he did not trust professional sports teams because he had encountered a great number of problems with them in the past. I did not want to gain that type of reputation. Yet, in spite of my best efforts, we still had some issues over the years.

One player incurred an inspector's wrath when he told him he was an American citizen. It turned out that he had applied to be an American but he was still a Mexican citizen because he was born in Mexico. The department did not take kindly to anyone misleading them. We had no choice but to release the player. He barely made it back into the United States, where he had lived for years. He would have had even greater problems re-entering Canada.

Another bizarre situation occurred when performer Rockin' Ray and his performing dog, Skyy Dog, were coming to Winnipeg to perform at a game. I received a call from the border that they were being detained because Ray, who had been given bad advice from someone, had told the border inspector that they were entering the country for a visit. The signage on the side of his vehicle was a dead giveaway that visiting was not likely the purpose of the trip. I pleaded with the immigration department to allow them to enter the country because we had heavily advertised their appearance. Permission was granted to allow them into Canada for 24 hours, provided I offered assurance that they would leave once the performance was over. This was likely one time where my relationship with the immigration officials benefited the Goldeyes.

Crossing the border has become increasingly more difficult in recent years, which has become a serious challenge for teams in the league. And it doesn't appear that this trend will be reversed any time in the near future.

Operating a business with the size and diversity of the Goldeyes required tight control over finances. Each year I was required to create a budget. Even with the constant changes that were occurring, the budgets came pretty close to the real numbers at the end of the year. I usually tried to have the actual bottom line a little better than budget. Owners seldom complain if you make slightly more money than predicted. In Winnipeg, this was a normal occurrence.

Being a general manager in the Northern League also meant having some fun at the park. On occasion, I would agree to do things that seemed downright goofy. Sometimes it was good for staff morale and sometimes it may have helped entertain the fans. As long as everything was done in fun, I was usually game to participate.

I still look with amusement at a picture taken some years ago when the Goldeyes brought "Sport" to the park. Sport was a mascot who toured the continent performing at sporting events. Dave Raymond was the original man behind the mascot and I really liked Dave. He put his heart into his work, liked to have fun, and was a great performer. He asked me during his performance in Winnipeg if I would help him with a skit. All I had to do was find a gentleman who was losing his hair. I took my hat off and smiled. Raymond immediately asked me if I would participate. All I had to do was sit in a chair. I agreed, and because I had my back to him, all I know for sure is that Sport put a plunger on my mostly bald head as part of the skit. A picture was taken to ensure this shining moment in Goldeyes' history was captured for eternity.

During the first few years, we asked people to sing Take Me Out to the Ball Game during the seventh-inning stretch. Unfortunately, I was asked to sing once in a while. I love to sing in the shower but somehow it was much different over a microphone. Some days, the rendition was downright scary and with some encouragement from some friends, my wife, and even my mother, I had to draw the line and inform all of the staff that I would not sing over the public address system any more. Funny, but I never got an argument from anyone.

Baseball was critical to my job. I understand and love the game. I don't think I could have handled the hours and the stresses of the position, particularly during those first formative years, if baseball had not been a part of the equation.

I was interviewed a lot during my career. I became comfortable speaking in public and I knew all interviews were good for the organization. One, however, stands above the rest.

The Goldeyes had great success on the field and made the playoffs every year I was there. The Winnipeg Blue Bombers Football Club, on the other hand, had a bad run in 1998. They started the season 0-10. During that streak, I was interviewed by Mike Beauregard on CBC television just prior to our first playoff game in the post season. I enjoyed Beauregard's humour and frequently watched his sports broadcasts. We were live on air and Beauregard started the interview by stating a few facts.

The interview went something like this. "So John, let me get this straight. You've been the general manager of the Goldeyes for all five years they've been in existence, right? (I smiled and nodded.) And the Goldeyes have made the playoffs all five years, right?" (Another smile and nod.) He then paused and asked, "Do you know anything about football?" I burst out laughing and it took a few moments before I was able to say, "No Mike, I know nothing about football."

Every year, my dream job would take a toll on my body and my sanity. At the end of the season, I would meet with the staff to discuss their futures, and with Katz to discuss my own. I loved the Goldeyes' staff (and the Canaries' staff for that matter). I looked forward to their written evaluations at the end of the season, which they were asked to produce. I would review each evaluation thoroughly and discuss it with each staff member in person. Listening and then acting upon their comments and recommendations was important to having staff members who were positive about their role with the organization. Many of their ideas were incorporated into the operating philosophies and procedures over the years.

Negotiating my own contract every year was a real treat. After the 1994 season, we seemed to be on top of the world. We had been far more successful than anyone had predicted. We had won the Northern League Championship and had gained respect as a professional sports franchise. I just assumed the owners would be pleased. When it came time to negotiate a contract, I knew I needed a raise. I was hired to fill a part-time position and the job turned out to be far more hours than any full-time job I knew. Even with the raise I had received after two weeks on the job, I was seriously underpaid during the first year and the situation needed to be rectified.

Katz had a different perspective. He pointed out everything he could think of that went wrong. His criticism caught me off balance. While I realized there was room for improvement, his personal criticisms were all out of proportion. He also wanted to change my title to business manager instead of general manager. He was never able to verbalize exactly why he wanted to do that and I was adamant that the title remain unchanged. The term "general manager" is recognized throughout baseball circles and was the title used by every other team in the league. I was hired as the general manager and I was not interested in another job title.

I knew in my heart that I had done a good job during that chaotic first season. I became resentful. I had busted my butt for very little money and this was the gratitude I received from the guy I worked for. It looked like my job as a baseball general manager was going to be short-lived. After a particularly colourful exchange with Katz at a restaurant, I returned to the office and started cleaning out my desk. I had filled one box with personal belongings when Kevin Moore walked in. He had worked for Katz for a few years and knew Sam better than I did. I told him I was sorry but I could not accept the personal criticisms I had received. Moore realized I was serious. I wasn't even angry any more, just disappointed in how I was being treated and with the realization that my "dream job" was coming to an end after one short season.

Two minutes later, the phone rang. Guess who? It was Sam Katz. He asked me what I was doing and I told him I was packing up my stuff and leaving. He asked me why I took things so personally and I told him his criticisms were personal and unjustified. He retorted that he was just trying to make the point that we, as an organization, could get better. I never did have an argument with that statement. He then offered me the job as general manager for the 1995 season at thousands of dollars more than his last and final offer. I was stunned. After hanging up the phone, I just sat at my desk and stared out the window as I tried to figure out what had happened.

I found out later that Moore had called Katz and told him he was about to lose me. Moore was a supporter of mine and he, no doubt, argued that Katz should do something immediately to keep me. Katz must have decided that he wanted me to stay and everything else had just been part of negotiating a contract. This was a foreign approach to me and gave me a new perspective. If this was negotiating, I had inadvertently played my ultimate card by packing up to leave. While contract time was never a lot of fun for me, no negotiation in the future was ever as tough as that first one. Maybe, that's because I had my eyes open a lot wider.

Negotiating with the rest of the staff was much different. I would meet with each of them and then recommend salaries to be placed in the budget for the following year. One thing I learned quickly was that people always wanted to be paid more money. In all my years as a general manager, I never had anyone come into my office and tell me they were overpaid. Usually, Katz would agree with my recommendations but sometimes he would cut things back. I don't think he ever paid any office staff more than I recommended.

I wasn't even sure how closely he read my charts and recommendations until one day when he called me from an airport. He had taken my 2000 year-end report on his flight and was reading over the salary recommendations. Almost all employees were recommended to have a small salary increase. When he came to communications director Jonathan Green, my comment was, "Let's fire him, he has started to date my daughter." Katz told me he broke out in uncontrollable laughter and that other passengers on the plane thought he was crazy. I then knew that he read my reports. Green has done a lot of good work with the Goldeyes and remains with the club as of the 2006 season. He is no longer dating my daughter.

After a few seasons, I came up with the idea of asking all of the staff to evaluate me in their year-end reports. I highly recommend this to managers. Some of them were uncomfortable evaluating their boss while others relished the opportunity. I never regretted the process because I learned a great deal about how I was perceived. The most important issue that came to light was that they wanted to be recognized more if they were doing a good job. For some people, no matter how many times they were praised, they could use more reassurance. Others were not as sensitive to this issue and assumed that no news was good news.

By analyzing these evaluations and privately discussing the concerns with everyone, I was able to find a better way to interact with many of them. The fact that I was prepared to listen may have been the most important message of the exercise.

Hiring people for the Goldeyes was a time consuming job but something I also enjoyed. We were fortunate to have minimal turnover in staff. One of my favourite job interviews took place when we were hiring a group sales coordinator in 1998. I had interviewed eight people one day when Lorraine Maciboric walked into the room. I started the interview with some standard questions, trying to make her feel comfortable, and then we got down to business. A part of every interview included an explanation of the tremendous number of hours the staff worked in the summer. If the applicant still wanted the job, we would continue the interview.

Maciboric was different. I was so taken with her enthusiasm and energy that shortly into the interview, I threw my question sheet away and sat back in my chair. She asked me if something was wrong. I said, "No, not at all. Please keep talking." Her energy and zest for life was exactly the kind of passion we needed in the office. Maciboric had been a school teacher, a mother, and had sales experience. I offered her the group sales position at less money than she was hoping for, which gave her some common ground with everyone else who worked for the Goldeyes. Hiring her was one of the best staff decisions I made during my tenure with the Goldeyes.

The network of people she knew was amazing. At any function I went to with her, she would know people. If she met someone, she could immediately put them at ease. She also had an excellent memory and she could recall a lot of detail about a person's life when she met that person again. That was a great asset in sales. She was aggressive, which could ruffle the odd feather, but she was a warm and caring person, which shone through. I loved working with her and exploring her ideas. Lorraine was invaluable to the Goldeyes for many years, until she left prior to the 2006 season to pursue other opportunities.

On another occasion, I had gone through the interview process and I was leaning towards hiring a man in his 50s in the ticket office. He was far older than anyone else I had interviewed. I finished the interviews late one afternoon and the next morning I was on my way to the Baseball Winter Meetings in Anaheim, California. That evening, I was sitting on a ride at Universal Studios next to Sam Katz. I asked him how he would feel if I hired a guy who was quite a bit older than me. He said, "The best person gets the job, John." I smiled and said, "Great, I know who I'm going to hire for our vacant sales position." Dennis McLean has been with the Goldeyes ever since and has sold countless thousands of ticket packages.

There was a lot of love in the office. We lived in close quarters 14 hours a day in the summer, under some serious pressure. Of course, there was the odd office conflict. I tried my best to have the disagreements dealt with openly and resolved quickly. It seemed like every year at some point, I would have to pull out the "A" speech at a staff meeting. I couldn't use this speech often, but on occasion it was useful.

Basically, it included a teamwork theme. There was one special rule that I expected everyone to abide by. No one was permitted to talk about a staff member to another staff member unless the person being talked about was in the room. Anyone could come to me with an issue about another staff member but my response was usually to get both parties in the room and have it out until we were at peace. People are people so sometimes they broke the rule. I believe, though, that having that philosophy helped the office flow as smoothly as possible.

Many people were a part of the Goldeyes' success story. They should all feel proud of their contribution. Some came to the organization for a short time and then moved on to bigger and better things but many stayed for years. A lot of people were a part of the Goldeyes' success story. They should all feel proud of their contribution. Some came to the organization for a short time and then moved on to bigger and better things but many stayed for years. The friendships that were forged while I was at the Goldeyes will never be broken. They were my extended family. How else could we spend 14 hours together at the ball park and then frequently hang out together after that?

The job was never dull. There was always something unique to challenge the mind. Interacting with the vibrant people in the industry kept me feeling young at heart. Every day, year after year, I woke up in the morning and was happy to go to work. How much better does it get than that? I had a key job in professional baseball, the game I have loved my entire life. I was one lucky guy. I lived a dream.

Staff dressed up on Psychedelic 60's Night

1998

1994

John and Bob Kipper

Sport and John during infamous skit
That is a plunger on John's head!

Bev and John Hindle
GM of the year award

Sheriff John

Chapter 5: The Northern League

A New League is Created

The Northern League (NL) was resurrected in 1993. A soft spoken, casual, and unassuming man by the name of Miles Wolff was the driving force behind that resurrection. To meet him, you would never imagine he was the strong personality behind the rebirth of an independent baseball league. He recruited the individuals who were to become the first owners and he met with local municipal officials in various communities to pave the way for professional baseball to return to the north central part of the continent. He gained the respect of everyone affiliated with the Northern League.

In fact, Wolff had a lot of respect throughout the sporting community. He was chosen in 2005 as one of the top 10 owners in all of sports by ESPN 25. The publication, written by Charles Hirshberg, celebrates the network's silver anniversary. Wolff placed eighth on the list, which included four Major League Baseball owners, three National Football League owners, and two National Basketball Association owners. The baseball owners on the list were George Steinbrenner (New York Yankees), Peter Magowan (San Francisco Giants), Ted Turner (Atlanta Braves), and the late Ewing Kaufmann (Kansas City Royals). Wolff was the only minor league owner listed. This was an amazing tribute to the man who was instrumental in changing the face of professional baseball across North America.

In addition, he was also selected as the 79th most important person in baseball history by John Thorn and Alan Schwarz in the eighth edition of Total Baseball: The Ultimate Baseball Encyclopedia. Total Baseball was launched in 1989 and is the most compelling and exhaustive reference series ever devoted to baseball. As a former owner of the Durham Bulls, Miles is credited by many as bringing vitality back into minor league baseball. He also owned Baseball America, the highly respected baseball publication. Suffice to say, the Northern League was very lucky to have Miles Wolff as its first commissioner.

"I don't know of anybody in baseball who is more honourable than Miles," said Mike Veeck, president of the St. Paul Saints. "Even though several of his rulings went against us, I always respected his decisions and knew he was doing what he thought was best for the league. What more can you ask of a leader?"

I agree with Veeck whole-heartedly. Wolff was one of the outstanding people I met in baseball. A very respectable man, he brought class and stability to the fledgling league. I feel lucky to have been able to get to know Miles Wolff.

As the league's first commissioner, Wolff and the other owners took a risk when they started an independent league in the early 90s. They recognized that the north central part of the continent was an area that did not have much minor league baseball. After years of preparatory work, the reborn Northern League threw out its opening pitch in June of 1993. It consisted of six teams in that first year: St. Paul, Duluth, and Rochester, Minnesota; Sioux Falls, South Dakota; Sioux City, Iowa; and Thunder Bay, Ontario.

I refer to the league as resurrected because over the years there had been a league called the Northern League no less than three separate times, dating back to as early as 1902. It symbolized a lot of baseball heritage because many of the greats played in the league, including Steve Carlton (Winnipeg), Orlando Cepeda (St. Cloud), Lou Brock (St. Cloud), Duke Snider (St. Paul), Roger Maris (Fargo), Denny McLain (Duluth), Roy Campanella (St. Paul), and Jim Palmer (Aberdeen).

Earl Weaver and Cal Ripken Sr. managed at Aberdeen, as did Walter Alston in St. Paul. Many other NL notables, who later played and/or managed in the Major Leagues, include Leo Durocher, Miller Huggins, Gene Mauch (St. Paul), and Joe Torre (Eau Claire) – a great deal of heritage indeed.

The current Northern League has been in constant motion since its inception in 1993. The Rochester franchise was disbanded after the first season. Miles Wolff knew he needed Winnipeg in the league for the 1994 season. Winnipeg was the second largest city in the geographical area. Sam Katz had attended a meeting prior to the 1993 season but did not confirm that he wanted a franchise in the NL. Wolff had also had a number of discussions with Winnipeg Enterprises Corporation. Things finally came to a head after the 1993 season.

"I flew to Winnipeg and signed a deal with Winnipeg Enterprises to operate a Northern League team for the 1994 season," said Wolff. "I could no longer wait for Sam to make up his mind whether he wanted in or not."

Three days later, he got a call from Katz, who told Wolff he was going to be a part of the Winnipeg organization. Sure enough, Katz purchased a 25-percent ownership in the club and became the president of the Goldeyes. A few years later, he would buy the WEC shares.

In 1993, the league had six teams, played a 72-game schedule, and had a salary cap of $72,000 per team. Compare that to the 2005 season when the league had 12 teams, played a 96-game schedule, and had a salary cap of $100,000-plus. Two veteran players did not have their entire salary charged to the cap, so, depending on their salaries, the cap was somewhere between $100,000 and $120,000 per team.

Franchises have come and gone over the years due to a movement in the Northern League from smaller cities to larger ones. As of the 2005 season, three of the original six teams were gone – from Thunder Bay, Duluth, and Rochester. Madison, Wisconsin, which entered the league in 1996, along with Fargo-Moorhead, lasted only until 2001, the same year a team emerged in Lincoln, Nebraska.

It's important to note that these changes were always made in a professional manner. Even if a team was on the verge of not meeting its payroll, that was never visible to the public. All movement within the league was conducted with proper notice and I think the league can thank Wolff for that. In Rochester, Thunder Bay, Duluth, and Madison, he injected his own money on a temporary basis to make sure the league was always placed in the best possible light. That is so very significant because during the same time frame that the Northern League has existed, several other independent leagues have been formed and disbanded. I believe lack of leadership was often the key factor in their demise.

The Northern League has since expanded to other cities, including Schaumburg, Joliet, Gary, Kansas City, Edmonton, and Calgary. There is talk of expansion to cities as far away as Detroit and Cleveland. In 1993, none of the owners would have dreamed the league could be so successful and expand to such far away places.

Is expansion a good trend? Maybe it is just a natural evolution for a successful sports league. In a way, it is flattering that teams want to be a part of the Northern League. On the other hand, as travel costs grow, expansion puts a lot of pressure on the smaller-market teams. It's a little sad that by the 2005 season, three of the original six teams were gone. I hoped that no more would be lost but those hopes were dashed for the 2006 season when the league drastically changed geography, which I will discuss later.

Since 1993, the make-up of the league has also been in constant flux. While it started with six teams, it has played seasons fielding six, eight, 10, 12, and 16 teams. In 1999, the NL formed an alliance with teams on the east coast. The Northeast League was absorbed and the Northern League created two conferences, the East and the Central. Teams in the East Conference, for the most part, did not have the same attendance figures as the teams in the original Northern League, which made up the Central Conference, and were not perceived to be comparable operations. I saw only a few games at their parks but those games revealed some of the differences between the two conferences. Besides lower attendance numbers, the eastern conference teams did not have nearly as many newer, quality ball parks.

The 2000 Northern League all-star game was held in New Jersey at Yogi Berra Stadium. That stadium was one of the best in the east. It was built in 1998 and was also home to Montclair State University, which just happened to win the NCAA Division III National Championship in 2000.

Communications director Jonathan Green and I arrived for the all-star game a day early and took the short drive to Allentown, Pennsylvania, to watch an eastern conference league game between the home town Ambassadors and the New Jersey Jackals. We were interested in observing the game operation of one of our new partners. The stadium in Allentown was small; including the dimensions of the park where the deepest part of the field was 375 feet. The distance between home plate and the back stop was much less than the recommended distance.

There were a good number of fans in attendance, however, and they seemed to be enjoying themselves. We were treated well and given good seats behind home plate.

During the game, there was a particularly close play at the plate and the umpire ruled against the home Allentown team. A middle-aged gentleman was so enraged by the call, he literally climbed onto the backstop netting and was uncontrollably screaming at the umpire. I was somewhat taken aback by the intensity of this man's reaction.

Shortly thereafter, I asked the Allentown general manager, Dean Gyorgy, what the story was with the guy climbing on the backstop netting. He replied, "Oh, that's our owner; he gets pretty wrapped up in the games." Pretty wrapped up! This was way over the top, I thought. I have sat with Goldeyes' owner Sam Katz at many games and he was very passionate and expressive when he watched our team, but I just couldn't imagine him climbing on the backstop to protest an umpire's call.

The experiment with the Northeast League lasted four years. During that time, the Eastern Conference representative inexplicably won all four post-season championships. Adirondack defeated Duluth-Superior in 2000 while the other three victories came at the expense of the Winnipeg Goldeyes: in 1999 against the Albany-Colonie Diamond Dogs, and in 2001 and 2002 against the New Jersey Jackals. The argument that the original Northern League was better in all aspects seemed to be weak. The players, at least, appeared to be comparable. It could be argued they were even superior in the Eastern Conference.

I suppose one could also argue that the Goldeyes would have won three more Northern League Championships if the amalgamation with the Northeast League had not occurred. The reality is, though, they were officially runners-up all three of those seasons.

The relationship between the two leagues disintegrated after the 2002 season. The agreement was tenuous from the start and it was maintained on an interim basis. It was essentially a licensing agreement that allowed the Northeast League teams to use the Northern League name.

I discussed the amalgamation with Sam Katz because he was in the owner's meetings and was part of the discussions. He told me in the beginning that it was likely agreed to because Commissioner Miles Wolff was a big supporter of the concept. Wolff is a visionary. He believed the move was the initial step to seeing independent baseball take on a more significant role in the overall baseball community. Independent clubs would have a stronger voice if they were aligned. The term "independent" had always been used in baseball to describe a team that was not affiliated with any Major League Baseball club. It did not mean these independent, unaffiliated teams could not align themselves with each other.

The initial agreement was for three years. Before the arrangement was to become finalized, which would have occurred after five years, the NL owners demanded a payment from the Northeast League owners to finalize their franchises in the NL. The former Northeast League teams did not agree with that approach. While economics may have played a role in the ending of the relationship, it does not appear to be the only reason for the break. The relationship was simply inequitable. Seldom can a partnership work when one side looks down upon the other. That was the case with the original Northern League owners. It was as if they felt they had married beneath their stature.

Teams in the east understood that some of the facilities were inadequate and changes were on the horizon. It should not be forgotten that the Northern League had also gone through a significant metamorphosis since its inception in 1993. Rochester, Thunder Bay, Madison, and Duluth were all a distant memory by the 2003 season.

Some of the owners in the former Northeast League were also very successful businessmen. I wondered how they felt about the attitude they were receiving. Floyd Hall, as an example, was the owner of the New Jersey Jackals. He had been the CEO of K-Mart Corporation from 1995 until he retired in 2000. His company, Floyd Hall Enterprises, had built Yogi Berra Stadium and Floyd Hall Ice Arena on the campus of Montclair State University in Little Falls, New Jersey. He was obviously a very successful businessman, and a real gentleman in all the dealings I had with him. Other owners in the east were also successful, including of course, Miles Wolff himself, who owned Les Quebec Capitales.

But even though affiliation with the Northeast League ended, expansion was still front and centre in the NL. The 2005 season saw Edmonton and Calgary, Alberta, join the league, swelling the ranks to 12 teams. With two six-team divisions, reaching the playoffs became that much more difficult. Four teams still made the playoffs but 12 teams were competing for those four spots. From an objective perspective, having all teams reach the playoffs on occasion was good for the league but the incredible streaks that Winnipeg and Fargo put together in reaching the playoffs were not an incentive for fans in other cities to buy tickets. After working in Sioux Falls in 2004, I witnessed first-hand the difficulty fans had in believing that their team had a real chance to make the post-season. Everyone loves a winner, and it's a problem when fans think there is no hope of their home team ever being one.

The Northern League is not alone with this problem. Major League Baseball has to deal with the same issue. Realistically, most teams do not have a chance to reach the post-season. That must hurt attendance in those cities, but the fact Major League Baseball also has the problem does not make it less of a problem in the Northern League. The original purpose of the salary cap and player classification rules was to maintain competitive balance in the league. To date, it has not worked very well. The fact, however, that Gary beat the mighty Fargo-Moorhead Red Hawks in the 2005 championship series might be a glimmer of hope for the other teams in the league, which have seldom, or never, made the playoffs.

I held the belief that the league was as strong as its weakest link. As a general manager, anything I could do to help teams that were struggling was a priority. There was no way Winnipeg was going to try to stop winning pennants or setting attendance records. It was up to the other teams to catch up as best they could in their own markets.

Most, if not all of the things we did in Winnipeg, or that the Saints did in St. Paul, would work in other centres. I felt the sharing of ideas and promotions between teams was an important part of the success of the league. When Winnipeg was a new franchise, I drew from the knowledge and expertise of the established and proven general managers. That was a huge benefit to the Goldeyes. After I had a successful track record, I felt a strong desire to share information and help others. Not all teams felt the same way.

Miles Wolff personally asked me to stay in close contact with my counterpart in Thunder Bay and to help him in anyway I could. We were the only two Canadian franchises at the time so there was a natural connection between the two teams. Unfortunately, it requires an open mind to accept someone's help. I did not find open minds in Thunder Bay during the last couple of years that the Whiskey Jacks were in operation. With that type of attitude, it was easy to predict their demise.

In 2005, a Northern League roster was made up of different classifications of players. Each team had to have five rookies who had never played professional baseball. The roster could only include four veterans, who had unlimited baseball experience and four LS-4s or LS-5s, who had four or five years professional experience. The first year in the Northern League did not count when computing years of experience. Therefore, a rookie coming to a team directly from college was still a rookie if he returned to the Northern League for a second year.

I believe these rules were designed to help control salaries, player's attitudes, and mostly, to ensure competitive balance in the league. Younger players were paid less and were usually so happy to be playing baseball, and getting paid to do so, they never thought to complain. The eligibility rules made for some interesting team chemistries. They were good for the rookies, who were able to play along side established players and learn the game quickly. But don't ever think the Northern League is a developmental league. One of the reasons the independent league concept has worked is because the local team is trying to win. Fans really appreciate that aspect of the league.

In affiliated baseball, teams are ordered to play "bonus babies" or other high draft picks because the Major League club has so much invested in those prospects. The big club is not as interested in minor league teams winning baseball games as they are in the development of the players. Anyone in baseball can tell you stories of players in horrible slumps that were kept in the line-up only because the Major League club insisted.

Sometimes there was good reason to be patient. Some pretty fair ball players did not start their careers off too well. Consider Sandy Koufax or Mickey Mantle for example. Thank goodness someone did not give up on them. They both struggled early in their careers but soon became dominant Hall of Fame players. Baseball is not an easy game to master.

How many other players, however, were not given the same consideration and were discarded from their teams without having a fair opportunity to show their talent? That was one of the reasons why good players were available to the Northern League. Injuries and lack of opportunities were two of the most common explanations I would hear from players when they were asked why they were released from an organization.

A trade in the Northern League was not like a trade in Major League Baseball. The Northern League had the player eligibility rules. Sometimes a team would trade a veteran player for a rookie. The veteran may be a better player but because the team had another veteran waiting in the wings, they were really getting two players that they wanted while only giving up one. This was sometimes difficult for fans to understand when they were trying to evaluate a trade. On the surface, it could appear that the trade was not equitable but it might just be a classic "Northern League trade." What you saw on the surface was not the entire story.

The Fargo-Winnipeg Rivalry

Fans in the NL get caught up in the rivalries that have been created between teams and cities in the league. Winnipeg initially had a rival in Thunder Bay because it was the only other Canadian franchise. The biggest rivalry, however, began in 1996 when Fargo-Moorhead was granted a franchise. The Fargo-Winnipeg rivalry is a natural. On account of the distance between the two cities which requires about a 3.5-hour drive, there has always been significant cross-border travel between them. When Doug Simunic left Winnipeg after the 1995 season and took the manager's position in Fargo, the rivalry intensified.

Simunic was an ideal interview for the media. If you talked to him for just a few minutes, he would have something controversial to say, which made for good copy. The media ate that up. His comments often fueled the competitive fires between the teams and created increased awareness and intensity among the fans. In other words, Simunic was good for attendance.

Fargo and Simunic were blamed for anything bad that happened to the Goldeyes. Sometimes the correlation took a great deal of imagination to follow. The most bizarre case of this occurred in 2002 when Fargo was accused of calling the

Oakland Athletics to inform them about the exploits of Winnipeg pitcher Bobby Madritsch.

Madritsch was a dominating pitcher in the NL and, no doubt, Fargo's playoff hopes looked brighter if he were no longer in Winnipeg. Don't think other teams, including the Goldeyes, have not recommended players from other teams to Major League organizations. Managers might phone around to find their players a chance with an organization, but that usually happened once the Northern League season was over. In-season they were trying to win and losing their best players to an organization did not increase their chances of winning. Jeff Bittiger, who was the pitching coach in Fargo at the time, did have a relationship with the A's and he may indeed have told them about Madritsch. His exploits were not a big secret. Winnipeg fans and the Goldeyes' organization, however, were outraged.

At the same time this was happening, the Northern League ruled that the Goldeyes had violated the salary cap. It fined the Goldeyes and determined that they would have to finish the season with only three LS-4s (players with four years professional baseball experience) instead of the usual four. That was a serious blow to the Goldeyes, forcing them to release pitcher Steve Thomas, their all-time saves leader.

Unbelievably, the Winnipeg media blamed Fargo. Day after day, the two stories were woven together in the Winnipeg newspapers. Fargo was trying to destroy the Goldeyes. Exactly how Doug Simunic or the Fargo organization could be responsible for Winnipeg's overspending on the salary cap was never made quite clear. Fargo owner, Bruce Thom, was on a league committee that evaluated the information but that hardly made Fargo responsible for the violation.

Most people reading those stories in 2002 believed that somehow Fargo was to blame for everything. Even now, Simunic laughs at the incident. He couldn't believe the stories were written in the first place and was even more amazed that people believed them. Doug Simunic and the Fargo-Moorhead Red Hawks like nothing better than to beat the Winnipeg Goldeyes. They would take whatever advantage they could against their arch rival. Simunic, however, has nothing to do with what Winnipeg pays its players.

The rivalry between Winnipeg and Fargo is real. Fans from both cities frequently follow their team to the games in each other's cities. Year after year, the two teams seemed to meet in the playoffs. After Fargo came into the league in the 1996 season, the Goldeyes and the Red Hawks, unbelievably, met in the playoffs six consecutive years. And equally amazing, the Red Hawks won every series played during the even-numbered years and the Goldeyes won all three series played in the odd-numbered years. The string was finally broken in 2002 when the Red Hawks and Doug Simunic missed the playoffs for the first time ever. They did, however, resume the rivalry in 2003, with Fargo winning the championship series in four games. Fans in both cities look forward to future clashes.

The rivalry escalated to a frightening level in Fargo during the playoffs in the 1996 season. I liked the people of Fargo and they passionately supported their baseball team. That passion, however, spilled over during Game 3 of the 1996 series, fueled by a long rain delay when the beer kept flowing at the concession stands.

I was sitting near a "gentleman" throughout the game, who kept referring loudly to our all-star first baseman, Terry Lee, as Sarah Lee. He commented a few times that Sarah could not hit a baseball hard enough to dent a cupcake. Now, the occasional intelligent comment from the home town fans might be considered cute, but loud, continuous, and repetitious stupidity quickly crosses the line from cute to obnoxious.

Andrew Collier was sitting next to a couple of fans whose target for their unruly statements was Winnipeg field boss Hal Lanier. The comments were personal and idiotic and were getting louder and louder as the game progressed. Finally, Lanier said something back to one of them. He walked towards the grandstand near the Goldeyes' dugout and suggested that the fans go sober up or come down to field level and tell him what they thought to his face.

Before you could blink an eye, Goldeyes' staff, including Collier, had come to the defence of their manager by confronting the fans. Third baseman Vince Castaldo led a charge of the players on the field to the area on the first base side where Lanier was standing near the Goldeyes' dugout. The fans responded with a barrage of nasty comments. "Go home foreigners" was one of my favourites, since almost all of the players on the Winnipeg roster were Americans. When racial taunts were screamed towards our black players, I realized just how dangerous the situation had become. I was sickened to hear a comment like, "Hey nigger, you will be lucky to get out of here alive." Statements like that have no place at a sporting event or anywhere else in our society. Everyone was standing and pushing forward. The situation was explosive.

John Dittrich was the general manager of the Red Hawks. He hastily ascended to the press box and over the public address system he pleaded with the Fargo fans to return to their seats. Dittrich said something like, "You've been great fans all season. Please don't ruin Fargo's reputation for being the best fans. Return to your seats and show the good sportsmanship we are known for."

It was like someone punctured a balloon with a pin. Immediately, the atmosphere changed. You could feel the tension lift throughout the facility. I always liked John Dittrich but on that night, I was very proud of him. He was faced with a difficult and dangerous situation and he performed quickly and decisively. His prompt action may have prevented a serious situation from erupting.

Since the atmosphere was always more charged when Winnipeg played Fargo-Moorhead, both teams, thereafter, had extra security around the visitor's dugout to protect the players and prevent any future occurrences of bad sportsmanship by unruly fans, especially near the end of the game. Rivalries were good for the league but they needed to be kept under control.

League Office

The relationship between the league office and the individual teams was interesting. Miles Wolff was the initial commissioner and Tom Leip was the original executive director. The league office was located in Minneapolis and I spoke with Leip a great deal at the beginning. He had some good baseball experience on his resume and he shared his knowledge with us willingly.

Kevin Moore and I met with Leip in 1994 at a restaurant in Minneapolis. It was late at night but Leip was always prepared to talk about baseball operations. He liked our enthusiasm. We talked into the wee hours of the morning, with the meeting ending only when the restaurant kicked us out because they were closing for the night. At the beginning, to have someone with experience to bounce questions off of was very good for the Goldeyes' organization.

Sam Katz often seemed frustrated with the league officials. He told me several times that he felt their decisions were biased against the Goldeyes. I believed they were acting in the best interests of the league as a whole, so I seldom saw a problem with their decisions, even if they were not always what the Goldeyes wanted to hear. The league office had a tough job trying to keep all teams and all owners happy.

I was told stories of owners who would call league officials at home in the early hours of the morning to complain about an umpire, or about some other decision that had been made the previous day. Being fair was my only criteria for a good decision. I did argue vehemently with league officials on occasion but I had a lot of respect for the people who worked at the league office, and I never called anyone at home at one o'clock in the morning. As a result, I had a great relationship with them.

The only real disagreement I can remember was regarding their recommendation that the general manager wear long pants at every game. The Goldeyes disagreed with this philosophy. Neither Sam Katz nor I believed it was necessary or even beneficial. We had a casual relationship with our fans and sometimes wearing shorts in hot weather was a better fit. It seems like a pretty small thing but it came up many times over the years.

When the league asked me to be on the three-man committee to create operational guidelines for teams, I argued against putting the requirement to wear long pants in the manual. I imagine it was added after they received our recommendations, but I left the Goldeyes before the manual was distributed. Those guidelines are still in use in some form or another in the Northern League and other independent leagues.

League Meetings

Dan Moushon replaced Leip after a couple of years. Moushon had been the general manager of the Watertown Indians in the New York-Penn League and the Fayetteville Generals in the South Atlantic League before taking the position as executive director of the Northern League in 1995. I liked Moushon and I felt he was honest and fair. Because he had worked in baseball for many years and had been a successful general manager, he understood the operational issues that clubs faced.

Moushon was a very organized person, which was great at league meetings. Our agenda would flow and the information we shared was invaluable. During my working career, I have sat through my share of meetings and frequently could not wait for them to end. Not so with Northern League general managers' meetings. I enjoyed them so much that I was always disappointed to see them end. I was like a kid in a candy store as I shared ideas with my colleagues. From my first to my last meeting, I was very keen to learn and to share information about our successes or failures.

Moushon would coordinate the rotation of the meetings to different league cities. Each meeting would include a tour of the host ball park. The meeting dates would also coincide with some other sporting event in that city. The host general manager would arrange tickets to that game so we would spend an entire weekend together. This was a great way to develop relationships throughout the league, which proved to be a huge benefit. It was much easier to call one of my counterparts to discuss an issue when I felt we were friends. To this day, I am still friends with many of them.

We had a lot of fun at those meetings. I was treated to some new experiences at sporting events in many different cities. One year we attended a University of Wisconsin football game, along with 80,000 other fans in Madison. Bill Terlecky, the Madison Black Wolf general manager, was a great host. He showed us the town after the meetings and arranged tickets to the football game. The University of Wisconsin was playing an early, nationally televised game against Iowa. The only difficulty I experienced was the expectation that I should be able to drink beer and eat bratwurst at 8:30 on a Saturday morning.

When we arrived at the gate to enter the game, I was informed that someone had miscounted and there were only 12 tickets for 13 bodies. I was the last guy in our line and Terlecky stood at the gate and waved the tickets and loudly counted bodies until we were all inside. I never did see a ticket for the game. The bleacher seating in the stadium was so cramped it didn't leave a lot of room for body movement without jostling the guy several seats down. I watched a lot of the game standing.

For anyone who has not attended a NCAA football game, I can assure you, there is a lot of atmosphere. I was amused to see entire sections of the stadium filled with students, including a huge band. The students yelled out cheers in unison and were really into the game. I was surprised by the intensity. I have since realized that this is quite common at NCAA football games all across the country, but my first game was a real eye-opener.

Our meeting in Schaumburg was another great trip and the Flyer's general manager, Rick Rungaitis, was also a terrific host. He drove like Mario Andretti so we were able to squeeze a lot into two days. We ate at Harry Caray's restaurant and were given an inside tour of famous Wrigley Field where the Chicago Cubs play. What a special treat!

While attending other meetings at various league cities, I also enjoyed an NCAA football game at the Fargo Dome, a CBA basketball game in Sioux Falls, an NCAA hockey game in Duluth, and minor league hockey games in Albany, New York, watching the Albany-Colony River Rats, and in Chicago watching the Chicago Wolves. If not for the league meetings, I would not have had those unique experiences.

A real bonus at the meetings in Albany was the opportunity to visit the National Baseball Hall of Fame in Cooperstown, New York. It was fun to be with a bunch of baseball guys and visit the "shrine" together.

I asked Moushon what he felt were the strangest incidents the league had to deal with when he was president. He told me that the municipal workers strike in Thunder Bay was one of the most difficult situations. The baseball park there was owned and maintained by the City of Thunder Bay. In 1998, the Whiskey Jacks had to take their spring training on the road and actually played regular season league games in Fargo, Grand Forks, and Wahpeton, North Dakota. The Goldeyes were the first team to play the Whiskey Jacks in Thunder Bay that season.

The municipal workers were still on strike but the Whiskey Jacks had decided to play anyway. The game was played in less than ideal conditions. No one was maintaining the field.

The grass was so long it was top heavy and simply laid on the ground. No telephones were installed because the telephone workers were not prepared to cross the picket line, so only cellular phones were being used. As the players arrived at the park for one of the games, a striking worker yelled, "Go home, you bunch of has-beens." Long-time Goldeyes' outfielder Chris Kokinda, who was never short of words, yelled back: "You have us confused. We're the never was's!" While no serious incidents occurred, it was an uncomfortable situation. The strike ended soon after the Goldeyes left Thunder Bay.

Another unusual situation was the umpire strike. Mike Pilato was the umpire-in-chief for the league in 1995. He was looking for compensation for an incident that occurred in St. Paul when he was attacked by a Saints' player. The confrontation occurred during a game and the Saints released the player immediately. The league subsequently suspended him indefinitely. That action appeared to make it clear that the league was backing its umpires and had no tolerance for such behavior. Pilato didn't see it that way. He convinced all of the Northern League umpires that they should support a wildcat strike and not work the games the following night.

Miles Wolff was on a plane flying from Fargo to St. Paul. In Fargo, he had met with a potential ownership group to discuss the possibility of a new franchise for the 1996 season. A meeting with Pilato was scheduled in St. Paul that evening and the umpires were waiting to hear the outcome. Meanwhile, the teams with home games were in a panic. Who was going to umpire the games that night?

The league found itself dealing with Thunder Bay first because the Whiskey Jacks game started an hour earlier than any other. That was the only team in the league in the Eastern Time zone. At the last moment, Thunder Bay was able to find local umpires to handle the game. We had a similarly tense situation in Winnipeg. The meeting between Wolff and Pilato resolved the issue and fortunately everything was back to normal the next day, but it was one frantic day as everyone tried to find alternate umpires.

While I did not agree with the umpires' position, it did emphasize their importance. It is hard to play professional baseball games without them. Every time an umpire makes a close decision, there's a good chance someone on one side or the other will feel it's a bad decision. It was necessary that the league back the umpire to some degree if complaints were lodged. Umpires were held accountable for inappropriate behaviour but, inevitably, they initially received the benefit of the doubt in the event of a complaint about one of their calls. I believed this attitude was necessary if a league wanted the good umpires to return year after year. You couldn't call yourself the pre-eminent independent baseball league without quality umpires.

Change in the Northern League Office

In October of 2001, in Lincoln, Nebraska, Miles Wolff walked into the Northern League meeting and announced that he was intending to step down as commissioner. Jaws dropped around the table. In Miles's words, "It is not fun anymore. I looked around the table at my last meeting and there were too many lawyers in the room! The sense of community spirit was gone. After 10 years, I felt that my energies could better be spent with my own club and in helping the Northeast League." The man who had been instrumental in the formation of the league had had enough.

The league set out to find a new commissioner and eventually appointed Mike Stone, former president of the Texas Rangers. Moushon and Wolff still ran the baseball operations for the league for the 2002 season, handling player moves and team rosters. After the 2002 season, however, the location of the Northern League offices moved to Fort Worth, Texas, where Stone lived. This decision was reached at an owner's meeting and was not unanimous. It appeared that the new teams wanted to separate themselves from the past and start anew. That was a significant event in the evolution of the league and one that inched the wedge between teams a little deeper.

Stone didn't know all of the history of the NL and that created some problems for him. Winnipeg was in the middle of a situation that created some controversy during the 2002 playoffs. Goldeyes' veteran Harry Berrios was injured and the Goldeyes asked permission to bring in another veteran player, Bubba Smith, to replace him during the playoffs. Initially, Stone agreed and Winnipeg flew Smith in to play.

After receiving complaints from other teams, an emergency conference call between owners was arranged. That call resulted in a 9-1 vote to suggest to Stone that his decision was inappropriate. He immediately reversed his decision. That would not have happened when Miles Wolff was Commissioner because no team had been allowed to do what the Goldeyes were proposing since the inception of the league. Stone finally made the right decision given the league's history, but not before causing expense and anxiety for the Goldeyes' organization.

On two separate occasions, Mike Stone asked me if I would be interested in being the president of the Northern League. I should have been flattered but I mostly felt a sense of frustration. The problem was his timing. The first time he called was late in the fall of 2002. I had left the Goldeyes at the beginning of 2002 and I was operating my sporting goods business, Home Run Sports. While I found his offer intriguing, after serious soul-searching I decided I could not move to Fort Worth at that time. I did ask if the job could be done from Winnipeg but that was not an option for Stone. Less than a month later, I received an offer to purchase my business. Since running the business had been the primary reason I turned down the job, I immediately contacted Stone and asked him it was still available. He told me the position had just been filled.

In the fall of 2003, I received a call from Mike Veeck, who asked me if I might have an interest in being the general manager of the Sioux Falls Canaries. At the same time, I also received an inquiry from a team in the Northeast League that was looking for a senior executive in its organization. That was an exciting couple of weeks around my house as I weighed the pros and cons of moving away from Winnipeg and getting involved again in professional baseball. My wife, Bev, was going to stay in Winnipeg, at least for the first year, which made the decision even more complicated. After the interviews and lengthy discussions, I had pretty much decided to go to Sioux Falls.

But first, I thought that I would make the effort to contact Stone at the league office to make sure no job opportunity was available for me there. The timing of our last discussion was so bizarre, I felt it was prudent to make sure nothing like that could ever happen again. Stone told me outright that there was no position available. At least I knew and could make the decision to go to Sioux Falls with all the facts on the table.

I agreed to go to Sioux Falls and packed up some suitcases and headed south. I had been there for a couple of weeks when the phone rang. It was Stone and he asked me if I had taken the job in Sioux Falls, which must have been obvious since he had called me at the Canaries' office. He said things had changed in the league office and he wanted me to come to Fort Worth. He told me he would contact the Sioux Falls' owner and convince him I would be more valuable to the league in the office than as a general manager of one of the teams. He suggested that if I came to Fort Worth, I would be groomed to take over his role as commissioner after the remaining three years of his contract were fulfilled. Sam Katz also called me to encourage me to take the job in Fort Worth.

The Sioux Falls' ownership was really upset and refused to release me from my agreement with them. I did not blame them. The search for a general manager for Sioux Falls had ended when I accepted the position. There was also a significant cost in securing a visa for me to work in the United States, since I was a Canadian. In essence, I felt that it was too late. How unbelievable was this? Twice in the space of one year, circumstances had prevented me from taking a job in the league office.

As of the 2005 season, the Northern League seemed to be doing okay. It continued to gain popularity, attendance was strong and more expansion was on the horizon. The quality of the players and the organizations, for the most part, appeared solid. There was some concern about the two expansion teams in Edmonton and Calgary, which struggled in 2005, but they were both great cities and everyone hoped the organizations would grow stronger.

My only hope was that all the owners could work in harmony and make decisions that benefited the league as a whole. Decisions that solidified the long-term rather than the short-term benefits had to be the focus. The only thing that could bring down the Northern League was the owners themselves.

I wrote this chapter in early 2005. Little did I know how prophetic my comments would be. In October of 2005, four teams pulled out of the Northern League, including all three of the remaining original teams. St. Paul, Sioux Falls, and Sioux City joined Lincoln in a venture to start their own league. That decision rocked the foundation of the Northern

League. It was a devastating blow to the "most pre-eminent independent baseball league in North America." It is hard to imagine that the Northern League in 2006 will not have a single team from the original six that started in 1993. The news was so significant that I added an additional chapter at the end of the book.

In December of 2005, another offer presented itself from the newer and smaller Northern League. Stone was stepping down and a search was on for a new Commissioner. I was offered a position handling the contracts for all the remaining eight teams. I was told that the job could be done from my house. The league appeared to be significantly cutting back on the responsibilities of the position. This time, I had no other job and I did not have to relocate. I did think about taking it but in the end, the time commitment required, combined with the salary offered and the lack of responsibility were not a fit for me. It was difficult to walk away from a job in baseball but I have no doubt that it was the right decision.

Miles Wolff

Dan Moushon presenting all-star award to pitcher Ryan Halla

Chapter 6: Cast of Characters

Baseball, and probably the entire entertainment industry, attracts more than its share of characters. This was certainly the case in the Northern League. High energy people with strong personalities were the norm. Northern League and individual team meetings were always exciting because few people were shy about expressing their opinions.

Sam Katz

When I think of the characters I met during my years in professional baseball, the first name that pops into my mind is the mayor of Winnipeg, His Worship Sam Katz. Working for Katz was quite an experience. I first met him and was interviewed by him at his house on a Sunday, so I should have realized that life working for him would be different.

Katz was thinking about work day and night. He worked countless hours and had no problem if his staff did as well. I would not describe him as the easiest person to work for because he was so intense. He would call at almost any hour day or night to check on information or to discuss some new idea that had popped into his mind. I even remember getting numerous calls from him while he was away on vacation. We had many staff meetings at nights or on the weekends.

His cellular phone rang constantly and I doubt that there were many people who were on the phone more than Sam. It was a little frustrating to be sitting in a meeting with him and have the phone continually interrupt our conversation.

Katz has non-stop energy and when he thinks he is right, there is no holding him back. They say you can't fight city hall, but I think you could argue that Katz fought city hall over the building of CanWest Global Park and won. How ironic that he now is city hall!

I jokingly comment to people that Sam Katz is the first mayor I ever helped get elected. I was in Sioux Falls at the time of the Winnipeg civic election in 2004 so I didn't work on his campaign or even vote in the election. However, part of my job when I was with the Goldeyes was to make the organization and its owner look good whenever possible. I think I did my job pretty well. We were a family and it was important to present a positive image at all times. At any of my presentations, I would always speak positively about Katz.

I witnessed many times how Katz loved to be in front of a camera. He was very charismatic and wanted to be the public face of the Goldeyes. He was media savvy and had long had aspirations to be in politics. He was comfortable speaking in front of a microphone and the positive public image that was associated with the Goldeyes looked good on him.

His image changed dramatically over the years. At Winnipeg Stadium during the first five years of operation, he would show up at the ball park part-way through a game wearing his softball uniform. He was very noticeable as he meandered through the crowd. To say he dressed casually would be somewhat of an understatement. He became far more fashion conscious in later years.

As the ball club gained popularity, Katz's reputation and image skyrocketed. No longer was he thought of as a concert promoter. His name was linked with the warm fuzzy feelings that people associated with the Goldeyes. His popularity was confirmed with his election as mayor of Winnipeg in 2004. Would any of this have been possible without the Goldeyes? I guess we'll never know.

The Goldeyes were very important to him but at times they were not his top priority. His attention to other projects never really affected my job because I treated the Goldeyes like they were my own. If a situation developed that I thought had the possibility of affecting the public perception of Katz or the organization, I would inform him immediately. Otherwise, I think he assumed no news was good news.

Katz was a good negotiator. I never saw him get the worst of a negotiation. Coming into a deal after Katz had started it could be difficult because he seldom put things in writing. More than once he would drop a crinkled piece of paper on my desk with some scribbled notes and tell me to turn it into a legal contract. I would smile because I knew there could be a very valuable contract on the page. Sometimes that process was complicated since there would be two interpretations of exactly what had transpired in previous discussions. There was no doubt, however, that Sam Katz was a good salesman. He sold the Goldeyes and he sold himself extremely well. He was also a talented problem solver and he could usually find a way to make things happen.

Katz is a great baseball fan and sitting beside him at a game is an experience and a lot of fun. He is certainly not afraid to cheer loudly for the Goldeyes. He has learned much about baseball since 1994 but, inevitably, during a game he would ask me a question or two regarding some inside part of the game. After giving him an answer, Katz would look at me and ask, "How do you know stuff like that?" I would just look at him and smile.

Over an eight-year period, I witnessed a great deal of change in Sam. I believe he became somewhat gentler and softer around the edges after the birth of his beautiful daughter, Ava. He had always believed in family values and he was very affectionate towards his own relatives. I found that one of his most endearing characteristics. Since the year Ava was born, Goldeyes' fans in attendance were treated to a free ice-cream treat during one game each year to celebrate her birthday. He was a very proud father.

I asked Sam to recall his fondest memory of the Goldeyes. He said, "I guess there are really three of them. Opening Day in 1994 when we threw out the first pitch; the night we won the Northern League Championship in 1994 was a special moment for a lot of people, including me; and the day we opened CanWest Global Park, which was the culmination of a hard fought battle that had been won."

While I could write much more about the man who was my boss for eight years, his name is woven throughout the book as an integral character in many of the chapters. I would sum this up by saying that working for Sam Katz was an unforgettable experience. He is such an interesting man. He is smart, has a good sense of humour, and he can be downright kind and generous. He is driven to succeed and decisions he makes are designed to advance that success. The approach has served him well. He has climbed all the way to the mayor's office.

Mike Veeck

What must it be like to be the son of a baseball legend? Few people in the world know the answer to that question but Mike Veeck, the son of Hall of Famer Bill Veeck, is one of them. His father owned three Major League Baseball clubs – the Cleveland Indians, the Chicago White Sox, and the St. Louis Browns. Bill Veeck was not happy with the status quo. At times, he created animosity among his fellow owners with his progressive ideas. He related well to the common man and he went out of his way to provide entertainment for the fans instead of relying solely on the baseball game to draw people into the park.

The scoreboard in a Major League ball park, or minor league park for that matter, is a centre of attention during games. It was Bill Veeck in 1960, with the introduction of his $350,000 exploding scoreboard at Comiskey Park in Chicago, who changed its importance for fans. Fireworks exploded from the scoreboard, along with various and magnificent sounds, which included a cavalry charge and crashing trains.

Other accomplishments that Bill Veeck is attributed to bringing to Major League Baseball include signing the first black player in the American League (Larry Doby) in 1947, signing the oldest rookie player (Satchel Paige) who was 42 years of age, and signing the shortest player (Eddie Gaedel). He was also known for outrageous or lavish giveaways at the gates, planting the ivy on the outfield wall of Wrigley Field, placing players' names on the back of their jerseys, promotional stunts such as hiring Max Patkin, "the clown prince of baseball," to coach at third base, and fireworks. Bill Veeck could be described as a man who was in favour of any promotion, even if it was a little off-the-wall, if he thought it would bring joy to the fans.

Funny, that is exactly how I would describe his son, Mike Veeck. Fun is a big part of the equation when Mike is involved. Baseball needs people like Bill and Mike Veeck. It was no surprise that good attendance followed them wherever they went.

I got to know Mike Veeck during my tenure in the Northern League. After I left the Goldeyes and then my baseball business was purchased, I found myself unemployed in the summer of 2003. Mike Veeck was one of the people who called and asked if I would be interested in working with him. Veeck is not your average guy – he is just a bit different. When he called me, he frequently used an assumed name. The first time he called, he told me he was Mike Weir, the great Canadian golfer. I was disoriented for a moment because he woke me from a nap on the couch where I was resting while watching a golf tournament on television. (For me, napping is a big part of watching a golf tournament.) I had to check to see if Weir was still on the leader board. I didn't think he would be calling me to ask for advice on his golf swing.

Veeck was calling to see if I would be interested in going to Sioux Falls to become the general manager. He was a big fan of the city of Sioux Falls since he lived there when he first bought the Canaries in 1999. He convinced me that Sioux Falls would be a good fit for me. While I actually negotiated my contract with principal owner Ben Zuraw, it was Veeck I relied on some days for advice or a dose of humour to lighten the day.

When I worked in Winnipeg, I was not sure what to think about Veeck. He seemed a little crazy at times and because he was the president of the famous St. Paul Saints, it was easy for people to take shots at him. I learned a great deal more about him when I worked in Sioux Falls. Veeck gave a lot of credit for his success to Marv Goldklang, the man who contacted him and offered him a job in baseball after Mike had been Ignored by the powers that ran Major League Baseball for many years. Veeck first worked at the Miami Miracle where the attendance was so low when he arrived, the players had trouble giving away their free tickets.

The Goldklang group of baseball teams, to which the Canaries were affiliated, conducts its own seminar each year. In 2003, it was held on Sanibel Island in Florida. I found a great family atmosphere existed throughout the meetings. People who worked for all the various teams were happy to share information, but they also seemed happy to hang out together and have some fun. I was welcomed with open arms by everyone, which was a good feeling.

When he spoke publicly, Veeck would often talk about some of his failures, which he believed people found more interesting than successes. "I've been fired from more places than I can remember. Hell, even my own Dad fired me when I worked for the White Sox," he would say. Everyone who has followed baseball closely over the years is aware of the debacle between games of a double header at Comiskey Park in 1979. Disco Demolition Night was Mike Veeck's idea. He asked fans to bring their old disco records to the ball park and he would have them blown up on the field between games.

The biggest problem with this promotion was that it worked too well. A mediocre Chicago White Sox team in 1979 was not drawing large attendance numbers. It was hoped that a successful "Disco Demolition" promotion could draw an additional 5,000 fans more than a normal game. The White Sox attendance averaged about 16,000 fans per game at the time.

Over 50,000 people showed up for "Disco Demolition" night! The Sox also turned away thousands of people who hung out in the parking lot or snuck into the park somehow. So many fans arrived with disco records; they stopped collecting them for the promotion, which turned out to be a big mistake. During the first game of the scheduled double-header, fans started throwing the records like Frisbees onto the field.

This was not a normal Comiskey baseball crowd. The attitude in the stands was more like a rock concert. "I knew I was in trouble when the first fan jumped onto the field," Veeck told me. The fans tore up the grass and ran rampant between games until Chicago police officers dressed in riot gear cleared the field. Sparky Anderson was the manager of the visiting Detroit Tigers and was not prepared to play the second game because of the damage to the field and the nature of the unruly crowd. The game was eventually forfeited which was only the fourth time that happened in Major League Baseball history. Mike Veeck was crucified in the newspapers and black-balled for years by other baseball owners. All because a promotion worked too well!

Veeck is a pretty big believer that any media coverage is good for a club. He asks all of his teams to be on the lookout for any opportunity to receive national exposure. Many of them have. I appreciated that philosophy but I was somewhat more conservative than many of my counterparts in the Goldklang organization. However, Veeck's calling card, "Fun is good", was something I could openly embrace.

What I grew to respect was Veeck's love for the game of baseball. He was cognizant that the game itself was paramount. No matter how wild the promotion, he did not want it to affect the game. That also put us on the same page. In 2005, when the Kansas City T-Bones and the

Schaumburg Flyers wanted to have the outcome of the first two innings of a league game be determined by two fans playing a computer generated baseball game, Veeck was opposed. At first, that surprised me because he was such a proponent of outrageous promotions, but that was when I first learned about his love for the game. Having a computer game count as the actual score in a league game was definitely affecting the game between the lines.

He would also talk about his family, which was so dear to him: how is wife, Libby, supported him and had been a source of wisdom in his life; and how their beautiful daughter, Rebecca, had shown such courage in dealing with a rare eye disease, a form of retinitis pigmentosa called cone-red dystrophy. Veeck was also quick to give credit to others. Combine all of these appealing characteristics with the fact that he was funny and entertaining and you can see why I liked the man.

Veeck believed it is imperative that the experience at the ball park remain fresh and vibrant. The St. Paul Saints are renowned for their off-the-wall-antics for the purpose of maintaining a fun environment. Every year I would look at the Saints' promotional schedule and shake my head in admiration of their imagination. Veeck told me he had a long list of potential promotions that he had not yet tried. He was just waiting for the right opportunity. That was one of his ways of keeping things fresh and vibrant.

Ed Nottle

Not as famous but a celebrity in the Northern League nonetheless, was the manager of the Sioux City Explorers, Ed Nottle. Nottle came from the old school of baseball. He did not beat around the bush but was blunt and opinionated. When asked what he thought about a woman, Ila Borders, playing in the Northern League, he said it was ridiculous. He did not believe women had the physical skills to compete with men on a baseball field. Nottle was a baseball guy. He did not work in the public relations department. He did, however, eventually learn to appreciate Borders' will to succeed as a ball player.

Nottle was the manager of the visiting Explorers when a Winnipeg Enterprises' staff member turned out the lights at Winnipeg Stadium at the end of the ninth inning of a tied game so that a fireworks show could be seen. Nottle sarcastically told me that in all his years in baseball that was the most screwed-up promotion he had ever seen.

During his first visit to CanWest Global Park in 1999, Nottle and I had a bit of a run-in. The home team was responsible for providing balls for batting practice for both teams. On the first day the Explorers were in town, over a dozen balls went missing after the Explorers were finished practice. That same night, Explorer's players were trying to use those balls to trade for hotdogs and other food from the vendors. I went to tell Nottle about the problem and he yelled at me. He said he had been in the game for over 30 years and ball players had always tried to buy food with baseballs. I told him I could accept that but I was looking out for my costs and Sioux City could provide their own batting practice baseballs from then on if any more went missing. He turned away in a huff, obviously upset with me.

That night, not one baseball was missing from the batting practice balls. Prior to the game, Nottle called me over to his dugout and told me he appreciated my passion for my job and respected me for standing up for what I believed was right. He told me there would be no more missing baseballs. Ed Nottle was a square shooter. He loved baseball and he loved the independent leagues. But he did have a few vices. Nottle was the only person I know who smoked in the dugouts, which was against Northern League rules. And I'm not suggesting he liked his beer, but the odd time he was kicked out of a game in Winnipeg, our per capita sales on beer would go up!

I loved listening to him tell stories. I even had the chance to listen to Nottle sing on occasion. He is a good singer and at the all-star game in Sioux City, he was the entertainment at the reception the night prior to the game.

Andrew Collier was involved in a good story about Nottle. The Goldeyes' staff communicated through two-way radios during games. In the early years, the radios didn't have head phones so anyone standing close-by could hear what was being said. Since staff members were constantly moving through the stands, I had to remind them to be careful what they said over the radios so no fans would be offended.

Barb McTavish, who coordinated game day promotions, was frequently on the field or near the dugouts. One night, she radioed to Andrew Collier in the press box to ask if a particular song could be played at the next break in the action. Collier blurted out over the air that her request should be no problem because Sioux City would be changing their struggling pitcher right away. Ed Nottle was standing close to McTavish and heard Collier's comment. Nottle yelled to Barb, "Tell that guy to do his job and let me do mine." We still laugh about that incident. After it happened, Collier was very careful what he said over the radio and soon thereafter, we purchased head sets to eliminate that type of communication hazard.

Ed Nottle was one of the most colourful characters to grace the Northern League. He became an owner in Sioux City for a while but he seemed more at home on the field than he did in the boardroom. I asked Mike Veeck what it was like at the beginning, as the league was being created. He told me that he looked around the table at an early meeting and saw Ed Nottle. He looked at Ed's weathered face and thought to himself, "This is what this independent league is all about. A baseball lifer like Ed Nottle who dearly loves the game has a chance to manage again." Veeck told me he ribbed Nottle many times that even Veeck had lasted longer in Major League Baseball than Nottle had.

Vince and Rosie

Vince and Rosie were two fans in St. Paul who spent more time tailgating in the parking lot than they did watching Saints' games. The St. Paul Saints have created an amazing phenomenon that occurs prior to their games. People come to the ball park from miles around, many of them hours prior to game time, to barbeque and party in the parking lot. It's affectionately called "tailgating". The parking lot next to the ball park is literally full hours before the stadium gates open.

In 1995, I decided to go to St. Paul to attend a game and witness what was new in the Saints' operation first hand. They were the pride of the Northern League and I thought surely I could pick up some good ideas to bring back to our park, as I had done the previous year. A few family members, Goldeyes' staff, and some friends also made the trip. When we arrived at the park an hour and a half prior to game time on a Friday night, it was amazing and exciting to see the parking lot completely full. Smoke from barbeques and the wonderful smell of grilling food greeted our aroused senses. The atmosphere was like a carnival.

We decided to try joining the fun. We purchased some wieners from a convenience store and headed to the park early Saturday afternoon, armed with our wieners and buns and a cooler full of drinks. We were hoping we could befriend some locals and ask to use their barbeque. Within the sea of vehicles, barbeques, and mass of humanity, we chose to ask a jolly looking fellow for the right to use his barbeque.

How could I ever forget his reaction? He grabbed the package of wieners out of my hand and promptly threw it in the trash can. "No one is putting wieners on my barbeque today," he touted. I wondered how anyone could be so bold and so rude. While we were standing there in a state of shock, Vince let out one of his deep roars of laughter. "Rosie," he bellowed. "Get some more plates. We have company from Canada here to eat with us."

Vince was a prize. He had received the shocked reaction he was looking for and was now about to become the most amazing host anyone could imagine. As he opened up the lid to his barbeque I was astonished to see what looked like a 25-pound turkey. It barely fit under the lid. We had stumbled across the "tailgaters extraordinaire." Every person in the parking lot seemed to know them and there turned out to be quite a few people who were affiliated with his group. I look back now and realize how fortunate we were to have picked their barbecue. That incident was the beginning of a wonderful friendship that still exists today.

Vince was a loud and fun-loving individual. When he found out the people he had befriended from Winnipeg included the Goldeyes' general manager, he was very pleased. Someone told him that visiting players were annoyed that by the time they arrived back at the hotel at the end of a game, there were very few places for them to eat. Vince decided to solve the problem during the team's next visit to St. Paul.

He asked me if the players would come to the parking lot after the game if he would agree to feed them. I knew the players would stampede there if free food was involved. I told Vince he was being too generous but he insisted. He would not let us pay or contribute any food to the occasion.

What a spread he put on! He barbequed tons of meat and provided salads and a full compliment of beverages, including kegs of beer. The players were ecstatic.

Vince and Rosie continued to provide food for the Goldeyes' players on their visits to St. Paul for a number of years. Sometimes he would allow me or the players to contribute to the food costs but often he would do it all himself. All Vince could say to me was, "Your players are so polite. Every one of them thanked me for the food. What a class bunch of guys you have and a class organization you run."

Over the years, everyone who came down with us from Winnipeg to a Saints' game was treated like family. All our staff knew of Vince and Rosie's exploits and would join in if they traveled to St. Paul. Two young guys who had won a trip to St. Paul at a Goldeyes' game during our "Pack Your Bags" promotion were stunned. They were so happy just to be in St. Paul, but after they stopped to say hello at the tailgating session, they were dragged into the middle of the festivities and treated like royalty. That made their trip even more memorable.

In searching for a way I could repay the hospitality, I convinced Vince and Rosie and a few of their entourage, including Sister Rosalind, the nun who gave massages at Saints' games, to come to Winnipeg and be our guests. I met Sister Ros' at a game in Fargo in 2006 where she threw out the first pitch. Although it was eight years earlier, she immediately recalled how wonderful the experience had been in Winnipeg. We were still playing at Winnipeg Stadium at the time so the best VIP treatment I could offer was a place in the press box. We prepared a room with seats and catered in quality food. Hal Lanier had the players all sign autographed balls and other memorabilia and we provided Vince and Rosie with some programs and merchandise items. They thought they were the king and queen of Winnipeg. To this day, when I see Vince, he has to tell the story and remind me how good he felt when he was at our park. It was a very small payment to make for some very special people.

Garth Brooks

Throughout my tenure in the NL, I had an opportunity to meet some very famous people. Garth Brooks came to town for a concert performance in 1996. I represented the

Goldeyes at the press conference during the afternoon and presented him with a Goldeyes' jersey with his name on the back. We hoped he would wear it on stage during his performance to bring added awareness to the ball club. I wore the cowboy hat I had purchased in Nashville, Tennessee, during a baseball seminar and presented him with the jersey. He was very gracious.

Just before I left, I spoke briefly one-on-one to Brooks. He told me he liked my hat. I casually asked him if he wanted to come to the game that night and if so, he was welcome to sing the national anthem. He laughed and pointed out that the last time he publicly sang the national anthem was at the Super Bowl to an estimated audience of over a billion people. He had no plans of doing so again in the near future. He had a genuine warmth about him. If you can know anything about a person in a few moments, I believed Garth Brooks to be a nice man.

Susan Auch

Susan Auch is a famous Manitoban who was very gracious when she was honoured at the ball park. She won Olympic medals in speed skating at an incredible three separate Olympics in 1988, 1992 and 1996. I was quite taken with her. She had such a pleasant attitude, was drop-dead gorgeous, and was a fierce skating competitor. I had a great deal of respect for her accomplishments which were a tribute to her tremendous ability to maintain her focus over a long period of time. I consider her to be one of the premier Canadian athletes that I have ever had the privilege to meet.

Ed Nottle

Vince Jeanette-master tailgater

Susan Auch & John

Mike Veeck

Sam and John

Sam Katz

Chapter 7: Don't Call Me Coach

In professional baseball, there are managers and there are coaches. The manager is the boss. Once someone reaches the position of manager, he usually doesn't take kindly to being called a coach. Every year, some unsuspecting rookie would inadvertently refer to manager Hal Lanier as "coach". Lanier would notice but he was not really offended and would never say anything. Then a coach or veteran player, as an initiation, would convince the rookie that he had offended Lanier, who was really upset with him. This rookie would sheepishly go into Lanier's office and ask for forgiveness. Lanier would smile and tell him not to worry about it. "Just call me Hal," he would say. The rookie would then return to the clubhouse, to roars of laughter from the other players who were in on the joke.

Doug Simunic

Doug Simunic is a beauty. Baseball is filled with characters, which is an important part of the lore of the game. Simunic will certainly go down as one of the most colourful figures in Northern League history. In every city where his team played, he was welcomed raucously by the home town fans. They knew who he was and they were not shy about telling him what they thought of his team, his weight, his heritage, or his ancestry. Simunic told me during one of our many lengthy philosophical discussions that if the opposition fans were yelling at him, at least they were not yelling at his players.

First, let me talk about "Simmy's" record. As of the midway mark of the 2006 season, he had managed in the Northern League for 14 years. He spent one season at Rochester, two at Winnipeg, and 11 at Fargo-Moorhead. He has won three Northern League championships and his team has made the playoffs 13 of his 14 years in the league. He has the highest winning percentage of any manager in the history of the Northern League. Those are pretty impressive stats.

Now let's talk about Simunic, the guy. When he was in Winnipeg, Simunic was constantly in motion. This motion included his body, which could be seen rocking in the dugout during a game, and his mouth, which was never silent for long. I came to the conclusion that if things were going too smoothly, Simunic felt obligated to shake things up. He seemed happier if there was a little crisis going on. That drove me crazy. The job was tough enough at the beginning without creating issues where none existed. There were very few quiet and serene days when Simunic was in town.

He was also a little paranoid. In the early years, Simunic thought someone was after his job: our coaches, myself, the popcorn seller, anyone. He would make the wildest accusations and there didn't have to be a speck of evidence to back up any of his allegations. He believed someone was trying to take advantage of him one way or another.

Simmy prided himself on his knowledge of the game of baseball and his ability to evaluate players. History has shown that he was very good at both. Far be it for some Canadian, particularly one who had never played at the professional level, to offer him any advice. One time, I questioned him during a long losing streak why he was not holding infield practice before our games. I was curious. It seemed like an innocent question to me, but not to Simunic. He described for me at length his baseball pedigree and his understanding of the job. That understanding did not include the general manager asking him baseball questions. I was disappointed in his lack of respect for my baseball knowledge.

Simunic fought for everything he could get for his players. He wanted free reign to do whatever he figured would strengthen the baseball club, which is common among managers. Hal Lanier and Doc Edwards were the same way. On one particular trip to Duluth in 1995, the bus left Winnipeg at 8 a.m. and arrived in Duluth about 3 p.m., which was four hours before the scheduled start of the game. Simunic complained that his players had sore backs from the long trip and were at a great disadvantage. He asked me how we expected him to win under those conditions. I informed him that that type of travel was a reality in the Northern League, since the league dictated the hotel schedule.

The home team paid for the visiting team's hotel rooms and the league did not schedule rooms the night before the first game in a series, unless the team was already on the road or the distance was too great. When Duluth or other teams came to Winnipeg, they had the same travel issues. Simunic was not satisfied. His complaints were reported in the newspaper, which of course, immediately got Sam Katz involved. Katz had initially requested that I keep bus and travel costs to a minimum. As soon as this issue hit the paper, however, he changed his mind. He reported publicly that the situation was simply an oversight by Goldeyes' staff and he had instructed them to correct the problem. I felt stupid trying to defend the team's actions only to have him change our position without telling me first. I read about our policy change in the newspaper.

As a result of the situation in Duluth, the Goldeyes never drove again on the day of a game, except to Fargo, unless the schedule made it absolutely necessary. The budget was increased so that the team left a day early and the organization paid for the extra costs of the bus and the hotels. We were the only team in the league that left a day early on a routine basis. We considered it a cost of doing business. Most of the other teams saw no need for extra costs for hotels or buses and they would arrive in Winnipeg a few hours before game time. The funny thing was, the Goldeyes handily won the game that night in Duluth.

For other teams, trading players with Simunic was always a challenge because he was so good at it. Trades usually worked out best for his club. Simunic has complained over the years that no one would trade with him. No one wanted to evaluate a trade and think they got the short end of it, and Simunic had a way of making that happen. He knew his teams and his players. He knew when someone looked better on paper than he really was and when a player was not playing to his potential. That skill was a part of his success.

In 1994, several trades during the season were instrumental in the Goldeyes winning the Northern League Championship. Simunic traded pitcher Scott Freeman to Duluth-Superior for outfielder Steve Dailey. Dailey hit .340 for the Goldeyes and played a solid defensive outfield. Freeman was 1-1 with an excellent 2.45 ERA when he was traded but finished up the season with a 2-10 record and much higher ERA. Simunic also traded popular Warren Sawkiw and Ted Williams to the Thunder Bay Whiskey Jacks for pitcher Tim Bruce, who pitched well for the Goldeyes in 1994, including being the winning pitcher in the championship game.

Simunic was always in motion with his team. "It's time to back up the cut bus!" was one of his favourite sayings. Players never took their situation for granted in Winnipeg. Things could change in a hurry. Making 40 player moves a season, though, is expensive and affects team chemistry. With his best teams in Fargo, there were very few player moves. I guess if you get the right talent at the beginning of the season, have few injuries, and have few players sold to Major League organizations, you don't have to make many changes. That's the ideal situation for the team, the fans, and the organization.

Did I mention that Simunic could be volatile? He had an opinion about everything to do with the game. He believed that once the players arrived for the season, the general manager should spend far more time worrying about them and less about sales, promotions, or any other part of the job. He was a strong advocate for the players. I guess that's the way it should be. It was part of his way of building his own team chemistry. While many conversations still stick out in my mind as if they were yesterday, there was one situation that changed our relationship forever.

At the conclusion of games, I was frequently so wound up I couldn't sleep. I needed to wind down a little, which, on occasion, included refreshments at our favourite haunts. A restaurant/bar close to Winnipeg Stadium that we frequented in the early years was called Grapes Leon's Centre. One night after a particularly stressful day at the office and a ball game, I was sitting quietly at a table with a couple of other staff members when I saw Simunic come storming into the bar and march straight towards me. He was talking loudly before he even reached the table.

Now the crazy thing is, I can't remember what he was concerned about. I just know he was upset and wanted action. I asked him to sit and have a drink with us, which just got him more riled up. By this point he was literally yelling in the restaurant. I could feel myself starting to react. I had dealt with a multitude of issues during the day and his concern was not even on the top of my list for the next day.

I got to my feet and in a tone and volume comparable to his, I informed him that I would not discuss the issue with him until the next day. Furthermore, I would not stand for him coming into a public place to talk to me like that, and that it was time for him to sit down and join us or leave.

Not only did Simunic calm down, but the way we regularly communicated changed that day for the better. There were limits and he had found mine. After he left the bar, I sat down and was somewhat traumatized and completely worn out. That was not my preferred style for settling conflict. I shook my head and muttered something about the craziness that I was currently living in. I doubt Doug will even remember the altercation. When you are high strung and live in constant turmoil, you seem to let things go and easily move on to the next crisis.

If the truth be known, I really liked Doug Simunic. He had a huge heart, loved the game of baseball, and was a very passionate person. Sometimes he talked too quickly, which got him in trouble, but it was that passion that I found appealing. He was portrayed as the arch villain in numerous situations but in reality, most of the time, he was doing the same thing for his club that many other teams, including the Goldeyes, were doing for theirs. It was just his brazen style that drew attention.

Simunic has been blamed in Winnipeg for everything from raiding Goldeyes players to being responsible for Winnipeg violating the salary cap. He was the brunt of rude, crude, and sometimes boorish insults at visiting parks throughout the league. Because he was never at a loss for words, the media loved him and always used his quotes to get everyone riled up when his team was coming to town. That was great for Winnipeg, where the rivalry with Fargo was the strongest.

While I tried to foster this rivalry between Fargo and Winnipeg, I did have my limits. I was once asked to sign a card that some fans were sending to Simunic after the birth of his baby girl. The card questioned the intelligence of him becoming a father and I could not see the humour in it. It was personal and, from my perspective, way out of line. I refused to sign it.

In fact, anyone who sees this big teddy bear when he is around his wife and daughter will see a warm and caring side of him they might not otherwise know. Simunic's wife, Stefanie, and daughter, Allasyn, are both terrific and fun to be with.

Simunic stayed two years in Winnipeg. His outbursts in the newspapers were a real stress for Sam Katz and the organization. Near the end of the 1995 season, he made a mistake. I was walking past the dugout a couple of hours prior to a game when I heard him say to a reporter that the problem with the fans in Winnipeg was that they were not educated enough in baseball to know when to cheer. Simunic was upset that Winnipeg fans would cheer a good play made by the visiting team or cheer louder for a promotion than during the game. From his perspective, that was not what fans should do. Regardless of what he thought personally, he should never have criticized the fans out loud, and especially not in front of a reporter.

The Goldeyes' organization, like every other team, valued the support of its fans. Criticizing them in the media made no sense. They were welcome to cheer in any way they wanted to. Besides, I was always proud of Winnipeg fans and I loved the way they expressed themselves during games.

When I heard Simunic make his comment, I quickly stopped and asked the reporter not to quote him because he was just kidding. I instantly recognized the danger of his remarks. With his usual flare, Simmy brushed aside my interjection, repeating his statements and even expanding upon them. I shook my head and mumbled that I could not protect him from himself and I left. The next day his comments were printed in a Winnipeg newspaper. I believe that influenced Katz, who did not offer to renew Simunic's contract for the 1996 season. He told Simunic that he needed to think about it. Simunic was not interested in playing that type of game and found a job in Fargo-Moorhead with the new expansion team immediately after the 1995 season. He has flourished in Fargo, winning two Northern League Championships and making the playoffs 10 out of 11 years.

One of Simunic's most used expressions was, "You're killing me!" His blurting that out, usually accompanied by a grin, always made me laugh. I started using the saying and soon it was a staple throughout the Goldeyes' office. That day in the dugout in 1995 when he spoke to the reporter about Winnipeg fans, Simunic really was killing me, but there was nothing humorous about it.

He still calls me "John Boy". I think he uses it as a term of endearment. He used to chuckle and say, "John Boy, you know I love you," to which I would retort, "Well then why are you driving me crazy?"

After Doug left Winnipeg, we seemed to get along even better. We would visit at league functions and he would call and give me his State-of-the-League address from time to time. During each call, we would pursue all possible conspiracy theories throughout the league and then he would hang up, satisfied that his position had been expressed.

"Simmy" is a tough competitor. To be good at what he does, you have to be. He believed strongly in the place of independent baseball in the overall baseball community. The Northern League has been a better place because Doug Simunic has been in it.

Hal Lanier

In the late fall of 1995, the Goldeyes were looking for a new manager. Several names had been tossed around, including John Cerutti from the Toronto Blue Jays. One day, I received a call from Katz. He asked what I would think about Hal Lanier as a manager. I blurted out, "If Hal Lanier is available, why are you on the phone talking to me?" I didn't know Lanier personally, but I was very aware of his successes as a coach with Whitey Herzog in St. Louis and as a manager in Houston. He seemed like a great catch for the Goldeyes, no pun intended.

One of the reasons Katz hired me was because he needed someone who knew baseball. This was one time it may have paid off. He talked to Lanier immediately and signed him to a contract before someone else could. Soon after, Lanier was on his way to Winnipeg for a press conference. The press conference was held in January and it was freezing. We were in the middle of one of Winnipeg's really cold spells, even for the locals. The temperature was near -35C (-31F) and it felt even colder with the wind chill. After the press conference, where Lanier came across really well, we went out to eat. Walking from the parking lot to the restaurant was enough to freeze anything exposed and chill anything that wasn't – especially when you were wearing summer socks and shoes.

Lanier's first question to me was, "What kind of jackets do we get for the players?" I laughed and told him not to worry; it would be a few degrees warmer by the time May rolled around. It was a good thing he had already signed a contract because I think he was having second thoughts. Lanier lived in Florida and he had only read about winter weather like that. Fortunately for the Goldeyes, Hal and I began a real friendship that night and soon the weather was not an issue. He had many questions about Winnipeg and I was a passionate ambassador for the Goldeyes and the city. I'm sure some of my passion rubbed off on Lanier. He went back to his hotel that night and placed his feet on the heat register to get some feeling back into his toes.

Right from the beginning, Hal and I could talk about baseball for hours. He would tell stories about Willie Mays or Willie McCovey and I would listen, but in my mind I kept saying, "He's talking about WILLIE MAYS!" It was hard to believe that a baseball guy like me was talking to someone who roomed with one of the greatest players in the history of the game. After all these years, I still never tire of Lanier's stories.

I was a little concerned about our relationship at first. Here was a guy that played in the Major Leagues for 10 seasons with the San Francisco Giants and the New York Yankees and who had then gone on to coach and manage in the Majors. What would he think of a baseball guy from Winnipeg? My answer came quickly and what a treat for me. Lanier learned to value my opinion, including input on baseball decisions. He treated me with the utmost respect. Together, we became a powerful team working on behalf of the Goldeyes.

And did we have some fun! We golfed together, hung out together on the road when I traveled to watch the team, and had a few barbeques at my house during the season. Lanier is a charmer. He lights up a room when he comes in and loves to have fun with people wherever he goes. After a few seasons, everyone in town seemed to know and like Hal Lanier. In particular, he charmed a local Winnipeg lady and convinced her to marry him. Pam and her daughter, Krissy, were a welcome addition to the Goldeyes' family.

I would say our relationship was built on mutual respect. Lanier knew how hard I worked for the organization and he knew me as a voice of reason during stressful situations. I tried to take care of him, his coaches, and his players to the best of my ability. I'm sure he appreciated the effort. From my perspective, Hal was special. The Goldeyes were lucky to have him. He was a great baseball man and a real ambassador of the game.

While attending the Baseball Winter Meetings in Nashville, Tennessee, Lanier and I ran into Tommy Lasorda, long-time manager of the Los Angeles Dodgers. We went for lunch with Lasorda and he had such glowing things to say about Lanier. He told me the Winnipeg Goldeyes were very lucky to have someone of his calibre managing the club. It was a lot of fun listening to the two of them swap stories.

On another occasion, the Toronto Blue Jays brought their caravan across the country and stopped in Winnipeg for a luncheon. I sat at the luncheon with Blue Jays' coach Nick Leyva. He worked with Lanier in Philadelphia with the Phillies and told me Hal was one of the most knowledgeable baseball men with whom he had ever worked.

But possibly the greatest praise came from Whitey Herzog during the 2001 Northern League All-Star game. Whitey was one of the greatest baseball managers of all-time. No less than six times, he led his team to the playoffs, winning the World Series in St. Louis in 1991. Hal Lanier was one of his coaches in St. Louis. Whitey looked me in the eye and said, "This guy (pointing to Lanier) is one of the best baseball minds in the game. You should treasure that he is here." I always did treasure Hal. I still do.

Lanier, however, is a person just like the rest of us and, therefore, does have the occasional flaw. He was not a good loser. You could argue that trait comes with the territory in professional baseball. After all, it's not youth baseball where winning should not be the most important factor. Lanier was paid to win and win he did. Eight straight years his club made the Northern League playoffs. Consistent excellence is the mark of a great manager in my book.

But I learned that if there was any way an issue could wait for 30 minutes after a tough loss, it was in both of our interests to let it do so. To Lanier's credit, though, I can say that no matter how stressed he was at the conclusion of a game, he would always compose himself if I needed to deal with something immediately. Usually, he just needed a little space. I previously mentioned that I was wound up at the conclusion of a game myself, but Lanier was much more wound up than I was.

Why do I think Lanier was a good manager? Obviously, his record speaks for itself. After watching him call games for all these years, I can only marvel at his intuition and skill. For example, he is uncanny at predicting when the opposition is going to steal. When he calls a pitch-out, he has usually guessed correctly which gives his club an excellent chance to throw out the runner who is trying to steal a base. He sees everything on a baseball diamond. His mind is always calculating the percentages at every point in the game and what could be happening in the later innings. He consistently gave the Goldeyes an advantage with his skill at managing a baseball game.

I know those of you who have watched many games in Winnipeg can remember a circumstance where Lanier did not pull the pitcher soon enough or waved a runner home to try to score only to have him thrown out handily at the plate. Baseball is a great game for second-guessing. We all know the saying that hindsight is 20/20. After watching hundreds of games and using my 20/20 vision, I am still convinced that Lanier is great at managing a baseball game – one of the best I have seen. Many years during the Major League playoffs in October, when Lanier was home in Florida, I would call him to ask his opinion on a manager's decisions. I was convinced he would do a better job than many of the Major League managers.

What fans do not sometimes recognize are the limitations teams are under in the Northern League. They operate with a 22-man roster. Major League Baseball has a 25-man roster, plus the ability to bring up players from farm clubs if someone is injured. This is assuming, of course, that the team has a full roster and no one is hurt. A team has to have a back-up catcher so, with nine guys in the line-up that leaves only one or two other players on the bench besides pitchers. Seldom does a team have the entire pitching staff healthy at the same time either. If a starting pitcher is pulled in the first couple of innings, there are not always adequate healthy arms to carry the load for the rest of the game. This especially applies if the team has recently played extra-inning games or has gone to the bullpen pitchers often in preceding games. Only the manager and pitching coach have all of this information. It's a great part of the game to be able to second-guess, but I usually gave the manager the benefit of the doubt, especially when the manager was Hal Lanier!

That does not mean I never questioned Lanier or asked him to explain a decision. I love the game, too, and was sometimes curious as to why he made a specific decision. I had many good conversations with him as he explained to me what he was thinking in a given situation. He always had solid reasons for his course of action. One of the great aspects of baseball is its inside intricacies. Discussing the finer points with Lanier was great fun for me.

Hal knew how to play the game. He didn't play 10 years in the Major Leagues because he hit a lot of home runs. He played great defence and he did the little things that a manager loves. When you do all the little things correctly, your manager notices. As a manager, Lanier noticed all the little things that happened during a game. Fans frequently notice the statistics. Managers like Lanier notice much more.

Scott Neiles, a local Manitoban and former Goldeyes' coach, once told me the best part of his time with the Goldeyes occurred during games when he would be able to discuss baseball strategy with Lanier. They would stand together in the dugout and discuss the options available to them. Neiles told me that while Lanier would discuss the specifics of the inning unfolding on the field, his mind would be racing to the next time around the batting order and potential moves many innings in advance.

I had the privilege of watching Lanier play on a baseball field once. During spring training, the Goldeyes agreed to play a softball game in Eriksdale, a small town in the Interlake Region of Manitoba, against players from the local area. Goldeyes' catcher Troy Fortin was from the Interlake and we wanted to support this charitable endeavour. Lanier played second base and Scott Neiles played shortstop. It was just a fun exhibition game but to watch these two turn double plays and flip the ball around the infield was a real treat. The visions of watching a younger Hal Lanier turn double plays on a Major League diamond were dancing in my head.

Since a common theme in this book is to illustrate why the Goldeyes have been so successful, I should point out the obvious. The Goldeyes have always had a great field manager. While I know Lanier would have loved to go back to the Major Leagues, he was very happy in Winnipeg. The one travesty during his 10-year tenure in the city was that he was never named the Northern League Manager of the Year. That was ridiculous. Every team voted on the award and for some reason Lanier was never chosen. I believe there was a little jealousy at the beginning, since he was a Major League talent, but how people could justify their votes year after year is beyond me. He clearly deserved the award on more than one occasion.

Lanier's reign in Winnipeg came to an end after the 2005 season. Granted 2005 was a poor year on the field for the Goldeyes but there was still some risk in making the change. Time will tell. Katz was quoted in a team press release when they announced that Lanier was leaving the Goldeyes as follows: "I wanted him to stay with the Goldeyes, as did a lot of other people, but I respect his decision to accept the position with Joliet and I speak on behalf of everyone in the Goldeyes' organization when I wish him and the Jack Hammers all the best."

If Katz really wanted to keep Lanier in a Goldeyes' uniform, he could have done so. Hal called me after he accepted the manager's job in Joliet to thank me for my friendship and my work with him when I was the Goldeyes' general manager. "I've been around for a while," he said. "I know when someone wants me. No offer was made to me that indicated that I was wanted back in Winnipeg." That says it all for me.

I personally believe that after 10 years in Winnipeg, if he was not wanted back, the Goldeyes' organization should have simply told him they were making a change. He deserved that. It was only after they failed to announce a decision on Lanier's future, and deadline after deadline passed, that he found himself in the position of having to look elsewhere. He then landed the job in Joliet.

Scott Neiles

I have known Scott Neiles for many years. He played baseball in the St. Boniface organization in Winnipeg as I did. He also played professionally in Australia for five years. Neiles was one of the best players I had the privilege of playing with on a baseball diamond. He could hit and he was an acrobatic shortstop.

I always liked Neiles because he had respect for the game and the players with whom he played, for or against. I am nine years his senior, so when he came up from the junior ranks to play for the St. Boniface Native Sons, I had been around for a while. Neiles was confident but respectful of the other players when he came into the league. I admired him for that because he was likely the best of the graduating junior players during all the years that I played.

I introduced Hal Lanier to Neiles shortly after Lanier arrived in Winnipeg for his press conference. The two of them hit it off immediately and while I was not initially sure if Lanier would like a local guy as a coach, he was very open to the idea. They worked together with the Goldeyes for five years. Neiles knew the game and was able to contribute on and off the field. He enjoyed discussing player moves with Lanier and sometimes they would work themselves into a frenzy during a losing streak to come up with all kinds of scenarios to make the team better.

"Trader Scott" would have our infield, starting pitching, the trainer, and the remainder of our stock of baseballs all going to another team for some player if he thought it would strengthen the ball club. Sometimes Lanier would just laugh and sometimes he would agree. I almost always agreed with whatever they came up with but on the odd occasion, I would voice my concerns and insist that they sleep before making any decision. A couple of trades of very popular Goldeyes' players were prevented in this way, when rested minds decided in the morning not to complete a trade.

Neiles would coach first base during the games, help throw batting practice, work with hitters, and be a sounding board for Lanier. He was a very useful guy to have around. Right from the beginning, Lanier gave Neiles a lot of responsibility. It added a lot of enjoyment to the job and made him feel he was useful and a valuable part of the coaching staff.

Neiles was a little frustrated that Sam Katz didn't appear to see the same value in his contribution. One of Katz's favourite rants when he was negotiating contracts was that "he could find 100 guys who would do the job better than you for half the money you were asking for." I don't believe there were many local baseball guys who could have done what Scott Neiles did for the Goldeyes. I tried to explain to him that the comments were just Katz's way of negotiating with everyone, including me. Since Neiles' departure from the Goldeyes' coaching ranks, the club has always brought in a coach from the United States to fill the vacancy.

My life and Neiles' life became permanently intertwined when he came to work for me at Home Run Sports, which turned out to be a good move on his part. He met his future bride, Carla, at Home Run Sports, even though I told him when he was hired to keep away from her. He listened to some things I said, but not that one. Carla and Scott were dating for some time before I found out. They married in 1998 and, being a good sport, I agreed to be the master of ceremonies at the wedding reception. Four years later, the two of them, with a couple of partners, bought the business.

Rick Forney

Over the years, the Goldeyes have had a great deal of stability on the coaching staff. The fact that the team reached the playoffs 10 out of their first 12 years could be correlated to this stability. As of the completion of the 2005 season, they have had only two managers, the two most successful managers in the current Northern League. Rick Forney took over for the 2006 season.

Forney was a great starting pitcher for the Goldeyes and still holds some team records. He loves to have fun and is a positive guy to be around. Forney was respectful of the Goldeyes' organization. Of all the characters who have worn a Goldeyes' uniform, he is one of my favourites. His sarcasm and sense of humour keep everyone around him on their toes.

After the 1998 season, Northwest Airlines was on strike. Since most players flew in on Northwest, we were scrambling to get the players home. Jonathan Green drove two players, Tony Chance and Rick Forney, to Minneapolis to catch flights on other airlines. Forney told Green he was going to play for Fargo for the 1999 season. Green believed him and was still upset by this revelation after he arrived home in Winnipeg. I had to call Forney to have him confess to Green that he was just joking.

Forney was a player/coach in 2000 and made the switch to full-time pitching coach in 2001. He excelled in that position. The Goldeyes rewarded him by naming him their manager for the 2006 season, replacing Hal Lanier. He appeared ready for the challenge.

Other Goldeyes' coaches

In the area of pitching coaches, the Goldeyes have also been blessed. **Jeff Bittiger** doubled as a player and pitching coach the first two years under Doug Simunic. Bittiger could pitch but he also had a good demeanor off the field and was a good partner for Simunic. He led the Goldeyes pitching staffs to ERAs of 4.36 in 1994 and 4.83 in 1995. These were solid numbers at Winnipeg Stadium, where the left field wall was a scant 300 feet from home plate.

Bittiger was also Simunic's sidekick. He was his sounding board and the sense of reason during some of Simunic's more intense moments. I always liked Bittiger and he moved with Simunic to Fargo in 1996.

One of the best games ever pitched in the Northern League was a duel on July 9th, 1994 between Bittiger and "Oil Can" Boyd, who was playing with the Sioux City Explorers. It was a classic pitching battle. Bittiger deservedly outlasted Oil Can for the win in a 1-0 game played in two hours and 16 minutes. Bittiger recorded 15 strikeouts and allowed only three hits in the contest, compared to three strikeouts and nine hits for Boyd.

After Bittiger, came **Bob Kipper**. Kipper was a left-handed ex-Major League pitcher. He was a good man and brought a real professionalism to his approach to pitching. Kipper was instrumental in the Goldeyes' success in 1996 and 1997. His tutelage of an inexperienced Jeff Zimmerman was invaluable to Zimmerman on his rise to Major League stardom.

Kipper would go to the mound when a pitcher was struggling. He would put both of his hands on the pitcher's shoulders, demanding eye to eye contact. He was a strong advocate and teacher of the mental side of baseball. Preparation and mental toughness were two subjects he liked to discuss. Bob Kipper left the Goldeyes to join the coaching ranks of the Boston Red Sox.

The Goldeyes have had a number of other coaches who contributed over the years, including **Arnie Asham** of local curling fame and former Goldeyes' shortstop, **Chad Thornhill**. I attribute the signing of long-time shortstop Max

Poulin, out of the 2001 local try-out camp, to "Thorny", as Chad was lovingly called.

Doc Edwards

I had the pleasure of being the general manager in Sioux Falls for the 2004 season when Doc Edwards was the manager. Doc played in the Major Leagues for seven seasons and managed the Cleveland Indians from 1987-1989. He is another character who loves to tell baseball stories about his Major League teammates or players that he managed. The stories would never stop. One of his favourites occurred in 1963 when he was catching for the Kansas City Athletics. They were playing in Yankee Stadium in front of a full house on "Mickey Mantle Day".

During Mantle's first at-bat, there were two strikes when the A's pitcher threw a beautiful pitch that, according to Doc, was completely over the plate in the strike zone. Umpire Ed Runge called it a ball. Talking over his shoulder without turning around, Edwards said, "C'mon ump, he doesn't need any help."

Runge slowly stepped around onto the field, leaned over and started brushing off the plate. His eyes were looking directly into Edwards' eyes, who was sitting in his crouch behind the plate. "Listen kid," he said. "There are 70,000 people here and none of them are here to watch you or me. And they sure as hell aren't interested in watching Mickey take a called third strike, so just shut up and catch."

"That's when I learned a lot about how the game is played at the Major League level," said Doc. "From then on, when a sure Hall of Famer received the benefit of a close call, I kept my mouth shut. He had earned it."

Another of Edwards' best stories tells of the circumstances of his first at-bat in the Major Leagues. Again, Yankee Stadium was the scene of the crime. Edwards was in the Cleveland bullpen during the 1962 season when manager Mel McGaha called down to get him to pinch hit for the pitcher. Edwards felt okay in the on-deck circle until he looked up at the crowd. He told me that staring at 70,000 people in Yankee Stadium was a little overwhelming for a 25-year-old rookie. He told me he was wondering if there were that many people in the entire part of the State of West Virginia where he grew up.

When he got into the batter's box, his heart was beating so loud he thought he could hear it. His arms felt like they were made of lead. He was facing none other than Hall-of-Famer-to-be Whitey Ford. Whitey threw the first pitch just outside the plate and Doc wanted to swing but he couldn't get his arms to move so he took the pitch for ball one. The exact same thing happened on the second pitch. Edwards gave himself a talking to and on the third pitch, he managed a feeble swing but missed the ball. He was so upset with his poor effort that he froze and was physically unable to swing at the next two pitches, which were both called balls. As he trotted down to first base, he wondered if Whitey Ford thought he had a good eye when in reality, he had wanted to swing at all five pitches but was too up-tight to do so. Welcome to the Big Leagues!

Hal's welcome to Winnipeg billboard

Hal Lanier

Hal Lanier, Scott Neiles, Bob Kipper

Doug Simunic, Jeff Bittiger, Joe Aiello

Rick Forney

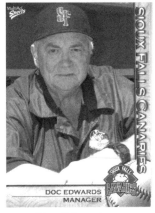

Doc Edwards

Chad Thornhill, Hal Lanier, Rick Forney

Chapter 8: Check the Line-up Card

Dealing with the players was a rewarding part of the job for me but it was also quite challenging. Jokingly, I have referred to it as being the den mother to 22 guys. I had to get them to Winnipeg (or Sioux Falls in 2004), ensure they had Canadian and American work authorization documents, find them a place to stay, order bats, helmets and uniforms that would fit them, look out for them so that they were happy while they were in town, and get them home at the end of the season, or sooner if necessary. Every year, I would personally have to loan players some money to get them through to the next pay cheque. Some of them even paid me back!

Sam Katz had previously operated a professional basketball team and he told me about some of the nightmares he had dealt with, like his players causing damage and getting into trouble. The Goldeyes' organization rarely had that type of problem with players. I think it's because of the type of person who plays baseball and, to some degree, the type of player who was recruited to play in Winnipeg.

I dealt with everything you could imagine. Travel, accommodation, immigration, and "Canadian" issues were stock items that affected all players. Family issues, money borrowing, bad tempers, large egos, language issues, and a host of personal problems were also common. Personal issues ranged from homesickness; difficulty adjusting to big city life; cultural differences; phobias, like fear of flying; and manias like kleptomania and egomania.

More than once, the organization was served with papers to garnishee a player's wages because of a paternity suit. Some of the players weren't being paid enough for it to amount to much money but we did what legally requested of us.

Arriving in a new city and a new country can be stressful, so we tried very hard to make the players feel comfortable immediately. Living in Canada for the first time required orientation. What was a "loonie or a toonie"? What was required to cross the border and work in Canada? Where should I bank? Did I get paid in Canadian or American dollars? Where did I park my car? The questions seemed limitless.

The orientation also included what the organization could do for the players and what the players were expected to do for the Goldeyes. Hal Lanier also insisted I talk to them about other cultural differences. Every year, he would remind me to tell the players about the flashing lights at pedestrian crosswalks throughout Winnipeg. I guess in some American states, pedestrians fend for themselves. To make it worse, in Winnipeg, once they push the button to activate the flashing lights, many pedestrians just start walking across the street, assuming the vehicles are going to stop. It would not be good to hit a pedestrian in one of those corridors. One of my stock lines during player orientation went something like this: "Hitting a pedestrian in Winnipeg in a pedestrian corridor can get you in serious trouble. In fact, hitting a pedestrian at any location is not a good idea!"

Most players were not paid much money. The minimum player salary in 1994 was $600 US per month for a three-month season. By 2006, it had risen to $800 per month for a 3.5-month season. No wonder the players had to borrow money. The entire team salary cap in 1994 was $72,000 US for the season ($100,000+ in 2006).

It amazed me that negotiating a contract with a player could come to an impasse over $100 a month. When one thinks of the ridiculous amount of money paid to Major Leaguers, it seems bizarre to be arguing with a professional baseball player over $100. But such was the reality of the Northern League. One of the things I would change in baseball if I had the power would be to share the wealth of Major League players with the players who might not make it that far.

Knowing how much our players were paid was a big incentive to me to take care of them as best I could. It was amazing how appreciative they were when I arranged cold cuts, pickles, bread, crackers and cheese before every game. I learned that it didn't take much to please most of them. It was the little things that seemed to matter. Arrange a good room rate for their parents at one of our hotels, or pick up someone's wife at the airport if the player couldn't be there, and you had a friend for life. In fact, doing any favour for a family member seemed far more important than doing something for the player himself.

We did have the odd player that liked to gamble with what money he did have. John Salamon, a relief pitcher with the Goldeyes, left quite a legacy with his exploits in gambling. One night in Duluth, several of his teammates reportedly watched him win over $6,000 in a matter of minutes playing blackjack. Salamon never asked to borrow money from me.

Another of my favourite players was closer, Steve "Tiny" Thomas. Thomas was a fun-loving guy unless he was playing some contest for money. A leisurely golf game turned into a nail-biting contest as the final holes were played in a tight match. Usually, I would just watch Thomas and Hal Lanier go at it. I had enough problems with golf without adding more stress by playing for money.

Host Families

Accommodation was one of the most important things to a player. Using an idea I first heard about from the Sioux Falls Canaries in 1994, we implemented the host family program. Winnipeg families were invited to host a ball player for the summer. Restrictions were placed on how much they could charge and, for the first couple of years, I visited every home to assure myself that it was a good situation for the player. A wide range of homes were offered. Some, however, were really not a fit. For example, we had single women offering to let players stay at their homes because, presumably, they were lonely, which we never felt was a good host-family situation. Some players may have disagreed.

One of the most complicating factors with the homes was the location. Sometimes good accommodations were not usable because they were not near other host families. Every year, I encouraged players to bring a car to use for the summer. Those with cars were easy to place in homes but those without were frequently more difficult. Jonathan Green, who took over host-family duties after a couple of years, told me on more than one occasion to sign only players who owned a car and agreed to drive it to Winnipeg. I told him that Hal Lanier insisted that playing ability needed to remain a criterion for signing players! Although baseball has more statistics than any other sport, there are none for "drives own vehicle."

Host families are important to an organization because many players are more comfortable in the security of a home environment. The younger players are not paid much, so economics is also a factor. The host families, of course, attend a lot of games so they are a fixture at the ball park and are some of the team's biggest fans. They don't host players for money, but rather, have a real desire to be a part of the organization and to help them. Host families have a special bond with the club and many of them have maintained long-term relationships with players that lived with them.

The home of Julie Bubnick was the first Goldeyes' host family situation. She helped recruit a number of others in her neighbourhood and liked having players stay in her home. "They are just ordinary guys," she said. "Everyone checks their egos at the door."

The first player to stay at the Bubnick home was Warren Sawkiw in 1994. Sawkiw might best be remembered in Winnipeg for being the player who proposed to his girlfriend, Debbie, on the field prior to a game (She said yes) and was traded the next day. The Bubnick family was shocked. They traveled to Thunder Bay to watch Sawkiw play later in the year and also attended his wedding in Lakeland, Florida.

Some of the host homes were so beautiful I wanted to move in for the summer myself. While we seldom had a huge excess of homes, we always seemed to have enough to accommodate the players who were interested. Many of the families remained with the program for many years.

In 1998, Brian Duva, the long-time Goldeyes' second baseman, was undecided about returning to play. Bubnick was leaving for two weeks in the spring so she asked Chris Kokinda, another long-term player, to stay at her house and keep an eye on her two children, Brian and Lisa. In the meantime, Duva decided to return to Winnipeg so both he and Kokinda played father, big brother, and friend to the two kids. During spring training, the two players drove the kids to soccer and baseball games and even offered guidance regarding a harassment issue at school. Julie could not have been more pleased.

Bubnick heard everything from the players and years later she decided to reveal much of it to me. She wanted to know, for example, if I was aware that Brian Duva one year sprained his ankle by falling over a cooler full of beer on the team bus, and missed a few games because of it. I knew his ankle was sprained, of course, but I was not aware of the circumstances surrounding the incident until she told me. I know now, Brian. At the end of every season, Duva used to say, "I'm leaving home to go home," which pretty much described the close relationship he had with his host family.

I also visited with George and Rosemary Wylie, who were a host family from 1996 until the 2005 season. They had no less than 15 players sleep in their home. The Wylies were another perfect example of how the program was supposed to work. We had conducted a short presentation on the field at a game near the end of the 1995 season to recognize families who had put players up in their homes. The Wylies were in the stands watching and after the game they met me in the concourse at the stadium and asked what the program was all about. They volunteered to participate during the next season and were a host family for ten years.

They opened their home to strangers for all the right reasons. They loved baseball and being a host family made them feel closer to the ball club. They asked for very little in return. The Wylies have been season ticket holders for all these years so they didn't even need to receive free tickets from the players. They had a few house rules, like no smoking in the house, don't abuse the animals (two dogs), and no one-night stands. Basically, they wanted someone who would respect their home and appreciate that they were giving them a place to live.

The Wylie's first player in 1996 was pitcher Paul Magrini. Magrini was traded to Sioux Falls as part of the deal that brought Jamie Ybarra and Andy Wise to Winnipeg – a pretty good deal for the Goldeyes. The Wylies, however, were devastated. They had become very close to Magrini and it felt to them like their own son was leaving. They did host another player, Peter McHugh, during that season and the start of the 1997 season but were equally distraught when McHugh was released after only two games in the 1997 season. Many of the relationships forged between host families and players were extremely close.

When McHugh arrived for his first season, all he carried with him was two bags. One was filled with his baseball equipment and the other with some clothes. That was all he brought to stay for months. When they first drove him to the ball park, he just stared in amazement. He had never played in a park the size of Winnipeg Stadium. When he returned the next season, he brought everything he owned but the kitchen sink. His truck was so packed when he crossed the border, he was afraid he would never get it packed in again if the customs officers were to remove anything for an inspection.

In 1998, at the request of the player they hosted, Joe Montgomery, the Wylies allowed another player, Art Baeza, to join him and also stay at their house. It didn't work out very well. Baeza and Montgomery feuded constantly. They even argued about who would get to sit in the front seat of the Wylie's car when they were being driven home after a game. That was the one season where being a host family had caused a great deal of stress in their home.

On one occasion, a player's father almost stayed longer than the player. Infielder, Chris Peckham was hosted by the Wylies in 1997. Unfortunately, he was released after playing in only three games. His father had arrived in Winnipeg to watch his son play ball but because of the cost of changing his flight, Mr. Peckham ended up staying at the Wylie's for three days after his son had left.

The Wylies have witnessed a wide range of worldly knowledge among the players who have stayed with them. Gerald Parr, a young man who arrived at the beginning of the 1998 season, couldn't believe he didn't have to wear his uniform to the park or on the bus ride to Fargo for an exhibition game. He felt like he had made the big time when he realized he was paid a per diem even during spring training. Unfortunately, he drove to Winnipeg from South Carolina but never played a regular season game with the Goldeyes. On his way home, his car had a flat tire and, unsure of what to do, Parr called his host family to ask for advice. George Wylie suggested he use the travel money he had been given, to get a new tire. "Thank goodness, you had given him travel money for the ride home or who knows where he might have ended up," George told me.

While the Wylie's have enjoyed almost all of the players who have stayed with them, they seem to have a special spot in their heart for Brian Myrow. Not every day does a guy living in your house make it to the Major Leagues. Myrow became the first Goldeyes' position player to do so when he was called up in September of 2005 by the Los Angeles Dodgers.

The Wylies credit the Myrows for getting them started on computers at home. During his second season in Winnipeg, Brian arrived with his wife, Tara. The Myrows hooked up a cable Internet connection, which they encouraged the Wylies to maintain when they left in September. The Wylies promptly went out and bought themselves a computer, which they now use to keep in touch with the players they hosted.

We did have some other interesting characters among the long-time host families in Winnipeg. Bob Brown and family hosted players for years. Mike Hickey still fondly remembered his time at the Brown's home when I saw him 10 years later.

During the 2000 season, the Brown's hosted Jack Jones. Bob Brown made a bet with Jones that the shortstop would not hit four or more home runs in the first half of the season. Four home runs were the most Jones had ever hit during a season in his professional baseball career. He accomplished his goal so, at the ball park prior to a game, Brown paid his debt by having his head completely shaved by the all-star shortstop.

Another player the Browns hosted was Victor Hurtado, who arrived in Winnipeg from the Dominican Republic and stayed with them in 1999. He went out on the first evening after being introduced to everyone in the house. Upon returning home very late, he discovered he had no key and took it upon himself to climb onto the roof of the house from the rear deck and walk across the building to one of the bedroom windows. He then began knocking on the window where the Browns' son, Jerrad, was sleeping. Jerrad woke to the knocking and to the sound of someone calling the name "Bob". They found out later that "Bob" was the only name Victor could remember from the introductions to the family.

It wasn't until the next morning that Jerrad told his parents the story. Later that morning, when Victor got up, he sheepishly told them he had forgotten his key and it had taken him a long time to remember where they lived. When he finally found the house and realized he had no key, he was unsure what to do. He told them he had mostly feared walking on the rooftop in the middle of the night. He was sure some neighbour would see him, think he was a burglar, and report him to the police.

On occasion, we had some special needs for host families. In 2000, we signed two Cuban players, Alexis Hernandez and Juan Carlos Bruzon, who spoke only Spanish. We needed a host family that also spoke Spanish. We were able to find a wonderful family in short order.

A Japanese player, Yasushi Hirose, in 2001, posed somewhat of a tougher challenge but, again, we were able to find a great family for him who spoke Japanese. Winnipeggers are generous people and were always there to help us when we needed help.

Communicating with these players was another story. I thought it was funny when Alexis Hernandez, who was the Goldeyes' catcher, would go to the mound to talk to the pitcher. His English was very limited at the beginning. He would talk and the pitcher would nod, but I was never sure much communication had taken place.

Talking to Hirose was even more bizarre because he spoke only Japanese. Unbelievably, our receptionist, Brigitte Dumas, spoke Japanese so between her and the host family, I was able to communicate adequately with him throughout the season. However, communication on the mound during a game was a different story. Rick Forney, our pitching coach at the time, was unable to have Dumas go to the mound to interpret for him, so he was on his own. No doubt, this lack of communication with Hirose was frustrating for both sides and may have contributed to his release.

I soon learned that not every player was suited to a host family. People were opening up their houses to complete strangers. It only made sense that the guest would have to live within the comfort zone of the family. Usually, it only took a few days for everyone to get comfortable with the situation but one of the players put some real stress on the program in 1995. On his first night in Winnipeg, he was introduced to his host family and immediately decided to drop off his belongings at their house and go out to a bar. He arrived back at their home in the wee hours of the morning, waking everyone up in the process. He had female company with him and the host family was not impressed. First thing in the morning, I received a phone call voicing their concerns. The player was removed from the home and was not offered another host family.

Some players may have had live arms, or came to the Goldeyes with solid track records, but didn't show up with the right attitude. Some liked to go out at night. When players didn't perform as well as expected, and had a suspect attitude, that was considered two strikes. The next thing they knew, they had been released. They were not offered a third strike in Winnipeg because they were already gone. Doug Simunic used to call it "Back up the cut bus!" Hal Lanier would say, "Let's get someone in here who knows how to play this game. These guys are professionals and they should know how to act accordingly." Neither Lanier nor Simunic had a lot of patience for poor play.

I liked to have fun and played baseball my whole life. I dreamed of playing in the big leagues. It really upset me to see players come into the Northern League with tremendous talent but proceed to waste it by staying out all night and not being ready to play to their potential at game time. There was plenty of time for a professional baseball player to have fun and still be ready to play every day. We started charting player's performances on Sunday afternoon games to see if it changed dramatically. Some did, and we had to wonder if Saturday night activities had something to do with it. Wasting, or not fully utilizing talent is one of my pet peeves.

Most of the players I dealt with were quality people. Some of them were leaving home for the first time. Most of them were working in Canada for the first time. They were excited to be setting out on a new adventure and were willing to help the organization in any way possible. I really enjoyed helping out those young men.

There was, however, the odd player who challenged my good nature. In the spring of 2001, Lanier told me he was having discussions with my favourite player from the past. I joked that he could sign anyone he wanted as long as it was not Mike Meggers. An ominous silence filled the room. I couldn't believe it. The entire organization was so tired of Meggers' antics during his first stay with the club in 1997 that he was traded to Duluth at the half-way point of the season, even though we had won the first half and he was leading the league in home runs.

On his first day at the hotel, he had changed suites twice because the room he was assigned was not to his liking, much to the distress of hotel management. Then the next

107

morning he marched into my office and demanded a big-screen television and a recliner rocker in his room. As he left my office, he flipped the keys to the car we had given him to drive for the summer, onto my desk and told me to have it washed. He left me sitting in my office with my mouth open. No player had ever spoken to me like that.

I immediately went down to Katz's office and told him about the demands. He thought I was kidding. He said he would deal with Meggers directly. I was unsure what that meant because Katz dealt with some player issues in private. At least, I didn't have to deal with it.

My day got even better when another veteran came into my office and asked to have the same furniture. That was the only time in all of my years as a general manager that a player asked for such furnishings. I don't remember being rude to players very often but that day may have been the exception. I remember my parting comments included, "Get out of my office!"

Most of the players were reasonable and realized they were in independent baseball and not in the Major Leagues. I tried to oblige them as best I could, but every year I eventually had to say "no" to a couple of requests. Only then did they realize there were boundaries. That's one of the reasons I referred to being their den mother; they would push until they found our limits. I suppose that's human nature. For the most part, I enjoyed my interactions with the players and believed them to be quality people. They were also good role models for the kids who idolized them and I was proud to have most of them representing the organization.

I dealt with close to 300 players during my career as a general manager. A few of their stories stick out in my mind as particularly interesting.

Jeff Zimmerman

Jeff Zimmerman was so quiet and humble it was hard to believe he could compete at the professional level. A 90-plus-mph fastball and a vicious breaking slider, however, allowed him to compete with anybody at any level. His success story is truly amazing. Zimmerman was never drafted. He had never played professional baseball in North America prior to his arrival in Winnipeg. He was a classic example of where the Northern League gave a player an opportunity to make it all the way to the Major Leagues. Without the NL and the Goldeyes, Zimmerman would likely never have been noticed.

He joined the Goldeyes for the 1997 season and pitched so well his Earned Run Average (ERA) led the league. He was signed by the Texas Rangers at the completion of the season and pitched one full season in the minors, where he had one of the lowest ERAs in the nation in any professional league. He landed on the Major League roster shortly after the start of the 1999 season. He won his first nine decisions in 1999 with the Texas Rangers, which tied an American League record for most consecutive wins to start a career. He was rewarded by being assigned to the 1999 American League all-star team by manager Joe Torre. What a thrill it must have been! All that happened in less than two years from his playing days in Winnipeg.

In 2001, Zimmerman became the closer in Texas. He recorded 28 saves, which tied him for eighth in the American League, and he had a sparkling 2.45 ERA. As of the 2005 season, he has had the most success in the Major Leagues of any Goldeyes' player.

Zimmerman's story is unique. He called me late one day at the office. It had been a long day and I was a little worn out. The voice on the phone said, "Hello Mr. Hindle, my name is Jeff Zimmerman and I would like to play baseball for the Winnipeg Goldeyes." My response was, "You and a lot of guys would like to play for the Goldeyes. What's your story?" I realize that sounds a little abrupt but, fortunately, I can laugh at myself now when I talk about it with Jeff.

Zimmerman proceeded to tell me he was a pitcher and had played on Canada's National Baseball Team. I retorted, "Oh, you're a real baseball player." You have no idea how many calls we would receive from players with no baseball experience but who wanted to play for the Goldeyes.

Zimmerman was a very engaging young man. We had a great conversation as he filled me in on his pitching career. He had recently pitched in France, which surprised me because I knew nothing of the calibre of baseball there, but I was very impressed with his style and his exploits on Team Canada. I immediately contacted Baseball Canada to locate some of his pitching statistics. The person answering the phone in the Baseball Canada office checked the roster of the National Team in the applicable years and told me no one by the name of Zimmerman was on the Canadian roster. I thanked him for his trouble and thought to myself, some guys sure have a lot of nerve and will say anything to get a shot at pro baseball.

All night long, though, I could not stop thinking about it. Jeff Zimmerman had sounded so sincere and he had given me too much information to be a fake. There just had to be a mistake. I decided to call one of my baseball contacts in Saskatchewan. Jim Baba is currently the Director General of Baseball Canada but he had been the head coach of the Canadian National Team during the years in question and I knew I would get the real story from him.

Baba immediately lit up when I mentioned Jeff Zimmerman. It was obvious he liked him as a person and thought he was a good pitcher. Zimmerman had pitched three years in the National Team program and he had a great deal of success. Baba was convinced that a healthy Jeff Zimmerman could play at the Northern League level. He expounded on his exploits as a pitcher on the National Team, informing me that Zimmerman had once pitched against the mighty Cuban National Team and held them in check for many innings. That was more like it! Zimmerman had not been exaggerating. If anything, he had not sold himself enough on the phone.

My next call was to Hal Lanier in Florida. I told him I wanted to sign a Canadian pitcher who had pitched on the Canadian National Team. Lanier was a little skeptical but agreed that if Zimmerman came to the local try-out camp, he would evaluate his stuff. That would have worked out fine except Zimmerman wanted assurance that he was going to be given a real opportunity. He already had a contract offer from a team in the Western League in California. I knew I didn't want to miss the opportunity with a quality Canadian player, so I agreed to sign him to a contract immediately.

The rules in the Northern League allowed teams to sign up to 28 players prior to the start of the season. Only veteran or LS-4 players had to be kept on the team's roster for a minimum of 10 days into the season. Any other player could be released in the spring, so Zimmerman was still in the position of having to show the Goldeyes he could pitch at the Northern League level even though he was signed. He was assured by this action, however, that he would stay with the club through the main two-week training camp and be given a fair opportunity to make the club.

Zimmerman drove from Calgary to Winnipeg for the local try-out camp in the spring of 1997. There were approximately 50 players trying out and he was one of the first to warm up prior to live batting practice. When he walked out on the mound, I was excited to see what he looked like. He threw a mere three pitches when Hal Lanier excitedly said to me, "Who is this guy?" I told him it was Zimmerman.

Lanier watched a few more pitches and then said, "Go and make sure he has a place to stay. We want this guy. Look at that arm." "Zimm" was pleased and we announced to the media that we were signing him to a contract. The rest is history. What a phenomenal season he had with the Goldeyes in 1997! His meteoric rise through the minor leagues and up to the Texas Rangers sounds more like a story in a movie than real life. It becomes an even more surreal story knowing that his brother, Jordan, was also struggling to make it to the big leagues with the Seattle Mariners. They were called up to the Majors about a month apart in 1999 and actually pitched against each other in July of that year.

Did this kind of success change Jeff? Not in my opinion. He remained humble and appreciative of everyone who had helped him along the way. He returned to help the Goldeyes at their 1999 Holiday camp, alongside Corey Koskie, who was with the Minnesota Twins at the time, and was a big hit with the kids. He is a kind and generous person and he lights-up when kids are around.

At the Baseball Canada Awards Banquet Fundraising Dinner in Toronto in 2002, Zimmerman was one of the Major League players in attendance. He was honoured at the banquet with the Alumni Award for Achievement after leaving the Canadian National Team program. During his speech, "Zimm" singled out Scott Neiles and myself and told everyone in attendance that he owed a great deal of gratitude to us for getting his career started in Winnipeg. He has been a supporter of Baseball Canada for many years.

Zimm told me during his first spring training with the Rangers in '98 that Lee Tunnel, a coach in A ball, was his biggest supporter. "I hate to think what might have happened if you hadn't called Babs (Jim Baba) or if Lee hadn't gone to bat for me. It's not just all about being in the right place at the right time but also about having the right people believe in you," he concluded.

Zimmerman's unfortunate arm injury has kept him from pitching in the Major Leagues since 2001. I met him in Toronto in January of 2006 and despite five arm surgeries, he was still focused on getting himself, and especially his arm, in a condition to once again pitch in the Major Leagues. Everyone who knew Jeff Zimmerman would have been thrilled if he had succeeded.

David Lowery

David Lowery was the Goldeyes' second baseman during the first two years of operation in 1994 and 1995. He was a fun-loving guy who enjoyed playing the game of baseball. He hit .284 during his first year, which was respectable, but he was a streak hitter. When he was hitting well, everyone left him alone, which is pretty common in baseball. Even with a terrible swing, few hitters would listen to advice if they were hitting the ball well!

Lowery, however, would listen to anybody when he was in a slump. Few players over the years asked for my opinion on their swing. We had coaches for that and some players would not even listen to them. Lowery did ask for my opinion and I told him I thought he was being too tentative at the plate and was not aggressively attacking the ball. I certainly take no credit, but immediately after our discussion he started hitting the ball real hard. You just never know what motivates someone. Hitting a baseball is as much mental as it is physical. Believing you can hit and being aggressive at the plate are critical to success.

My best David Lowery story is one he told me. Lowery is a graduate of the University of Texas and was invited one year to play in the Texas alumni game. He was happy to be there and during his first time at bat he was facing none other than "Rocket" Roger Clemens. He told me he battled the entire at-bat and finally hit a ground ball right back up the middle past Clemens. As he was running to first base, he was thinking, "I just got a hit off of Roger Clemens, a sure Hall of Famer."

Suddenly, he realized there was going to be a play at first base so he turned on the speed and was relieved that he beat the throw by a step. Immediately, the umpire called him out. When Lowery turned to argue the call, the umpire stopped him flat and said, "Son, do you see who's pitching out there? That's Roger Clemens. And do you see who just made that great play at shortstop? That's Spike Owens (Major League shortstop for many years). Sorry son, but you're just David Lowery and You're Out."

Kris Cox

I left the Goldeyes in body in December of 2001. I have never truly left them in spirit. In the fall of 2002, I received a call from Bob Cox, the father of a prospective player. He wanted his son to have a chance to play professional baseball in Canada. "Why Canada?" I asked.

It turned out Bob Cox was born and raised in British Columbia. He was an athlete who had played major junior hockey in Canada and professionally in Europe for many years. He wanted his son to experience playing professionally in Canada. I referred Mr. Cox to the Goldeyes but he kept calling me back to ask what the chances were of his son playing in Winnipeg.

I had received a lot of calls over the years from parents and most of them had no idea of the level of play in the Northern League. These guys are good. Some of the players are only one or two steps away from the Major Leagues. Someone who had not played at an elite level of baseball was not likely to be able to compete with them. Parents want their children to succeed and to fulfill their dreams but they are seldom objective. Bob Cox was different, though. He had been a professional athlete and he seemed to understand the quality of the players who were in the Northern League.

Upon reviewing his son's resume, my curiosity was peaked. Kris Cox had played for top Division 1, NCAA schools at Old Miss and the University of Southern California. He had also played in the Cape Cod League, which was a tremendous summer league where many of the top college players in the U.S. were invited to play. Cox was near the top of the Cape Cod League in batting average, an impressive statistic considering the level of competition. He had also played for the Canadian National Team in Panama on the same team as Donnie Smith and Greg Morrison, who were both current Goldeyes' players. Both of them thought Cox was a great outfielder and could help the Goldeyes. I contacted Baseball Canada, received a glowing report of his talents, and became convinced that Cox would have a chance to succeed in a Goldeyes' uniform.

As luck would have it, I was taking a trip to Orlando, Florida, and intended to spend some time with Hal Lanier. Hal and I were and, hopefully, always will be good friends. I suggested to Lanier that he sign Kris Cox, or at least bring him in for a try-out. He was skeptical and did not get a ringing endorsement from Nick Belmonte, the Goldeyes' player procurement specialist. Finally, Lanier agreed that if Cox would find his own way to Winnipeg, he would be kept around for the main camp and be given a legitimate opportunity to make the club.

By that time, I considered Cox my find, so when he came to Winnipeg I spent some time with him and tried to make him feel at home. He was a really nice guy and was soft spoken, intelligent, and had a very disarming smile. He loved the Goldeyes' organization and the City of Winnipeg from the beginning. And he impressed Lanier enough at the try-out camp that he was signed to a contract.

In his first game in Winnipeg, Cox hit a single and a home run but he did not get much chance to play early in the 2003 season. He was struggling with the reality that he was sitting on the bench like many players do. Most rookie players who came to the Northern League were accustomed to being stars on their previous college teams. Sitting on the bench was a difficult transition for them to make.

A couple of weeks into the season, I received a phone call from his father, Bob, who told me Kris was a little discouraged about not getting a chance to play. The Goldeyes were in a home stand so that very night I asked Kris to go out with me after the game. We had a wonderful chat. He was indeed a little discouraged and not actually sure how to feel. He had left a good job and his wife, Christy, at home in Denver and was wondering if it was all worthwhile.

I told him the decision was his and his alone. It was his life we were talking about and how could I, or anyone else, advise him about what sacrifices would be too much to make in pursuing his dream of playing professional baseball. I did tell him that my experience in the Northern League had taught me two things. Nothing was for sure in baseball, and things changed very rapidly. Player moves were swift and numerous in the NL and you just never knew when you would get an opportunity. That was partly because it was a short-season league and all teams were trying to win. Players were sent packing if they went into a prolonged slump, even when their career track record indicated they should be having success. Cox seemed to enjoy our talk and when I dropped him off at his hotel, he was in a better frame of mind.

Unbelievably, change occurred the very next day. Shortstop Max Poulin knocked on his door the next morning to tell Cox that both Poulin and third baseman Pat Scalabrini were injured. Cox was given his opportunity to play. To his credit, he made the most of the opportunity. During his first at-bat, he hit a triple off the centre field wall and ended up playing the remainder of the season. He played so well, in fact, he was selected as the co-winner of the Northern League Rookie of the Year for 2003. And to think he was almost ready to go home!

Brian Duva

For six years, Duva played an exciting brand of baseball for the Goldeyes. Diminutive at five feet, eight inches tall, Brian played the game with a great deal of heart. He had a lot of fun in Winnipeg but he came to the park ready to play. His 1997 season was dominant. He batted .332, scored 82 runs in 80 games, had 111 hits and stole 55 bases. He was fun to watch. As he left at the end of the season, I shook his hand and thanked him for such an entertaining season. Duva amassed great statistics over his six years in Winnipeg but equally important was the fact he was the public face representing the players.

Duva's speed was a constant threat during a game. In my mind, the most exciting play in baseball is hitting a triple. Duva had 19 during his career. He also had 180 stolen bases, which, as of 2005, just happened to still be the Northern League record. Duva amassed Goldeyes' team records in many offensive categories, leaving his mark in the record books and in the hearts of the people of Winnipeg.

After he retired, Duva was honoured at a game on July 20th, 2001 – an honour that few people will ever realize. "Brian Duva Day" at CanWest Global Park culminated with his No. 5 being unveiled to the fans in its permanent place above the left-centrefield wall. No player shall ever again wear that number in a Goldeyes' uniform. What a wonderful tribute to a player who represented the organization with class and distinction and provided the fans with exciting baseball for six years. And as if that wasn't enough, Glen Murray, Winnipeg mayor at the time, pronounced Brian an honourary citizen of the city.

Chris Kokinda

Chris Kokinda was one of the most fun-loving players to ever wear a Goldeyes' uniform. He remembers his time in Winnipeg as one giant ride. He recalls the usual clubhouse frolics and the excitement of playing in front of 6,000 fans every night.

In May of 1999, the Goldeyes were putting the finishing touches on CanWest Global Park. When Fargo came into town for an exhibition game, however, the two teams were not able to take batting practice on the field, which was too fragile. Arrangements were made to use Whittier Park, an amateur baseball facility about 10 minutes away.

The Goldeyes finished hitting and the Red Hawks took the field. The last two Goldeyes' players who were leaving the park were Kokinda and Duva. An ice-cream truck was coming down the road so they stopped it and bought a couple of ice-creams for a pre-game snack.

Kokinda decided to have some fun so he convinced the ice-cream truck driver that the Red Hawks were potential customers. With a straight face he suggested the driver take his truck right out into the outfield to sell a whack of product. As he pulled away, Duva said, "No way is he going to do that." But sure enough, the truck proceeded directly through an open gate and drove right onto the outfield grass where the Red Hawks were stretching.

Doug Simunic stared incredulously as the truck, with music blaring, drove right up to the players. Duva and Kokinda were rolling on the ground laughing. Later that night Kokinda passed Fargo catcher Chris Coste in the tunnel under the grandstand. Coste looked at him and laughed. "That was a good one!" he said.

Another of Kokinda's favourite stories is about the night in Fargo that the players wrote out the words to the Canadian national anthem. During the first two games of the series, the anthem singer had made mistakes. Fargo was a little embarrassed and players in the Goldeyes' dugout offered to provide the Red Hawks with the correct words for the anthem, as follows:

O Canada!

Our home and native land!

True patriot love in all thy sons' command.

With glowing hats we see thee rise,
The True North strong and free!

From foreign wine,
O Canada, we stand by our tall trees.

God keep our hands glorious and clean!
O Canada, we stand on guard for thee

O Canada, we stand on guard for thee

O Canada, we stand on guard for thee

The poor anthem singer sang the words right off the sheet provided. When the line, "With glowing hats we see thee rise," was sung, Red Hawks manager Doug Simunic looked over at his coach, Jeff Bittiger, with a puzzled look on his face and pointed to his hat. Then he saw the players in the Goldeyes' dugout laughing.

Both Kokinda and Duva told me that was the hardest they had laughed all the time they played for Winnipeg. The players meant no disrespect. They were just playing a prank and never believed the words would actually be sung. To my knowledge, never again did Fargo sing the incorrect words to O Canada. They printed correct versions of the anthem and if there was any doubt that the singer for the game was familiar with the words, they simply played a tape of the music.

I asked Kokinda why he once ran around the bases at Winnipeg Stadium naked. He laughed and said, "How did you know about that?" It was after the last game the Goldeyes played at the stadium in 1998. It was a cool September evening and after sitting in the clubhouse enjoying a couple of beers, Kokinda went back out onto the field with a towel wrapped around his waist. He dropped the towel and ran around the bases. Maybe he wanted to be the last person to circle the bases at Winnipeg Stadium because the Goldeyes were moving to their new park for the 1999 season. He couldn't remember what motivated him to do it but he remembered being very careful when he slid into home.

One of his more bizarre stories occurred in Thunder Bay. A young woman offered her car to Duva and Kokinda one night while they were eating at a restaurant. She simply handed them her car keys. They went to the parking lot and were unsure which car was hers, so they started using the keys to try opening vehicles. Finally, they found a match – a Ford station wagon. They proceeded to cruise the town and didn't return until near midnight. As they pulled up to the front of their hotel, the woman who had loaned them the car was waiting on the street. "Where is my car?" she asked. All this time, they had been driving in someone else's car! Unbelievably, the keys had started the wrong vehicle.

Kokinda was a very popular player in Winnipeg. I asked him how it felt to be a celebrity. He told me he never thought of himself that way. He never took himself too seriously. I think that was part of his charm.

Mike Hickey

Most players who played in Winnipeg told us they were treated better by the Goldeyes' organization than anywhere else they had played. Affiliated minor league clubs were serious business. Players were being evaluated on their progress at all times, with an eye on whether they could be Major League ball players. I visited with former Goldeyes' third baseman Mike Hickey in his home town of Honolulu, Hawaii. Hickey was one of my favourite players. He liked to have fun but he was serious about being ready to play.

Hickey was one of the players who still dreamed of becoming a Major Leaguer when he played for the Goldeyes in 1997. He had played for five seasons in the Seattle

Mariners' organization before coming to Winnipeg. During the long bus rides so prevalent in the minor leagues, he would sit and stare out the window and dream of stepping onto a Major League diamond. He realized those 10-12-hour bus rides through the backwoods of North America were the cost of his dream.

Humble about his own talent, Hickey realized he was a solid player who could put up good stats, but he was not a "blue chip prospect" who would be given a myriad of chances to show his skill because the club had a lot of money invested in him. Hickey enjoyed the life of a ball player. Players could sleep in and play a game they loved while getting paid to do so. They were admired by thousands of fans and especially young women, who thought they were pretty special. All in all, he said he had a lot of fun during the years he was traveling the world playing baseball.

I asked him why he didn't make it to the Major Leagues and he said he had asked himself that same question 1000 times. Many players were bitter that they had never been given a real chance, but not Hickey. He had been given a fair opportunity while in the Seattle organization, he said. He had attended big league spring training with the Mariners and during one of his first games, he was playing third base. He dove to his right to catch a well-hit ball but then he stood up and threw the ball over the first baseman's head. Hickey heard Lou Piniella, the Mariner's manager, yell from the dugout, "Get me somebody in there who can play." What a discouraging thing to hear! Hickey had been given a golden opportunity to shine and had not performed to the best of his ability. Still, when he came to Winnipeg, he was hoping for one more shot.

Hickey realized, though, that he was in the minor leagues. He laughed at guys who acted like they were in "the show". He played his last year in the Atlantic League with the Newark Bears. He said the Newark team operation was too slack for his liking. He preferred field managers who took the players and baseball more seriously, like it was in Winnipeg. He believed it was not too much to expect players to show up on time for games and bus trips. He told me there were times when they didn't do that in Newark and no one ever seemed to be held accountable. It was then he realized it was time to hang up his cleats.

Try-Out Camps

Walking out on the grass for the first time every spring was always a thrill. As general manager of the Winnipeg Goldeyes, one of my best days every year was the day we held the local try-out camp. Try-out camp signaled the beginning of the season. All the long hours in the office throughout the winter were behind us and baseball had arrived. I would walk out on the grass at CanWest Global Park (or the artificial turf at Winnipeg Stadium) and watch the multitude of players trying their hardest to impress the coaches.

I had been in their place at other try-out camps and I knew the level of excitement and the anxiety they were feeling. I could see it in their eyes. I tried to treat everyone at these camps with the utmost respect. It was a special day for the players. Many did not have the level of talent we were looking for, but they were all on the field to do their best, with the faint hope that their best would be good enough to get them into a professional baseball uniform.

The try-out camp was, in part, a public relations exercise because it was the first day individual tickets went on sale, and we held an open house that included tours of the park. Still, there was baseball being played on the field and a few of the candidates out there even made their dreams come true.

Players who made the opening day roster and had been discovered at the spring camp from 1994 to 2005 include Andrew Halpenny, Ken Smyth, Jeff Zimmerman, Dale Ballance, Lindsey Dahl, Matthew Dahl, Kalam Paull, Brent Zulyniak, John Somrock, Todd Bargman, Jeff Danton, Matt Mason, Yasushi Hirose, Max Poulin, Kris Cox, Kelly Hoffer, and Jayson Magee. I have already expounded on the exploits of Jeff Zimmerman and Kris Cox. Max Poulin shines out from others on this list as a player who made a dramatic impact with the Goldeyes and, in the process, became a fan favourite.

Poulin's sixth year with the club is 2006. He is a defensive dynamo and has made several Northern League all-star teams. "Maxie", as he is so affectionately called, has speed to burn and is very acrobatic. The fans love him. He arrived in Winnipeg for an open try-out camp in 2001. While evaluating the talent at the end of the camp, it was coach

Chad Thornhill, a former shortstop himself, who fought the hardest to keep Poulin. He loved his speed, his arm, and his defence. Thornhill said, "We can teach him how to become a better hitter." So here is a big thank you to Chad Thornhill from the fans of Winnipeg for recognizing the potential. They love their "Maxie."

Player Quips

I often questioned whether players were ready to play every day. We would hear stories in the front office that would make you wonder. Winnipeg is a fun city and players were treated like celebrities, especially by the ladies. No matter what players believed, it was impossible to imagine they could play at their peak if they were out carousing most of the night. Reports surfaced after the 1997 season that one or more players had even been drinking in the clubhouse during games in the playoffs. No wonder the team didn't win.

Players could be broken down into a few categories. About half of them still believed they had a shot of making a Major League ball club; a few knew their realistic shot was over and they were playing out the end of their careers in the Northern League; a few knew that the Northern League was the pinnacle of their careers. The hungry ones, who were trying their hardest to be noticed by an organization, usually had the most success. Our main concern as an organization was having players in uniform who were trying to win a championship. That was the hope of the organization and the fans.

Brian Duva

Chris Kokinda always had fun

Jeff Zimmerman

Rick Forney

Mike Hickey

Kris Cox

Chapter 9: The Fans

When I was the general manager of the Goldeyes, I must have said 1000 times that "Winnipeg fans are the best!" Now that I no longer hold any official capacity with the Goldeyes, and I have seen even more games in more Northern League cities, I would like to say, "Winnipeg fans are the best!"

I guess it's easy to say this when the Goldeyes set new attendance records nearly every year, but when I talk about how much I love Winnipeg fans, I'm not referring only to numbers. There are numerous reasons to value the people who come out and support the Goldeyes.

For example, Winnipeg fans stay later than fans in other cities. So many times I would look at another staff member and comment, "Can you believe these people are still here!" The Goldeyes would be losing by a 9-2 score, the temperature would have dropped to 10C (50F) with a wind blowing, and the game would be over three hours old. Yet, thousands of people would still be in their seats cheering every pitch.

My experience in many other cities was that the fans would not even show up if inclement weather was forecast – never mind staying until the bitter end in less than ideal conditions. Maybe Winnipeg fans are just tough Canadians and are used to rough weather. They certainly seem to be a special breed.

A unique characteristic of the Winnipeg fans when I was general manager was their desire to cheer every good play they witnessed, even if it was made by the visiting team. Leon "Bull" Durham hit a massive home run at Winnipeg Stadium when he played for the St. Paul Saints in 1994. It hurt the Goldeyes' chances of winning the game but the fans were excited to see a recognizable name in Winnipeg and cheered his accomplishment loudly. Our players and coaches didn't understand. I tried my best to explain to them that the fans were just happy to be in the park and they were being good sports when they cheered the opposition. Some players never seemed to fully accept that explanation. The lack of respect for this aspect of the Goldeyes' fans became part of the undoing of Doug Simunic in Winnipeg. He was not a big fan of cheering the visiting team.

Hal Lanier, however, didn't have a problem with the fans cheering a good play by the opposition. He told me once, "Winnipeg fans are a lot like fans in St. Louis. They also cheer good plays made by the visiting team." Hal coached and won a World Series ring with Whitey Herzog in St. Louis, so he would know. I personally love the way Winnipeg fans cheer.

Many people are not comfortable cheering against the opposition but prefer to cheer for their favourite team. In baseball, you really can do this because both teams are active on almost every play. You can cheer for your batter to get a hit or for your pitcher to get him out. You can cheer for the hit ball to land safely or for the defensive player to make a great catch. You can hope for the great throw to record an out or for the runner to be fast enough to beat it.

I have a sportsmanship issue when fans try to distract a free-throw shooter in basketball, or a field-goal kicker in football. That's not what sports is all about and it runs contrary to my sense of fair play. In that sense, I am just like the majority of Goldeyes' fans. And yes, I confess that I too cheer a good play by the visiting team. Good baseball is good baseball no matter who makes the play.

Besides, there is never any doubt who Winnipeg fans are cheering for and who they hope will win the game. They are having fun and show it at every turn. They laugh at promotions, tap their feet to good music, cheer the opposition when they make a good play, and go wild over the Goldeyes. That is the way it should be. I think they are good sports and I hope they never change.

It was also the fans that created the demand for better coverage of the Goldeyes in the Winnipeg media. In my opinion, the media were the last to jump on the Goldeyes' band wagon. At the beginning, Sam Katz and I would have countless meetings with different media outlets asking for better coverage. It was slow in coming. I'm convinced that every call made by fans to a media outlet asking why the game was not being broadcast or asking for more information about the team really made a difference. Media outlets know that for every person who calls, there are many more who think the same way but do not pick up the phone.

Other than attendance figures, there was little hard data to indicate the team's popularity but being so close to the action, my "spider senses" told me that interest in the Goldeyes was growing exponentially during the 1990s. It was hard to prove until radio statistics came out in 2000 showing that huge numbers of fans were listening to Paul Edmonds on Goldeyes' radio broadcasts. The high ratings even surprised the Goldeyes' organization. The number of people listening to the broadcasts rivaled the number of those listening to the Winnipeg Blue Bombers Canadian Football League team – a number that no one would have predicted.

How was that possible? Where did the interest in the team come from? Perhaps, baseball has a wider appeal in the general population than some other sports. Males and females, young and old, people from all walks of life share in the enjoyment of baseball. Price is also a factor. Baseball is affordable. A professional baseball team's market is virtually everyone in the community. The entertainment value for the cost involved can't be beat.

In my role as a general manager of the baseball club, I felt limited in what I could say regarding other sports teams in the market. I did not want to be perceived as criticizing the competition. I personally like most sports, but if you are going to talk about professional sports as family entertainment, let's be candid. Hockey at the professional level allows fighting as part of the game. Fighting is not family entertainment. I spent a great deal of time and energy trying to explain to my kids how to solve conflicts without fighting. Yet, the premier professional sport in Canada allows fighting within the confines of the game.

Fighting has nothing to do with hockey. All you have to do is watch international hockey where fighting is not permitted to see how good the game can be without fighting. Or for that matter, watch a youth game prior to the age that fighting is allowed. It's a fast-moving and exciting sport. I believe fighting should be removed from hockey like it is in every other major sport. Until it is, hockey will not appeal to everyone and is, therefore, a harder sell as family entertainment.

Football, on the other hand, does not allow fighting but it is a very physical game. The crowds that attend Winnipeg Blue Bomber games are more aggressive than Goldeyes' crowds. Beer-spilling and loud and obnoxious behaviour are more common at football games. Professional baseball clubs do serve alcoholic beverages at their games but still, there is a much different environment. Maybe it's because more families with younger children are at baseball games, or maybe the nature of baseball games is more conducive to an enjoyable, laid-back atmosphere. All I know is that almost no problems with intoxicated or rowdy fans occurred at Goldeyes' games in the eight years I was there, or in Sioux Falls in 2004. I'm not saying there were no problems, just that there were almost none.

I was quoted in a local newspaper after receiving one of my Northern League General Manager of the Year Awards as follows: "Hindle credits fans for creating the energy to draw upon." I didn't always agree with the quotes that were attributed to me in the newspaper but I certainly did in that case.

Now, if you were to ask me what I miss the most, my answer would be the staff and the fans. We were at the park so much in the summer that we saw our fans as much as we saw our own families. Visiting and having fun with people at the games was a significant part of our social lives. Our organization prided itself on being close to the fans. That included the players signing autographs but also the relationship between fans and the front office staff.

Sam Katz would frequently sit in the seats with the fans, as would I. We would hand promotional items out at the gates on occasion and be available to whoever wanted to see us. Katz attended many games despite his busy schedule. I missed three games in eight years, one for a family wedding, and two when Katz took me to the Major League all-star game in Atlanta. It was very strange to be in Atlanta watching Sammy Sosa in the home run derby when the Goldeyes were playing at home. Katz was the boss and it was his idea. He said the Goldeyes could survive without me for a couple of days. Hard as it was for me to believe, he was right.

Because I was from Winnipeg and had played baseball my whole life, I knew a lot of people in the community. At every game, I met people from my past. Baseball games are social affairs, which is a part of their charm. Some days during a long home stand, our staff would become worn out but as soon as the fans started entering the gates, all the tiredness would dissipate. It was the fans that got us through the rough times. Our staff felt blessed to be a part of something so good for the community.

Many people now just remember the Goldeyes' experience at beautiful CanWest Global Park but I remember the allegiance of the fans at Winnipeg Stadium. How else can you describe it? Attendance averaged approximately 4,000 fans per game every year we were there – at a make-shift ball park created in a football stadium. It was that solid core of fans that, in some ways, made CanWest Global Park possible. Public awareness of the Goldeyes increased year after year; it was clear that the demand for professional baseball was real.

That demand and support was accomplished in a stadium where no one had to buy a ticket in advance. Seats were always available at game time. Even at our "world record game" in 1997, when we sold 22,081 tickets, you could still buy walk-up tickets. Ask anyone in the industry and they will tell you, if you are relying almost exclusively on walk-up ticket sales, you are doomed.

After CanWest was built, attendance saw a sharp increase. At seminars in the United States, baseball executives would approach me but when they heard I was from Winnipeg, they didn't believe I could understand the problems their teams were having with low attendance. I would point out to them that we came through the school of hard knocks at a 33,000-seat football stadium. I could understand everyone's problems. As the saying goes, "What doesn't kill you makes you stronger." The adversity of playing at the football stadium made the Goldeyes' organization much stronger.

I wouldn't be surprised if many other general managers in the league would say, off the record, that Winnipeg fans are the best. On the record, of course, they would likely praise their own fans. The truth is, large numbers of Winnipeg fans would tour other cities in the league while following the Goldeyes on the road. When I was in Sioux Falls in 2004, every game played against Winnipeg, especially on a weekend, brought out a number of Goldeyes' fans. No other team would consistently bring the same following, even though distance between the cities would be shorter than from Winnipeg. I have sat (or paced) during games in Fargo-Moorhead where hundreds of fans from Winnipeg were in attendance. Don't think Fargo didn't like the rivalry between the two teams!

It would be negligent on my part to not mention the attendance numbers. When we started in 1994, there was great apprehension among almost everyone involved about whether local fans would support independent baseball in Winnipeg. I was not one of those people. I was optimistic from the beginning that the Goldeyes would get support. That is one of the first things I told Katz during my "job interview". I was sure local baseball and softball players would find the ball park a fun place to be during Goldeyes' games.

When we first started, attendance figures enjoyed by the mighty St. Paul Saints seemed well beyond us. The Saints sold out 242 games in a row at home, over a five-year period (6,305 was a sell-out in 1994). They were the envy of every team in the league. Sell-outs were not a possibility for the Goldeyes at the football stadium. Our goal was to get as many people as possible to come to the games. When you look at the challenges we faced, you can appreciate the exhilarating feeling of fulfillment when we surpassed the Saints in per game average attendance in 2000. The seemingly impossible had been achieved. We had come a long way and it was all because of the fans that supported us throughout the journey. Winnipeg became the envy of every team in the league.

I don't mean to sound like a bad cliché, but our philosophy was simple. We wanted to treat each person like a special guest at our facility. We would welcome them when they arrived by greeting them, treat them to a wonderful fun experience while they were there, and say goodnight and invite them back as they left. There is no rocket science here. However, if it's so easy, why don't all companies treat people that way? The ones that figure it out usually thrive for the long term. I like to think that other sports franchises and entertainment activities in and around Winnipeg tried to copy the Goldeyes and if copying is the finest form of flattery, I guess the organization should feel proud.

Sam Katz is the king of the splashy one liner. "The answer is yes – now what is the question," for example. I actually had one fan ask for a free ticket for himself and 20 of his closest friends. When he was told they were $5 apiece, he remarked that he knew that what Katz had said was too good to be true. Katz was the front guy. The staff dealt with the day-to-day reality.

Katz also frequently said in television interviews: "The fans are the boss!" A disgruntled customer told me one night after a particularly bad game that if he was the boss, he wanted to inform our entire pitching staff that they were fired. I told him he was the boss metaphorically but I would convey his wishes to the manager and pitching coach. I thanked him for his passion and his comments, which seemed to satisfy him. He had been listened to.

Everyone did think of the fans as the boss to some degree if they wanted to work for the Goldeyes. The customers were not always right but they were always the customers and needed to receive special treatment. If a fan was not satisfied with an answer given by staff, the likely response was, "I'm going to call Sam!" If I had a dollar for every time I heard someone say they knew Katz or would call Katz, I would have enough money to buy the New York Yankees. (Well, maybe the Milwaukee Brewers.)

Katz was diligent at returning phone calls and he was very good with people on the phone. He was readily available to the fans, which was an important part of his success.

In 1994, the club was in its infancy and people were excited that professional baseball was back in Winnipeg. In the eyes of the fans, the team and the organization could do no wrong. During a game in June, we were scheduled to give away miniature bats. The bats were delayed and were not available on the scheduled date so we stood at the gates and distributed vouchers to everyone, which allowed them to receive a bat once they did arrive. They didn't arrive until late August, but I didn't get one complaint from anyone regarding the miscue. I think people were only prepared to think happy thoughts. If this had happened in later years, it may have been different. While the fans remained understanding, there was a higher expectation on the organization to deliver.

Fan excitement from the very beginning was critical to the success of the organization. It was the motivating factor that inspired us to keep getting better and better – an attitude that was contagious throughout the staff. Not every comment from every fan was positive, however. We lived in the real world, where it was not possible to make hundreds of thousands of people happy all the time. That was the goal, however, and we came very close to achieving it.

Sometimes there were screw-ups. I preached that what separated a good company from a bad company was how they dealt with the screw-ups. Most people could accept that on occasion something had gone wrong. What they wanted was results in fixing a problem quickly, which is exactly what they deserved. The Goldeyes would bend over backwards to accommodate someone when we slipped up.

While it is impossible to mention all the fans who touched my life while I was a general manager, there are a few experiences I would like to share. One beautiful summer evening, I was invited to a "Section F" party in Winnipeg. Fans who all sat near each other at the games decided to have a backyard barbeque and listen to Paul Edmonds broadcast an away game on the radio.

It was not uncommon for fans who sat in the same section to form a bond, especially when they were season ticket or mini-pack holders. It was a part of the camaraderie of attending the games. The "Section F" gang was hard-core Goldeyes' supporters. I cared what they thought about the team and listened to all of their suggestions. I believe we had a mutual respect for each other. They were surprised when I accepted their invitation to come to the party. That close personal relationship with fans made a positive difference over the years.

In 1996, we played an exhibition game. A season ticket holder who sat high in the grandstand at the old stadium cornered me. He was furious that we had let Simunic go to Fargo. He believed that Lanier would only be here for one season on his way back to the Major Leagues. Every time I saw that season ticket holder at the park, I smiled when I thought of the altercation. Lanier's 10th year as manager of the Goldeyes was 2005, so I decided to question that fan one night about our discussion so many years ago. He remembered his outburst and had to admit Lanier stuck it out in Winnipeg far longer than he had expected. He did point out, however, that Simunic had done okay in Fargo for the past 10 years as well. He was still a big Simunic fan. Signing Lanier turned out to be one of the best decisions the organization ever made. Whenever a manager, coach, or player move is made, you have to wait to see how he performs before you know whether it's a good move for the club. I think fans would all agree that signing Lanier turned out to be a good move.

Another fan story involves an acquaintance who buys season tickets and sits in the last row of seats at CanWest Global Park. He doesn't walk easily so, with no stairs to negotiate, that seat works well for him. He frequently has a nap during games as he lets the baseball flow over him. Many times, I have walked by and smiled as I saw him with his eyes closed.

A staff member called me on the radio one night because he thought there was a problem with one of our fans. I raced over to investigate and he pointed out this gentleman, who, he believed, had passed out. He wanted to know if we should call the medical staff. I smiled and informed him that the man was just having a little snooze. Sure enough, at that very moment the fans erupted with cheers as the Goldeyes scored a run. Our sleeping fan immediately woke up and began to clap with the others. He didn't miss a beat.

Some fans stood out from the crowd. Dancing Gabe is a fixture at most Winnipeg sporting events and the Goldeyes' games were no exception. Gabe is a very nice guy and we got along well. He would move around the ball park, mostly staying out of the way of people, and then he would get up and dance to the music during breaks in the game. Everyone in Winnipeg recognized "Dancing Gabe".

Another pair of fans that leap to mind is the "Duva boys", who were more aptly called Duvaneers. Brian Duva was the most popular Goldeyes' player with the fans in the first decade of the franchise. As of 2006, he is the only player to have his number retired and displayed on the outfield wall. Two young guys took it upon themselves to make up signs. One sign read DU, while the other read VA. They would race through the stands imploring the fans on each side of the stadium to take up their chant. DU – VA, DU – VA, DU – VA would ring through the ball park whenever the popular second baseman came to bat or performed some other feat on the field. It created excitement and was a classic unscripted act that brought character and history to Goldeyes' baseball.

Chris Kokinda, who was Duva's sidekick, also received a special salute. When he came to bat, a fan would call out in a booming voice – Koooooooooooooak! Both chants were carried by fans to other ball parks throughout the league.

Another unscripted event occurred after every strikeout a Goldeyes' pitcher would register against an opposing batter. Season ticket holder Steve Heller, or his designate, would display a K, the baseball scoring symbol for strikeout. The Ks would be displayed so that everyone in the park could see how many strikeouts the Goldeyes' pitchers had recorded during the game.

In Sioux Falls, they built a pulley system so when a strikeout is recorded, Jerry Bouman, a season ticket holder who attends virtually every game, hooks a K onto a wire. It runs down the wire and bangs to a stop at the end, behind home plate – a great place for all to see. If you are unaware of the tradition in Sioux Falls, the banging of the Ks can be a little startling until you recognize what is causing the noise.

In fact, that particular activity created a situation one day. I arrived at the office early one morning and, soon after, I was informed that a very irate fan was on the phone wanting to talk to me. The person was disgusted that we would allow the Ku Klux Klan to promote themselves at our games. I immediately knew what he was referring to because the previous night, our pitcher had recorded three quick strikeouts and thereafter the three Ks sat conspicuously on view for a number of innings. After explaining what the K symbol represented, the caller calmed down a little. I just never knew when I arrived at work what the day would bring.

In 2003, the Goldeyes put pictures of their fans on the season tickets. Every ticket had a different fan. That was a great idea and recognized the close relationship the organization had with its fans.

When I went to Sioux Falls, it was interesting to recognize the same types of fans at the park. I came to the conclusion that every minor league ball park has a similar cast of characters. I will do my best to list some of them.

First of all, the kids get their own category:

- Little ones squeezing a ratty old mascot doll that is obviously loved to death.

- Youngsters sitting with their moms or dads hoping to catch a foul ball, and wearing gloves that are much too big for them.

- Wide-eyed youngsters looking for their heroes and hoping to get autographs.

- Young ones with eyes full of wonder (accompanied by a gasp of breath) when they see the ball diamond for the first time.

- Young children who are more interested in the mascot than the ball game (unless the mascot comes too close, in which case, they hide behind mom or dad).

Then come the adults:

- Season ticket holders who keep score every game. Some of them could tell you every statistic imaginable for the current crop of players and how they compare with players from the past.

- Fans that pace with worry as the game comes to its climax (I hope they don't bump into me during the playoffs).

- Fans that drink just a little too much beer every game.

- Fans who think they are members of the front office. They always believe they have the inside scoop on anything going on with the club.

- Ladies who try to gain the attention of their favourite player(s).

- Sweet elderly folks who bring an array of cushions, jackets, and illegal snacks that they pass around to everyone in their section.

- Business people in suits.

- Fans who are "the walking souvenir store."

- Fans who make their own stuff and apply the home team's logo because the ball park store doesn't offer it, yet.

- Casual fans who just want to kick back.

- And the loud-mouthed goof.

All of these characters are sitting at every ball park on the continent. They are a microcosm of society. I love to talk to all of them. Everyone has an interesting story to tell and most are passionate baseball fans and supporters of the home team.

Fans are a part of the entertainment package at minor league baseball games. Between–inning contests throughout the game require their participation. Sometimes they arrive early just so they might be picked to go on the field and act goofy. If the team is handing out a souvenir giveaway item, a number of people will frequently be lined up prior to a game to ensure that they get one.

A unique activity at Goldeyes' games that amazes visiting teams is the seventh-inning stretch. Singing "Take Me Out to the Ball Game" in the middle of the seventh-inning is traditional in baseball. Almost every team on the continent does it. In most places, the fans join in the singing. Only in Winnipeg is there a choreographed stretch that goes along with the song. Kristen Hodkinson and Tracy Smith were leaders of the Storm Performance Company, which danced between innings during the first few years. They created the actions to go along with the words in the song. They would stand in front of the fans and stretch in unison as "Take Me Out to the Ball Game" was played. Soon fans started to follow along. Initially, the actions were a little complicated and included a spin. Fans were unable to do that in their seats so the actions were quickly modified to their current form.

Every visiting executive that comes to CanWest Global Park is astounded that so many people in the stands join in the stretch. You can't help smiling when you watch the multitudes of fans having so much fun as they try to keep up with the movements. For many years my elderly father would wait patiently for the seventh-inning stretch and then join in. It warmed my heart to watch him enjoy himself so much. There would likely be a riot if the Goldeyes were ever to try to stop the tradition.

To highlight another difference that set Goldeyes' fans apart, I need to discuss playoff games. Winnipeg has always drawn well in the playoffs. The goal all year for every team is to reach the playoffs, so why would the fans not come out and support the team when they reached that goal? In most Northern League cities in the United States, that is exactly what happens as the playoff crowds are sparse. Minor league baseball in the United States takes a back seat to football once September rolls around.

During the 1999 playoffs, the Goldeyes played the Sioux City Explorers, then the Fargo-Moorhead Red Hawks, and finally the Albany-Colonie Diamond Dogs. The championship series was heart breaking for the Goldeyes as they lost three games by the identical score of 7-6. Over 6,000 fans attended each of the final two games in Winnipeg.

The reaction of the Albany players and management was dramatic. For days after the series ended, I received calls and emails from players thanking me for the incredible experience. They wanted to express their gratitude to the fans who were frenzied supporters of the Goldeyes during the games but who stayed at the end of the last game and cheered the Albany team as they were awarded the Northern League Championship Trophy. That display of class and sportsmanship had a profound effect on many of the visiting players. I felt proud to be from Winnipeg.

While it is obvious where I stand, I believe the words in this chapter speak for themselves. Simply put – Winnipeg fans are some of the best you will find anywhere.

"World Record" 1997   Running the bases
Fans loved their Goldeyes

Chapter 10: Only on Game Day

Why have the Goldeyes been so successful? There is a multitude of factors: baseball is a popular sport; the price is right; they have a great baseball stadium; they have a winning tradition; they have a vibrant owner; they have dedicated staff; the organization has always been close to its fans. Sure, all of these statements are true, but I believe there is one primary reason why the Goldeyes have been more successful than anyone's wildest imagination could have predicted.

The quality of the game-day experience has been the difference. A great game-day experience is created by a magical combination of consistency and the totally unexpected. These two things may seem to be at opposite ends of the spectrum but really, they are not, or at least they are not mutually exclusive. A professional baseball club needs to provide its fans with consistent entertainment. If you mix that with a crazy promotion, have unexpected guests, or give the fans something to take home, then you just might have a winner. The Winnipeg Goldeyes have managed to come up with the right mix with remarkable consistency.

When I was general manager, the baseball club operated from a philosophy that required all staff members to put the customer first. When people went to Goldeyes' games, they had fun. That made them want to come back. The winning game-day experience was created by a lot of great people working together with a positive attitude.

We viewed a tape made by the El Paso Diablos ball club at an El Paso baseball seminar, which stressed customer service at games. We used that tape and the concepts it promoted to create a closer relationship between the fans and our staff. Every year the organization held a training session for all game-day staff prior to the start of the season. Year after year, I would stand up in front of these eager people and tell them if they wanted to come to the park and smile and have fun, then they were in the right place. If they were there to date the players, then they were in the wrong place. Most of them listened to me. Our hope was that our fans would see positive people who were happy to be working at the game – from the parking attendant to the ticket taker, fan services representative, and concession worker, the Goldeyes' experience was all about having fun.

Game day is an exciting time in a professional baseball club's office. Putting on "a show" 50 times per year never becomes commonplace. At every game, something different happens to keep things lively. While we tried to plan each game long in advance, inevitably some details needed to be handled the day of the game. That created pressure on the staff because the doors opened at a set time and we had to be ready.

I loved the buzz of activity. A staff member would be writing up a game script, which would be reviewed by a number of others. Some days, promotional items had to be prepared for giveaway at the entrance gates. Some days we were preparing costumes for the staff or planning the logistics for a special guest or performer. Everyone had a different job. Our full-time staff had to coordinate and assist the 100 or so game-day staff that would arrive prior to the gates opening. Parking, fan services, food and beverage, barbeques, suites, press box, game production, security, medical, facility cleaning, and grounds crew all used part-time game-day staff.

Over the years, as an organization we had to deal with a wide variety of issues during our games but smoking was undoubtedly the most controversial. While smokers are sometimes loud in defence of their rights, they are drowned out by the massive numbers of non-smokers who want to be isolated from second-hand smoke. Being outdoors did not minimize the demand to ban smoking at the ball park.

In 1996, the Goldeyes were the first sport's organization in Winnipeg to ban smoking in the seating area of the stadium. The trick then was to find an area in the park where smokers could go. There was a progression over the years to smaller and smaller areas of the facility until, finally, people had to exit the park entirely and go out to the promenade to smoke, where they were completely isolated from the game. Last I heard, the Goldeyes were considering providing the radio broadcast for the smokers, just as they do for patrons using the restrooms.

On occasion, we would have to deal with an irate smoker, but for the most part, smokers have resigned themselves to the fact they are being restricted throughout society. The non-smoking trend has recently gained steam with many provinces and states banning smoking in public places.

Noise-makers were another issue. Some fans like to bring artificial noise enhancers to games. These items might seem to be part of the game for some, but others sitting around the noise-maker complained that the noise negatively affected their enjoyment of the game. Like any item that generates noise, it was not really the item that was the problem, but the way it was used. If someone was constantly generating noise near another fan's ear throughout the game, there would be a negative reaction. But if it was used only after the home team scored a run, the noise largely went unnoticed.

The Goldeyes themselves distributed hand clappers, duck calls, and inflatable bangers at different games over the years. Hand clappers became a fan favourite. Winnipeg fans would attend away games and take their clappers with them. Hand clappers can make 200 people sound more like 2000. The people in Fargo didn't appreciate Winnipeg fans showing up with their hand clappers. I think that resulted in increased sales of the clappers in Winnipeg because fans traveling to away games wanted to ensure they had an adequate supply.

The Goldeyes made the controversial decision to ban any instrument that made excessive noise. I understand this was a little subjective and possibly stricter than rules at many other venues, but we decided to make the best decision for the majority of our fans. Some people could not understand why we would not allow air horns, cow bells, sirens, whistles, or laser-light pens. Laser-light pens didn't make noise but they could be very dangerous to players on the field. At times, we may have disappointed an individual for the benefit of the whole but we made every effort to maintain a safe and fan-friendly environment at our games. Those decisions were widely supported by the majority of fans.

In 1995, the first decision the Goldeyes made to try to control the game-day experience was to hire their own ushers instead of using Winnipeg Enterprises' employees. Immediately, the name "ushers" was dropped and changed to "fan services representatives", which more aptly described their function. At the time, the baseball club didn't control parking, security, concessions, or stadium operations at Winnipeg Stadium, but we could control the fans' experience while they were in their seats.

Fan services reps in Winnipeg were initially the dancers who performed on the field between innings. They would help people find their seats and after everyone was settled, they would change and go onto the field between innings and perform routines. Before long, we had to hire additional people because the duties during a game continued to grow.

Fan services reps became an integral part of the "show" that the Goldeyes put on at every game. A unique interaction developed between them and the fans in each section. The fan services reps would toss candy and other products to the fans in their respective sections, encourage "their fans" to get involved, and lead them in the seventh-inning stretch. Some close relationships were forged, which created more fun for everyone. Many comments from fans were placed in our suggestion box requesting that the same fan services rep be allowed to work in their section game after game. At the end of the season, some of them received gifts from fans in their sections, such as personal trinkets, hand-made paintings, and pictures drawn by kids.

We tried to make the fan services reps feel like members of the Goldeyes' family. We knew how important they were to the overall game experience. Some fabulous people came to work at the games over the years. Many of them were students looking for summer employment. Some, however, were older. They were housewives or workers who looked upon the games as a change of pace in their lives and an exciting way to spend a few hours. The fact that we were paying them was really a bonus for some.

Kim Robinson was the first fan services rep who was not a member of the dance team. She was a computer systems analyst whose high-tech job was very stressful. I met Kim when she was attending a game in August, 1995. Our "world record game" was fast approaching and we were in desperate need of more fan services reps to handle the expected 20,000 people who would be attending. Kim volunteered to work the game and then asked if she could also volunteer during the remainder of that season. Volunteers are usually welcomed by a professional baseball club.

I asked Kim why she wanted to work at our games and she raised her eyebrows and said, "Work! John, this is not work. I work during the day. I'm here to have some fun with these great people."

She told me a story that summed up her experience. After a particularly stressful day at work, she was volunteering at a Goldeyes' game in 1995 but was finding it hard to act happy; she felt she would rather be lying on her couch at home. A young fan came up the stairs in her section wearing a baseball glove that was much too big for him. As he reached the top of the stairs and the field came into view, his eyes grew as big as saucers and he let out a squeal of glee. "Look at that, dad!" he exclaimed, the excitement resonating from his beaming face. For the remainder of that evening, all Kim could do was smile. Telling me this story, years later, still brought tears to her eyes.

Kim worked at the games as an escape from everyday life, with a goal of enjoying the atmosphere! What a great way to look at the experience – a place to go and have fun! How many fans felt the same way? When "Cotton-Eyed Joe" or some other catchy tune would be played over the PA system, Kim would start dancing. The next thing you knew some of the people in her section would be dancing, too. Her positive attitude helped everyone around her have a good time. Many fan services reps after her, too many to mention, shared that joy of working at Goldeyes' games.

We started the 1994 season by using a number of different personalities to act as public address announcer at games. Sam Katz initially thought it would be good to have different local media representatives perform the duties. No doubt, he figured that would expose them to the Goldeyes and they might later talk about the club on the air. It became apparent to me, however, that the idea would not be effective in the long run. It was difficult to schedule the various people and as the game scripts became more complicated, the PA announcer's job grew in importance and difficulty. Having a different person every night was proved to be a nightmare for our game production.

One night, I was posed with two problems. The person doing the PA announcing was struggling with the fast-moving game script. Furthermore, we were playing an afternoon game the next day and we had been unable to find anyone to work. I found the solution to the problems sitting in the stands.

Ron Arnst was a baseball acquaintance I knew who had worked as the PA announcer at the World Youth Baseball Championships in Brandon, Manitoba. He had also been the emcee at a couple of functions I had attended. I had seen Arnst a few times at Goldeyes' games and this particular night, I sat and visited with him for a while. I asked if he could help us out the next afternoon. He agreed, and after listening to him for one game, Kevin Moore, who was responsible for game production, and I agreed we needed to convince him to come back. It didn't take much convincing.

Arnst celebrates his 13th year with the club in 2006. He has been an integral part of the Goldeyes' game experience. He loves baseball and it shows. At the beginning, he was very careful not to comment during the play of the game, which was a traditional approach for baseball. With a little prodding and encouragement, however, he began to interject the odd comment that added to the fan's enjoyment. Sometimes he explained what had just happened on the field and sometimes he simply boomed out over the PA system the name of a player who had made a great play. Fortunately, he was knowledgeable about baseball so he knew when it was most appropriate to comment and when it was not.

With Arnst's help, we encouraged our fans to get on their feet for the last out of the game, especially when two strikes were on the batter. It's a tradition in baseball and now it is a common practice at Goldeyes' games. Initially, fans were not aware what was expected of them.

The press box is a wild and crazy place during a game but sometimes the pace of the game allows time for idle banter back and forth between staff members. They can also become a little giddy during a long home stand. Arnst was usually in the midst of the ruckus. He liked to have fun and I liked hanging around the press box at times just to share in it.

I asked Arnst to tell me about some of his special Goldeyes' moments. He remembered many exciting plays on the field but surprisingly, what he thought of first occurred during rain delays. One of his favourite stories started with Rick Forney, who was a Goldeyes' pitcher at the time. Forney was sitting on a bucket and pretending to be fishing in the rain. He was sitting there in a rain poncho and pretending to cast onto the tarp that was covering the infield. The fans, who were waiting patiently for the weather to clear, found it amusing. One time, while Forney was pretending to be fishing, Marty Neff, a hefty infielder, came barreling along and slid head first on the infield tarp right towards Forney's fishing line. It was a hilarious sight and Arnst added to the fun when he commented over the PA system, "It looks like Rick has just caught himself a whale!" Such comments showed his great sense of humour and his ability to add to the fans' experience.

Arnst has made his mark by weaving his personality into every Goldeyes' game. Some of his most famous quotes:

At the start of every game, he would introduce the home club by blasting into the microphone, "Okay folks – Let's really hear it for your Winnipeeegg Goooooooldeyeeeees!" The longer he could hold the words, the louder the crowd became.

"Your attention please! If you own the vehicle with licence number _____, your lights are on. But don't worry, they will eventually go out by themselves."

(Somber tone) "Your attention please! If you own vehicle with licence number _____, (exciting tone) CONGRATULATIONS! "You have the dirtiest car in the parking lot. Go to the fan services booth to collect your free car wash coupon." Every game, year after year, he made that announcement. Every game, fans in the stands laughed. His delivery was the reason it worked.

Foul balls have always been a part of baseball but, as a general manager, they made me cringe because every foul ball was an opportunity for someone to get hurt or for a vehicle to be damaged. After a few seasons, my car looked like it had been in a hail storm.

On the other hand, foul balls were great for the fans. The value placed on retrieving a used baseball never ceased to amaze me. Fans would fall all over themselves in an attempt to catch a foul ball. And if someone succeeded, everyone else in the stadium cheered for them – all over a ball that was worth six dollars when it was new.

As a general manager, I thought it would be wise to capitalize on the phenomenon so we created a promotion that rewarded fans who caught foul balls before they bounced, by giving them a prize. I do love Salisbury burgers which have been the prize for a few years but my favourite prize was a three-piece chicken dinner. Not that it was such a great prize but, "Congratulations! That catch has just won you a three-piece chicken dinner," had a nice ring to it. The chicken-clucking sound effect was also a nice touch. The fans were rewarded for something they were going to do anyway, so I realized any prize would suffice to make the promotion work.

Several times per game a foul ball was hit completely out of the ball park. Some fans even stood in the parking lot waiting for a ball to come. Others hung over the railing and watched the action below. One night, a ball was hit into the parking lot and one of our parking lot attendants picked it up. The staff was under instruction to return balls to the security office but this time, the attendant succumbed to the cries of the fans from the concourse, who were leaning over the railing imploring him to give them the ball. He fired it up to the concourse and hit a woman square on the shoulder.

Courts have ruled that the possibility of being injured during games by a batted ball is part of the risk of watching a baseball game. A ball thrown by a parking lot attendant and hitting a fan was obviously not contemplated in that ruling. The Goldeyes could have been held liable. Fortunately, the woman was not badly injured.

I received another foul ball story from a very reliable source. When the Goldeyes still played in Winnipeg Stadium, a foul ball was hit into the crowd and struck a woman. According to procedure, fan services staff and medical personnel arrived on the scene immediately to assist if she was injured. Although she was hurting badly, the woman claimed she was fine. The staff took her at her word and returned to their stations. Days later, I discovered she had, indeed, been hurt and had a wicked bruise on her leg, which took a long time to heal. Immediate medical treatment at the time of the incident would have reduced the damage so why had she not admitted to the injury? It turns out she was embarrassed because she had not shaved her legs!

Another bizarre incident occurred when a fan was injured by a thrown article – an ice-cream bar. After "Take Me Out To

The Ball Game" was sung during the seventh-inning stretch, staff threw ice-cream bars into the stands as part of a sponsored promotion. One night, a well-meaning fan services rep threw an ice-cream bar up to a sky-suite. He really had to fire it with good velocity to reach that level and it struck a fan right below the eye. Imagine having to explain that your black eye was caused by an errant ice-cream bar.

I am a firm believer that you can learn from everyone. I attended many Northern League games in different cities. Since I became a general manager, I have been unable to sit and watch a sporting event or any other public event, simply as a fan or spectator. I am forever analyzing the production, whether it's a banquet, a Remembrance Day Service, a wedding, or another sporting event. Sometimes I think of the compulsion as a curse. The days of just kicking back and enjoying the atmosphere are over.

The key to good production of an event is to analyze what you are doing from the attendee's perspective. It sounds simple, but not everyone can look at themselves from an outside perspective.

Maintaining an open mind to learning is also a skill. It is easy to think you have all the answers when you are successful but, chances are, you don't. One staff member told me she didn't feel she had learned anything at a seminar we attended in El Paso, Texas. She had not maintained an open mind.

I attended a Northern League game in Duluth with approximately 1200 fans. In spite of the small attendance, I spent my time analyzing the entire facility and studying the game production to see if there was anything we could use. I found something in the concession stand.

The Dukes were selling sliced-up apples in a plastic container with a caramel dipping sauce. They were fantastic and I returned to Winnipeg determined to find some healthy food choices for our park. Our staff discussed the idea and the very successful fruit stand at Goldeyes' games was the result. A closed mind would not have found that gem.

Game-Day Incidents

When you put thousands of fans into the park day after day, some unusual events are bound to happen. For example, one night some guys renting a suite insisted on having the door locked. They said they would come out if they wanted a server to bring them anything. That had never happened before. Finally, staff used a master key to open the door and found two half-dressed women entertaining a group of 15 guys. The women had been invited as the feature entertainment for a stag party. While some of our younger male staff members were disappointed that they had not witnessed the show, we brought a quick end to the performance. It amazes me that people would think they could use a suite at a ball game for such a purpose.

Prior to another game, a newspaper reporter walked down to the Goldeyes' dugout and left a wire, not visible from inside, hanging in the dugout and connected to a tape recorder. I presume he was trying to get information or quotes from the players or coaches without their knowledge. A fan services rep saw what happened but could not immediately find a full-time staff member so she decided to act on her own. She went to the tape recorder and turned it off. When the reporter returned for his tape just prior to game time, he was puzzled, and disappointed to find a blank tape.

Every year, the Goldeyes would allow the Scouts to sleep on the outfield grass overnight after a game. Every year I was nervous about the event. We were responsible for the protection and well-being of a lot of children. I was adamant that security be extra vigilant and that the facility be in peak condition for the event. One year, the cleaners had come right after the game to clean up while the Scouts were watching a movie on the video board. They collected all the refuse generated during the game and placed it in a garbage compactor at the rear of the facility. Unfortunately, the compactor lid was not closed properly and the garbage all shot out onto the parking lot.

A "mountain of garbage," my sources tell me, was worked at for quite a while prior to my arrival in the morning, with the hope that I would not see the mess. No doubt there were many other incidents that I was not privy to during my tenure. Security, cleaning, and even the medical personnel, who were all staying in the facility throughout the night, pitched in to solve the problem.

Speaking of medical personnel, accidents do happen at baseball games. The Goldeyes had a fabulous team of qualified medical people stationed throughout the park. Stefan Zueff, who has led the team for many years, is a certified paramedic. I was proud that our organization had made the decision to ensure that top quality medical care was available to our fans. My career background before baseball was as a public health inspector and an occupational safety officer. Safety and health were important issues to me. The significance of these decisions became apparent one fateful night in 2002.

About 20 minutes prior to the beginning of a game, an elderly gentleman collapsed in the promenade at the base of the stairs. Medical personnel reached his side less than a minute later. No visible signs of life were present. There was no heart rate and he was not breathing. Immediately, someone was dispatched to call 911 and the paramedics began CPR (cardiopulmonary resuscitation). A large crowd had gathered around the man and additional Goldeyes' staff members immediately created a perimeter.

A defibrillator was used to restore the man's heart rate and a breathing tube was inserted to facilitate the efforts of staff who were still breathing for him. Two intravenous lines were also installed. The ambulance arrived approximately 15 minutes after being called and took over all emergency procedures. At the hospital sometime later, the man began breathing on his own.

Our medical people told me he would likely have died at the base of the stairs if the system and proper equipment had not been available. Few decisions over the years could be credited with saving someone's life, but it appears the decision to have good medical people and equipment in place did.

I asked Stefan Zueff for some comments on the successful outcome of the incident. These were his words: "A lot of things made this possible, the least of which was the EMS department's involvement... This was possible because of the Goldeyes' attitude towards fan safety with regard to medical care, specifically your attitude. Furthermore, you approved the purchase of the defibrillator (a device that was not cheap), as well as all the other equipment we needed to do our jobs."

While I appreciate those kind words, I disagree with Zueff in one regard. I believe that during that incident, and many others, he and the paramedics at the park proved they were first class, and it was the quality of the people who worked at the games that was the key factor in the success of the program.

During another game on a hot summer day, an incident occurred that taught us a lot about our fans. Someone reported to our staff that a dog had been left in a vehicle in the parking area and a window in the vehicle was only slightly open. The person was concerned that the dog was suffering and might become dehydrated if something wasn't done soon. We immediately announced the situation over the PA system and encouraged the person responsible to get back to the vehicle. The PA announcement reminded the person, and of course, everyone else in the crowd, how quickly the temperature can rise in a closed vehicle. The response was a gasp of horror from the fans.

Fortunately, the person responsible got back to the vehicle and the problem was resolved very quickly. That was when we learned our lesson. About 10 minutes after the initial announcement, a woman arrived at the fan services desk and demanded to know what had become of the dog left in the car. "Don't you realize there are literally thousands of people wanting to know if the dog is okay?" she asked. I think she was about to break into the vehicle and save the animal herself.

Fortunately, we were able to announce that the situation had been resolved. We heard a collective sigh of relief from our fans, followed by a loud cheer. From that day on, when any serious situation was announced over the public address system, we would also announce the resolution if at all possible.

There is constant pressure on the staff during games as they welcome thousands of people into the park. Because fan safety becomes the organization's responsibility, the Goldeyes hired their own security personnel. Since 1999, Paul Dartnell, who was a City of Winnipeg policeman for 30 years, has coordinated security. It was important to have security but recognize that we were mostly dealing with families and people out having a relaxing time at a ball game. Over the years, the odd incident involving missing persons, physical confrontations, attempted car break-ins in the parking lots, drug violations, and panhandlers did occur.

It was always important to have security in place for those rare occasions.

While it's not fun to think about, the worst case scenario at a public place is the abduction of a child, or even a child who cannot find his or her parents. In 2000, we implemented a program called "Code Adam". It's a widely known program created to help public facilities deal with this horrific threat. We first heard of it through our contact at the public library who had been to a conference where the program was presented. We received information and created a plan for the ball park. If a parent came to us and said his or her child was lost, the plan was immediately triggered. Exits were secured and the entire facility systematically searched.

We were always successful in re-uniting lost children with their parents but it was comforting to know that we had a plan in place. One day, a mother came to the fan services booth and informed our staff that her eight-year-old son was missing. Almost immediately, the exits were secured and a PA announcement was made asking everyone if they had seen the lost boy. Initially, it was assumed the child was just roaming the facility. We checked the restrooms to no avail and a couple of minutes passed but still no child appeared. The mother was becoming anxious.

I went on the staff radio and told everyone that we needed to act. A description was aired over the radio and I directed our PA announcer to make an announcement that really got people's attention. Ron Arnst was the announcer and he knew exactly what I meant. "Fans," he said. "Please pay attention. I have an important announcement to make. We have a lost eight-year-old boy. He is in the ball park. We need 6,000 pairs of eyes looking for him right now. He is wearing a striped blue and orange shirt and his name is Adam. (The name has been changed to protect the innocent.) We have a very anxious mother and we need to help her. Everyone please look around you."

Within seconds, Adam was found. He was happily eating the popcorn he had purchased, but was sitting in the wrong section. He had started to wonder why his mother was not in her seat.

Their joyous reunion was heart-warming to watch but it made me realize that a definitive plan in these circumstances was a valuable tool. Over the years, "Code Adam" was successfully used a number of times.

One strange day in 1998, the staff radios were used for a different purpose. At the conclusion of a game, we noticed that a staff member's purse had been stolen. We quickly determined that the person responsible had to be a visiting mascot. We knew this person was carting a huge bag carrying the mascot costume and had just walked over to Polo Park Shopping Centre, a large complex very close to the stadium. Immediately, several staff members converged on the shopping centre and searched for the suspect, staying in touch with each other by radio. Unfortunately, the search did not find the culprit but the staff member was impressed that we cared about her dilemma and had exploded into action.

Baseball knowledge was not a prerequisite for working for the Goldeyes. A case in point would be the first time I asked Lorraine Maciboric to stand at the fan services booth during a game and answer questions. One of her first clients came to the booth, looked around, then said, "Are there no line-ups tonight?" Without batting an eye, Lorraine responded, "No, it has been a slow night so far!" The fan gave her a strange look and left. She told Barb McTavish what had happened and Barb laughed and showed Lorraine the player line-up sheets that we had available for fans. "Don't ever tell anyone who works here this story," Barb recommended. I never heard it until long after I had left the Goldeyes.

On occasion, due to the intense nature of the job, the staff had to find ways to let off steam before or during games. Game 5 in a six-game series was frequently the most difficult. Many times, the tension could be broken in the office by making fun of the fact that someone had "Game 5 attitude."

I recall a few instances when we became downright giddy. One night, Barb McTavish called me on the two-way radio because the visiting manager was roaming the facility during the game and she was convinced he was trying to spy on the Goldeyes. She invented the code words "The Red Rooster Crows at Midnight." That meant some conspiracy could be brewing, so anytime I heard those words over the radio, I would search McTavish out to determine what was going on.

The first night I heard "The Red Rooster Crows at Midnight", the staff was concerned that Sioux City Explorers' manager Eddie Nottle was sneaking around the park and spying on the Goldeyes. Nottle had been thrown out of the game and was searching for someone he knew so he could borrow some money to buy some beer. He had no interest in spying on the Goldeyes.

Another night, some members of the game production staff were convinced that Darryl Motley, star slugger with the Fargo-Moorhead Red Hawks, was corking his bat. When I asked how they had come up with that theory, the only explanation was that Motley was under the grandstand during the game swinging a bat. He was the designated hitter and was simply warming up. I informed the staff that they had been watching too much television. We all laugh now at how serious they were at the time. The "Red Rooster" crowed a few times over the years.

McTavish created a number of other codes to keep herself and the other staff entertained. Code 56, for example, meant there was an unruly fan that no one wanted to deal with. I'm sure the codes came out more during Game 5 or Game 6 of a home stand when fatigue was getting the best of us. Every once in a while I would ask McTavish for a new code book so I could keep up to speed!

Chapter 11: Let's Have a Little Fun

As general manager of the Goldeyes, I received a number of comments from hard-core baseball fans that we were not about baseball because there were too many other activities at games. In case some of you cynics out there still think baseball should remain stagnant, proper, and completely traditional – wake up! There is a lot of competition in the world for the entertainment dollar. That's why minor league baseball teams run promotions. They want as many people as possible to come to games and enjoy themselves. There is also the added benefit of generating revenue with promotions, but a number of promotions may be cost-neutral or even cost the club money.

I consider myself a bit of a baseball purist. I believe, however, that we are few in number. In order for a professional baseball team to be successful, it has to appeal to the masses. That requires the organization to provide added entertainment once the fans show up at the park. All successful minor league baseball teams do it. The Goldeyes are no exception.

A complete entertainment package starts outside of the gates before fans even enter the park. A seasonal promotional schedule will include giveaways at the entrance gates, theme games, special entertainers, and some crazy promotional ideas. During every game, the team will conduct between-inning contests, during-game promotions, and product tosses into the stands.

In short, the fans are entertained by creating an over-all fun atmosphere. A fan told me one evening that he hated not showing up for a game because he was never sure what he would miss. It was music to my ears! Another season ticket holder told me facetiously that he was always watching carefully, in case a baseball game should break out. We tried to balance the need for entertainment with the reality that it was professional baseball. Most times, I think we succeeded.

In a positive environment, learning is contagious among people. At the end of the inaugural 1994 season, four Goldeyes' staff members went to the Minor League Baseball Seminar in El Paso, Texas. What an experience! I was amazed that personnel from so many minor league clubs would share all their successes and setbacks with their colleagues from other teams. There was a genuine desire among delegates to help all clubs perform better.

One night, after 10 hours of seminars and a social function, we were sitting in the hot tub at the hotel. One of our staff members was taking notes as we discussed what we had learned and how we would implement the many promotions at our games. His notes got wet and were hard to decipher in the morning, but we knew good ideas were on the page. The creative juices flow at all times of the day. I realize now that the desire to be "the best we could be" was one of the hidden secrets of the success of the Goldeyes.

Those seminars put a demand on stamina. They started at 8 a.m. and went through to 6 p.m. Then there would be a social function, where we would discuss everything we had heard all day with general managers and staff from other teams. Some of these functions lasted until midnight or later and then we had to start all over again at 8 a.m. It was a tough few days but someone had to do it.

At one of my first seminars, I had the pleasure of cornering Steve Shaad, general manager of the Wichita Wranglers. Steve was an exciting guy to be around because his passion for the job clearly showed. He seemed to like our representatives because we too were keen about the business and striving to get better. He told me a story one night that I referred to many times during my tenure as a general manager.

He began by telling me that the most important thing in the office was to make sure the lid was not put on top of the flea jar. After I looked at him incredulously, he explained that if you put fleas in a jar and then cover it with a lid, the fleas will begin to jump but after they hit their heads on the lid a couple of times, they will learn to jump just high enough so they don't reach it. Even if you then remove the lid, they will not jump any higher because they will have been conditioned.

Shaad said it was the same with energetic staff members with great ideas. If every time they brought up a new idea, they were met with resistance from others who had been there longer, they would soon stop bringing up ideas. That could spell big trouble for a business.

It's easy for people to say, "That won't work. We've tried it before. That will cost too much money. That's not funny or entertaining enough. That expense is not in the budget. (Note that a money reason made the list twice.) The list of reasons not to do something can be very long indeed. Without new ideas, however, game production will become stale. The energy and excitement will diminish. We found that very few promotions, no matter how good they were, would entertain the fans every game. New ideas were a must.

And just because an idea didn't work five years before, doesn't mean it won't work now. Likewise, if an idea is too expensive, it can be sponsored or altered to be less expensive. I found the best approach was to take ideas and let people work with them. Not everything was do-able but almost everything was worth exploring.

To give you some idea of the breadth of activities that came out of ideas spawned at those seminars, I have listed a few you might recognize if you were to attend a Goldeyes' game: baseball buddies, pop-up contest, library reading program, virtual reality baseball game, kid's club, run the bases, race the mascot, sumo, horse race, and theme games of all kinds. The list is lengthy.

To be sure, we molded an idea that was brought back from a seminar and made it our own. We also created some of our own contests and promotions, but the ideas that were gathered at seminars played an integral role in the product that the fans saw at our games.

The Baseball Winter Meetings were another story. During those meetings, baseball flourished in December. Since I was young, I thought the Baseball Winter Meetings were very special. Major League and minor league clubs were represented. When I took the general manager's job, the only question I remember asking Katz was whether I would get to go to the Winter Meetings. He promised me I would be expected to attend. As a baseball enthusiast, I had heard the news flashes, player signings, and trades that came out of the meetings and I thought it would be exciting to be there and mingle with baseball big wigs.

It turned out that the meetings were also home to the largest baseball trade show in existence. It took three days for us to go through it properly. You could find everything from unique merchandise to entertainment acts, giveaways, promotional ideas, and more. For the first few years, we would call the media back in Winnipeg and try to provide information that would be worth passing along to our fans. New merchandise and promotions were not as exciting as player moves but we tried to have something to report that sounded fun and newsworthy.

When we first went to the Winter Meetings, our manager would come also. We soon realized that the baseball side of our operation was not the focus of the meetings, so in later years, we mainly went to view the trade show. There were always people there to visit with and share ideas. The meetings turned out to be not as glamorous as I had originally thought but I enjoyed them nevertheless. I never went to a seminar or Winter Meetings without gathering some information that was useful to the organization. There was so much to learn and I was a very eager student.

When we first attended the seminars, we were a little in awe of the successful teams but it didn't take long before we were looked upon by others as equals. The exploits of the Winnipeg Goldeyes were known far and wide in baseball circles. How could you sell over 20,000 tickets to a single game? How do you get so many fans to attend play-off games? How beautiful is your new park because it sure looked good on television during the Pan-American Games? Do you really average more than 6,000 fans per game? There was a lot of interest in what was going on in Winnipeg.

Our only criteria for promotions was that they were fun and entertaining, which was a challenge at times if a sponsor was adamant that a promotion run a certain way. Usually, they also wanted the fans to be entertained. Once CanWest Global Park opened, a whole new world of technology was available to use with the new state-of-the-art scoreboard. Even then, we tried to mix up the new technology with some of the old standard fun antics on the field.

Firework's displays are a staple of minor league baseball. Fans will purchase tickets specifically to see the fireworks at the conclusion of the game. Very few promotions can make such a direct link to ticket sales.

Before the Goldeyes could ignite fireworks at Winnipeg Stadium, the fire department insisted that Maroons Road, which ran behind the right field fence, be closed down, and they had to ensure there was no one sitting far along the first base line. Once the club moved to CanWest Global Park, it became even more complicated. Not only did the street behind the outfield fence (Waterfront Drive) have to be closed down, but we also had to pay the Harbor Patrol to have water traffic on the Red River diverted from the area near the park. It was worth it, though, to see the fans stay until the end of the game and cheer spontaneously when the fireworks were over.

I love fireworks. I stood on the field with the fireworks exploding over my head and thought to myself that life was pretty good. I asked the firework's company to give us more light than sound for their presentation. That was my personal preference and one that I believed the fans would enjoy the most. I was also trying to eliminate complaints about the noise from surrounding neighbourhoods, especially on week nights.

Case of the Missing Pig

On occasion, a staff member would come up with a promotion that required the cooperation of another team. Communications director Jonathan Green did just that in 2000. One of his new corporate sponsors was a restaurant called Hog City and Green wanted a promotion in keeping with the name. The St. Paul Saints were frequently coming up with wild promotions so I knew they would cooperate with the Goldeyes if needed.

The Saints didn't have a mascot suit with a person inside at that time, but rather a live pig that had a ball bag attached to it. The pig would walk up to home plate throughout the game and take baseballs to the home plate umpire. The Saints received a lot of exposure for such a novel idea. Green came up with the idea that the pig should be stolen and Goldie accused of the theft. The Saints were coming to Winnipeg for a three-game series. The intent of the promotion was to raise awareness of the rivalry between St. Paul and Winnipeg and to draw attention to the upcoming series, along with two of our corporate sponsors – Hog City, and the Manitoba Pork Council which was sponsoring the third and final game of the series. I made a quick phone call to Saints' general manager Bill Fanning and asked if he would go along with the promotion. As expected, Fanning thought the idea was unique and fun.

The Saints sent out notification to all Northern League teams that their pig mascot, Hammy Davis Jr., had gone missing. The Goldeyes sent out press releases on two consecutive days. The pig went missing in the early hours of Monday, June 19, 2000. According to the press release, a swatch of yellow fur and a white glove, similar to the one Goldie wore, were found near the scene of the crime.

Included in the second press release was information from St. Paul that while the yellow swatch had turned out to be nothing more than a piece of someone's toupee, there was still no explanation for the white glove. The authorities were reported to have widened their search to include Canada. During each press release, the sponsorship of the Manitoba Pork Council and a pig barbeque for charity were mentioned. I was quoted in the second press release, stating that any possible link between the missing pig and the upcoming pig barbeque was purely coincidental.

One of the great things about Northern League baseball was the acceptance by the players and coaches that we were having fun and these promotions were a part of the experience. The baseball was serious, but the antics between innings and off the field were recognized as part of the entertainment.

Marty Scott was the manager of the Saints and when told of our promotion, agreed to participate. At the scripted time, he sent two St. Paul players over to confront Goldie and force him to try on the glove that had been found at the scene of the crime. With the O.J. Simpson trial still vivid in people's minds, the response from the crowd was one of laughter and excitement. Alas, the glove did not fit and Goldie was cleared of all suspicion. We then announced that word had come in from St. Paul that their pig had been found unharmed. All in all, it was a great promotion.

I'm sure everyone has favourite promotions they've witnessed at a professional sporting event. The following are some of my favourites, with some insight into why I like them.

Goldie

You might not think of a mascot as a promotion but from my perspective, he is the most important non-baseball activity at the park. For those of you who have not been to a Goldeyes' game, Goldie is the mascot. He is a big yellow thingamajig?! He has baseball ears, a trumpet nose, and a rotund shape. The first year he had a baseball base stuck to his derriere. It had to be removed, though, because it was an irresistible target for people to kick. It never ceased to amaze me that people forgot there was a person inside the suit – a person who could be hurt! We quickly realized there was a need for a helper to follow Goldie wherever he went for crowd control and also to double as a means of communication with him during a game.

Goldie does not speak. Communication is achieved by motion and expression. The Goldeyes have been very lucky in that just two individuals have worn the costume from Goldie's inception through the 2005 season.

Our first Goldie, Scott Hiebert, was a loose cannon. Hardly a day went by without someone asking over our radios, "Does John know he is going to do this?" Of course, if I heard that, I would storm around trying to find Goldie to see what he was up to. Usually, I couldn't find him because he was on the roof of the stadium ready to zip-line down onto the field, or he was sneaking around with his air gun looking for something to hit.

The air gun he built was ridiculous. I guess we were somewhat low budget during the first few years and couldn't afford a commercial gun for throwing things into the crowd, the way the Goldeyes do now. One day, Hiebert put a baseball in the gun and, while standing at home plate at Winnipeg Stadium, shot the ball over the left-centerfield grandstand onto Empress Street. If you stand in the northwest corner of the current Winnipeg football stadium (CanadInns Stadium) and look to see how far that is, you will realize the magnitude of that shot. I estimate it to be over 500 feet.

Scott Hiebert had a great imagination. He created a life-size dummy, on which he would put a visiting team's jersey and wrestle with it, which was entertaining, but I was very uncomfortable when he slapped or punched it. And when he kicked it between the legs, I was visibly upset. Hiebert and I had countless discussions about the Goldeyes being family entertainment and what constituted proper mascot etiquette. Unfortunately, we never came to a concise agreement.

The final air gun episode occurred between innings of a game when Goldie went to second base with the dreaded gun, which I thought had already been moth-balled. My annoyance turned to horror as I watched Goldie load it with a baseball and aim it towards the crowd along the third-base line. He was actually aiming at the dummy, which was tied to the chain link fence that ran in sections all along the third-base line and out to the outfield fence. He fired…. The ball hit the dummy and knocked down over 200 feet of chain link fence. Pieces of the dummy were everywhere. We had to stop the game and get staff to go and push the fence sections back up before the game could resume.

I can barely imagine what could have happened if Goldie's aim had been bad and he had shot the ball into the crowd that was sitting directly behind the dummy and a few feet higher. The gun was never seen again and the dummy was only used for skits that included dancing or hugging. I didn't have much hair left to fall out and did not need the stress.

While I do feel Hiebert crossed the line once too often, I had to marvel at his talent, ingenuity, and complete lack of fear. One night the Toronto Raptor, the mascot of Toronto's National Basketball Association franchise, came to Winnipeg Stadium and performed skits with Goldie throughout the night. He was a friend of Hiebert's and had agreed to perform at the last minute. The skits included jumping on a trampoline and dunking a basketball into a portable basketball hoop, which the Raptor was quite famous for. The Raptor had recently been named the best mascot in the NBA. Goldie was every bit as acrobatic and entertaining. The fact that he could interact all night long with the Raptor and look every bit as good, says a lot about his talent. Those two put on quite a show.

One of my funniest recollections of Goldie occurred at the old stadium. We were playing the Duluth-Superior Dukes. It was a hot afternoon game and Goldie had been interacting with the visiting team as he usually did. One of the visiting players snuck up behind him and dumped a bucket of water on Goldie. The visiting team thought that was funny but Goldie got the last laugh. At a certain point midway through the game, the Duluth manager called time and went to the mound to talk to his pitcher. Out of the corner of my eye, I saw the entire Duluth-Superior bench empty as the players went running into the left field corner through the bullpen behind the third base fence. There was Goldie with a huge pressurized water hose spraying water all over the players. As much as I am a traditionalist and did not want to impact the game, I could not stop laughing at the sight of the players scrambling for drier ground. As the manager turned to wave for his new pitcher to enter the game, no one was to be found. The players were all down the left field line cowering under the powerful blast of water.

Goldie has done some amazing stunts. Hiebert was schooled in karate and was a trained gymnast. He would enter the park often by jumping on a large trampoline and performing somersaults in the air before landing on some mats. At least he would usually land on the mats. Once in a while, he would miss and it would hurt just to watch him bounce on the artificial turf. While many of his antics alarmed me, nothing came close to the anguish I felt when he would zip-line from the roof of the second deck of Winnipeg Stadium on to the field. Killing Goldie might have received national exposure but it was not part of the family-oriented entertainment we were marketing. The first time he slid down, the crowd went crazy. I asked Hiebert how often he had done it before. He responded, "I was practising all afternoon!"

For several years, including all of the years at CanWest Global Park up to 2006, Chris Spradbrow performed as Goldie. Spradbrow was also very athletic. He was scripted throughout the game and earned his money every night. He was famous for his dancing on the dugout. Frequently, at some point in the game, he would dance to the song, Cotton Eye Joe. The fans were always appreciative. I think most people realized the effort required by the person in the suit. On hot days, Goldie has been known to lose four to five kilograms (10 pounds) during a game.

Spradbrow had some unique talents. He was a musician and it was not uncommon to see Goldie join the band playing on stage during the pre-game entertainment on the promenade. He loved to play the drums and it was a sight to see the big yellow, furry mascot pounding out a tune.

Everyone loves Goldie. He is a key figure, promoting the organization throughout the off-season and participating in as many events as possible. I have been with Goldie at a multitude of events and he is always a big hit with children and adults alike. The organization has been lucky to have dedicated individuals inside that costume, who take their job seriously. The Goldeyes introduce Goldie shortly before every game as the best mascot in the Northern League and I'm confident they are right.

The Best Theme Games

Every year, we titled a number of games as "theme games". These games created interest with the fans but were also enjoyable for the staff. Here are a few of my favourites.

Shirt Off Our Backs – This promotion saw nine fans win an official game jersey right off the player's back. Every inning someone won a jersey and as the player came in off the field, he removed his jersey, autographed it, and presented it to the fan. A second jersey was waiting for the player in the dugout.

Psychedelic 60s – Players and staff wore tie-dyed shirts throughout the evening. We played 60s music, wore head bands, and talked like hippies. "Hey man. You look groovy tonight," was standard lingo. It took a bit of convincing to get Hal Lanier on board with this promotion but when he heard I was going to wear a tie-dyed shirt in public, he agreed he would wear one too. But we couldn't run too many of this type of promotion or the players might rebel.

Dress-Up Theme Games – Any day the staff could dress up was a fun day around the park. During a few games each year, all of the staff would dress in costumes and try to entertain the fans. Fans could win prizes if they dressed in the spirit of the theme. A few would participate but not many. While I doubt extra tickets were sold for those games, they were part of the added experience for the fans once they arrived at the park. Medieval theme was one of the best because the costumes were elaborate. Hawaiian, Country (I got to wear the cowboy hat I bought in Nashville), M.A.S.H., Christmas, Halloween, and Frontier were other themes used. Theme games were good for staff morale.

Christmas in July – We would decorate the stadium with Christmas decorations donated by a local shopping mall. It would take all day to do because it's hard to make a huge baseball stadium look decorated. We gave out prizes during the "nine innings of Christmas", took pictures with Santa, and at the end of the game, we would make it snow. Initially, we tried huge portable fans, which we lugged up into the upper deck of the grandstand, along with heavy bags of potato flakes. Scoops of the flakes thrown in front of the fans would look like snow as it blew to the ground. Upon arriving at home after these games, our staff would have to take their "white" clothes off and have them washed immediately. While that was annoying, the flakes worked better than the year we dropped thousands of ping pong balls.

Scouts and Guides Sleepover – I can thank our good friends in Sioux City for this idea. Every season the Scouts and the Guides attended a game as a group. At the conclusion of the game, they pitched their tents in the outfield grass and camped overnight. A movie was shown on the video board after the game. In the morning, a light breakfast was provided and they were on their way. Some staff and extra security had to spend the night, which made for some very sleepy staff the next day, but I have great memories of these sleepovers. The campers had a great time and so did many of our staff.

Choo Choo Tuesday – This promotion became one of my favourites because it was somewhat personal. My brother loves trains and my Dad worked for the Canadian National Railway for 42 years. During the first Choo Choo Tuesday game, Gar Hindle, my dad, threw out the ceremonial first pitch. At the time, he came to almost every game and he was the oldest member of the CNR pensioners in that part of the country, so he was a fitting candidate. I was encouraged to catch the opening pitch, which I did. It was a very special moment for my family. This theme game became a staple on the promotional schedule and each year we gave away train-related prizes, including a fabulous train trip through the Rocky Mountains.

President Bush/John Kerry Bobble Head Giveaway – I became involved with this promotion when I worked in Sioux Falls. It was first proposed at the Goldklang meetings in Florida in November of 2003. All six of the Goldklang teams were to purchase bobble heads of both candidates for the 2004 U.S. presidential race. The stadiums were decorated in red, white, and blue and polling booths were set up in each stadium. Fans were asked to vote for their favourite candidate and received that bobble head.

The dynamics of the promotion were created by the connection of all the teams. Six different American states were represented: South Dakota, South Carolina, New York, Massachusetts, Minnesota, and Florida. We promoted the vote as a prediction of the upcoming election. We were very accurate, too; five of the six states voted the same in both elections. We kept track of the vote and fed information to a central number where we would find out how the votes were coming in across the country. We even announced the wrong winner in Florida and had to change it after a recount.

What astounded me was the intensity that the voters displayed. Many Americans take their politics seriously. Republican voters would not even look at the Kerry bobble head and Democrats would walk across the concourse to avoid the Bush bobble head. Voters in the U.S. appeared to be very polarized, even during our fun bobble head promotion. The Goldklang group was big on national exposure and the promotion was reported by the national media.

The Best Between-Innings Promotions

Horse race – The beauty of this promo was that it was low tech. Three employees holding sticks with horses nailed to them, raced around the outside of the outfield fence. If one of the horses took the lead at the beginning of the race and led wire to wire, it was a boring promotion. I suggested to the runners that they script the race so the lead changed hands at least three times. Over the years, the staff became quite inventive with new ideas for keeping the race fresh. When they came up with the idea of stopping at the Moosehead beer bottle outfield sign at CanWest Global Park to have a drink, it cracked me up.

Dirtiest car in the parking lot – This promotion was executed every game for eight years. Few promotions can survive and be entertaining every game. Usually, we would run promotions every second or third game. The public address announcer, Ron Arnst, made it sound like something bad had happened to the car and then would change his voice and announce the owner had won a car wash. Every game for eight years the crowd would laugh. That has to be the definition of a good promotion.

Baseball Buddies – Prior to the game, a team of young boys or girls dressed in their ball uniforms would run out onto the field as they were announced by the PA announcer and stand beside a Goldeyes' player during the singing of the national anthems. The shining eyes and excitement on the faces of the youngsters before they ran onto the field would melt the coldest heart. If ever I was having a bad day, I would go down to field level and mingle with the Baseball Buddies prior to the game. It always made the day better.

The Best Entertainers

Sport: My all-time favourite performer was Sport. He was funny, talented and a real professional. He put on a great show and somehow even convinced me to sit in a chair on the field and have a plunger stuck on my head.

The Flying Elvises: Several Elvis impersonators jumped out of a plane at the end of the game with lights glowing on their suits and landed on the field. The first three jumpers landed gently near second base. The final Elvis had more lights on his suit and flew over second base, over the pitching mound, over home plate and landed feet from the backstop. For a moment, I thought we were going to have Elvis plastered half way up the net of the backstop, and let me assure you, he was no Spiderman.

Piano Man: The piano man was a unique act and a big hit at the all-star celebrations in 2001. He played the piano by dropping balls onto the keys. I was fascinated by his skill in handling the balls while playing at the same time.

Christopher: The Goldeyes were the first team to bring Christopher to the Northern League. Christopher is one guy attached to four life-sized puppets that all move in unison. The Village People and the Jackson Five were two of the costumes he used during his performances. You have to look very closely the first time you see Christopher to determine who the real person is as he dances around the field to the music.

Promotions That Did Not Work So Well

The most bizarre stories are about the promotions that didn't work so well. Some of them are funny now when I look back on them. These incidents brought home the realization that our games, including promotions, were live entertainment.

Polaris Snowmobile Race

This was the promotion that made the Goldeyes internationally famous. Or should I say infamous? Three go-carts were dressed up to look like snowmobiles. Three contestants would drive the snowmobiles in a race in foul territory close to the stands from first base around behind home plate to third base. Since top speed on the machines was seven mph. (11 km/h), it seemed there was little risk involved.

One of the first times we ran the promotion, a young boy was driving one of the carts and immediately I could see that something was wrong. First, he started steering directly at the pitcher's mound where the opposing pitcher was warming up. He got close enough that the pitcher stopped throwing and was ready to jump out of the way when the machine did a 180 degree turn and headed back off the field but directly towards the visitor's dugout between home plate and first base. The young lad's eyes were as big as saucers and his fingers were white from gripping the wheel as he drove full speed down the steps into the dugout.

My heart stopped beating. Fortunately for all concerned, a long-time former Goldeyes' player, Dan Guehne, then playing for Duluth-Superior, along with some of his teammates, cradled the machine as it plunged into the dugout, thereby cushioning the fall. When promotions manager Barb McTavish picked up the little guy, his biggest concern was whether he could get autographs from the players. He thought it was very cool to be in the dugout. Fortunately, he was not injured, other than a small scrape. What a huge relief. We showered him with gifts and comforted his mother.

A local television station filmed the entire incident. Within 24 hours, the segment was aired throughout Canada and the United States. I got calls from the league office and three general managers in other cities who had seen the incident on television. This was not how we had planned on becoming famous. Poor Barb took her job very seriously and I found her under the grandstand crying during the next inning of the game. It was very emotional for all of us but especially for her because she coordinated all of the game-day promotions, and she took her job very personally.

The next day, I received a call from one of my corporate sponsors, Grand Prix Amusements, which agreed to put kill switches on all three machines so that kind of incident could never happen again. From then on, every time the promotion ran, McTavish could be seen testing the remote kill switches before the race. As well, the race was conducted in the outfield where there was a lot more room for error.

Robin's Donuts Race the Mascot

Race the Mascot was an on-field promotion that involved a visiting mascot, who started the race at second base, and a young fan who started at first base. They raced around the bases until someone won by stepping on home plate. In Winnipeg, Goldie often interfered with the visiting mascot between third base and home plate, which allowed the youngster to race past them and touch home plate. Sometimes the interaction between Goldie and the other mascot was really comical. I enjoyed watching the little tyke running around the bases wearing a baseball jersey that was too long and almost dragging on the ground, as the crowd cheered him or her on to victory. At least, that is what was supposed to happen.

On occasion, a youngster would be so enamored with the mascots that he or she would stop to partake in their scuffle or to get up close and touch them or jump on top of them if they were rolling around on the ground. The biggest miscue occurred one day at Winnipeg Stadium. Goldie tackled the Robin's Donuts mascot as part of the skit and the robin's head came off and went rolling down the third base line. The look on the youngster's face was one I will always remember. It was not a good look.

Other Goldie Miscues

After years of live performances, it was inevitable that our mascot would get into some trouble. The time Goldie was most seriously hurt during my tenure, he had wrapped himself with duct tape and was rolling around on the top of the visitors' dugout. Part of his skit was to roll off the roof onto the field in front of the visiting players and flop around. When he rolled off, he fell awkwardly and ended up with a hairline fracture in his arm. We had to use a replacement Goldie for a few games. I'm not sure what he was thinking that day, or how he expected to brace his fall while he was all tied up, but then, I frequently couldn't figure out what he was thinking.

Another strange event occurred when the St. Paul Saints were in town during the 1998 season. A new Goldie was on his familiar perch on the roof of the visitors' dugout. The dugout had a metal roof and Goldie made the mistake of pounding on it, making an unbearable noise for the visiting team.

While I would have preferred that some team representative had come to me and asked for us to restrain Goldie from banging on the roof, the St. Paul catcher, former Major Leaguer Matt Nokes, took the matter into his own hands. He came out of the dugout and took Goldie's broom and placed it over his neck and seemed to be choking him. Nokes was a big strong guy and I was not sure how serious he was. By the time I ran down to the field to check it out, Nokes had left but Goldie was still upset. He was not hurt but was shaken up. My first thought was that it was a good thing this had not happened with our original Goldie, who was trained in karate. He might have laid a licking on Nokes in front of thousands of people, which was not the kind of image we had been promoting for Goldie. As fate would have it, league President Dan Moushon happened to be in attendance at that game and witnessed the entire event. He suspended Nokes for one game for his behaviour. Nokes had not intended to hurt the mascot in any way but his actions were unacceptable. He apologized to Goldie.

Every event that happened was an opportunity for another promotion. The next time St. Paul came to town, we billed it as the rematch. Matt Nokes was apprehensive and I received a call from his agent informing me that if we put Nokes in a bad light he would take legal action against us. That annoyed me because I believed Nokes had initially acted inappropriately and I was trying to fix the situation. My plan was simple. Nokes and Goldie would walk gingerly towards each other on the field prior to the game and when they reached each other they would shake hands, hug, and walk together in front of the fans. It would make Nokes look good and bring the matter to a conclusion. I convinced Bill Fanning that it was in everyone's best interests. He agreed and so did Nokes. The whole exchange went off beautifully to the cheers of the fans.

Night the lights went out in Winnipeg

Running the ball club out of Winnipeg Stadium presented numerous challenges. Operationally, the biggest issue was that the facility staff did not work for the Goldeyes. One night we were playing the Sioux City Explorers and planned for fireworks to be ignited at the conclusion of the game. Winnipeg was in front most of the contest but Sioux City scored in the top of the ninth inning to tie the game. The Goldeyes failed to score in the bottom of the ninth, so extra innings were in order.

Just as the Goldeyes started to run onto the field for the top of the 10th inning, the stadium lights went out. For a moment, I thought I was having a bad nightmare, but within seconds, the fireworks started to explode right on cue. Chaos reigned for a moment as I tried to get information from the press box. After what seemed like an eternity, I finally learned that the lights were turned off by accident. Because they were halogen bulbs, they had to cool down and it would take 25 minutes before they would come back on. We made an announcement to the fans and shot off the fireworks.

There was usually a lot of stress on game days back then, but that was over the top. I walked past Sam Katz on the concourse and exclaimed, "Could anything else go wrong tonight?" He calmly said, "Yes, my general manager could have a heart attack. Calm down." That was one of the nicer things Sam ever said to me. I guess the stress was showing on my face. I didn't like screw-ups and this was a big one. We had significantly affected the game, which had definitely not been our plan.

An amusing part of the story occurred on the field when I told Sioux City manager Eddie Nottle what had happened. Nottle retorted that he thought he had seen everything, but shooting off fireworks during a game was a first. Only in Winnipeg, he commented, would you try to pull off a stunt like that. He knew, of course, that we had not done it on purpose. I told him jokingly that we did it especially for him because he had been around for such a long time and we knew he would appreciate it.

However, while it was an experience, I still don't find it funny. It was a classic example of why we needed to operate our own facility.

Fireworks

While we are on the subject of fireworks, I should point out that fireworks are best displayed when it is reasonably dark outside. Opening Day, 2000, was played on May 26th before a crowd of 6,616. We were planning on big things in 2000. This was our second year in the new stadium and our sights were set on the St. Paul Saints' attendance records. There was a lot of energy in the park and we planned a huge fireworks show to kick-off the new season.

I really like Rick Forney. He was a great player and competitor for the Goldeyes. He treated me and the front office with the utmost respect and turned into a wonderful pitching coach and was promoted to manager for the 2006 season. On May 26, 2000, however, I had a few choice words for him under my breath. I realize it's hard to complain about an Opening Day pitcher who shuts out the opposition, with a little help from Shawn Onley in relief, but did they have to do it in just one hour and 59 minutes? I was never concerned with it being dark enough to shoot off fireworks on Opening Day because there was always a lengthy ceremony to start the season and all the players were introduced to the fans. Since the game started later than normal, there should have been adequate time for darkness to fall before the game was concluded. Not in 2000!

It was still much too light to shoot off the fireworks when the game ended so we decided to try entertaining the fans for a while. We delayed as long as we could. We broadcasted a long game wrap-up and player interviews over the public address system, played movie clips on the video board, and had Goldie perform a skit. Just when I thought the fans were getting too restless to wait any longer, I determined it was dark enough to let the fireworks fly. Conditions weren't perfect but everyone got to see the fireworks.

Gorilla Warfare

We found a gorilla act at the Baseball Winter Meetings. Five guys dressed in gorilla suits were running all over the trade show, creating a lot of energy. The cost of such acts was always an issue for us. We questioned whether it was worth spending thousands of dollars to bring them to the park. How many people actually showed up at the game because we were bringing in an entertainment act? We came to the conclusion after a few years that very few people were there because of the entertainment. Once they arrived at the game, they may have enjoyed the entertainers, but that was not the determining factor in their decision to buy tickets.

Gorilla Warfare had an unfortunate vehicle accident prior to arriving in Winnipeg. A couple of their cast members were injured and did not make the trip. As I watched their performance, I believed the quality of the show was compromised. The big problem, though, was one of their skits. I was standing on the concourse watching between-innings when they brought a large purple dinosaur, which looked remarkably like Barney, onto the field and placed him near home plate. They already had a gorilla riding around the field on a four-wheeler. Marketing director Devon Kashton was standing next to me and said, "I think they are going to run over and kill Barney." I said, "Don't be silly, they would never do that. They know this is family entertainment."

Sure enough, the gorilla roared around the infield on the four-wheeler, then we watched in horror as he ran right over the dinosaur. I was speechless. Not so the fans. I received several calls from upset parents in the morning. It seems that some children were traumatized as they witnessed the destruction of what they believed to be Barney. We were not happy with the gorillas.

The Famous Chicken

One time, we decided to bite the bullet and pay our largest fee ever for an entertainer. The Famous Chicken was a high profile performer who had received a lot of television exposure. He charged accordingly. His act on the field was professional but, unfortunately, on this night his actions behind the scenes were not. Entertainers provide their own music. One of his skits was noticeably cut short because we did something wrong with his music and the skit on the field ended abruptly. I was not pleased with the screw-up and went to apologize to the Famous Chicken. I also wanted to ensure him that the rest of his performance would go smoothly. I guess he was more upset than I was. When I walked into his dressing room, the first thing I saw was a chair being tossed clear across the room.

I had been informed just before I entered his room that as he left the field his language was very offensive and we had complaints from fans, who had brought their children to see The Chicken. He was still upset when I arrived and was flapping his wings and trying to get the head of his costume off as he repeated over and over, "The Chicken needs air! The Chicken needs air!" Our organization had little tolerance for anyone who used foul language (pardon the pun) in front of our fans. The Chicken was no exception and I told him so. I assigned someone to stay close to him no matter where he went for the rest of the night. He performed another couple of skits and signed autographs but there was no further incident.

Mini-Bat Giveaway

We were involved in a love affair with the fans in Winnipeg from the beginning. It seemed that in the first year we could do no wrong. One June evening in 1994 we were supposed to give away mini-bats at the gates prior to a game. We had ordered the bats but did not confirm shipping dates, nor did we follow-up adequately on the order. The bats did not arrive in time for the game. In fact, they didn't arrive until two months later. It could have been a very embarrassing situation for the organization. We stood sheepishly at the gates prior to the scheduled giveaway game and handed out vouchers for the bats. While I was very apprehensive about how this would look, our fans took the entire debacle in stride and I received virtually no complaints. I had worried for days for nothing.

Jake, the Diamond Dog

I love dogs. I took every opportunity to bring dog acts to the park. Rockin' Ray and Skyy Dog, the local fly-ball associations, and Jake, the Diamond Dog were some of the canine entertainers we had at our games. A bizarre situation occurred while I was the general manager in Sioux Falls in 2004 at a Canaries' home game.

Jake was a wonderful Irish Setter. He arrived at the park in the afternoon, along with his trainer, Jeff, and a young dog in training called Homer. I had fun on the field with both dogs as they went through some of their skits. I told Jeff it was okay with me if he wanted to use Homer for some extra promotions as a training exercise. I thought it would be added value for the fans and if something did not work perfectly, everyone would realize Homer was just learning the trade and be sympathetic.

Just prior to the start of the game, both dogs were on the field playing Frisbee with the fans and having fun. Jeff did his best to put on a good show for his clients. All of a sudden, a rabbit appeared and started running around the infield. Within moments, Homer saw it and gave chase. He might never have caught the rabbit if Jake had not got involved. Jeff was trying to call off the dogs to no avail. With two dogs in pursuit, the rabbit had no chance. They pinned it against the back stop and Homer grabbed it in his mouth and killed it.

I was standing on the field wondering what to do. Who was supposed to come and deal with this situation? I decided the best course of action was to walk over, reach down, pick the rabbit up and carry it underneath the grandstand. As I walked along the grandstand with the dead rabbit in my hand, a woman said, "Thanks a lot. That was just what I wanted my daughter to see." I didn't look at her but I thought to myself, "Does she really think we planned this?"

Unbelievably, another bizarre event occurred at the same game. At the end of the fifth inning, Jeff decided to let Homer race a young fan on the field. The youngster started at first base and was to run around second and third and then touch home plate. Jeff was to throw a ball into the outfield and Homer would race out, grab it, and return it to Jeff just after the young fan touched home plate. Jeff told me he was an expert at timing the length of the throw so the youngster always won in a close race. I felt a strange sense of foreboding as I watched Jeff throw the ball over second base and Homer take off in hot pursuit. Just as the youngster rounded second base, Homer hit him at full speed, clipping his legs out from under him and sending him flying.

My heart leapt in my mouth as I watched. Killing a rabbit was bad enough for one game. Hurting a young fan was definitely something I never wanted to see. What a trooper we had as a contestant, however. He looked around a little shocked, then jumped to his feet and started running again. He was determined to win the race. He was fine and we provided him with much better prizes than were initially scheduled. Homer was sent to the showers. He had created enough excitement for one day.

Strike-out Batter

When I first went to St. Paul and discovered that they had a strike-out batter promotion, I was annoyed. Here was an example of a promotion that could potentially impact the baseball game. The promotion has all the fans at the park winning something if the chosen opposition batter strikes-out. I believe that during the 1994 season, all the fans would win a two-litre bottle of Coke from a local store if the batter struck out. I have also seen half-price beer at the concessions for the next inning, free pancakes, and various other prizes.

Dan Bilardello was the Goldeyes' catcher in 1994. He was a former Major Leaguer and one of the leaders on the club. St. Paul named him the strike-out batter during the first game of a series. He didn't strike-out so no one won a prize. Not to be denied, the Saints named him the strike-out batter again for the second game. In fact, they named him the strike-out batter in all four games of the series. During his last at-bat in the fourth game, the Saints PA announcer told the fans that Bilardello had accomplished a worthwhile feat. He had not struck out in four straight games. The crowd gave him a rousing ovation and Bilardello removed his helmet and bowed to the crowd. When he did not strike-out during that last at-bat, the Saints announced they were retiring his number and informed the crowd that never again would he be chosen as the strike-out batter. His uniform number hung on the outfield fence in St. Paul for the remainder of the 1994 season.

Miscellaneous

Many times through the season, the Goldeyes offered prizes to lucky ticket holders. Program prizes were chosen at random before game time because they were printed in our game production scripts but the winner of any larger prize was not chosen until we had ticket stubs from the gates to choose from. That way, every fan in attendance had an equal chance to win, not just those who bought a program. Several times per year, I walked onto the field with a drum of tickets and picked the winner in front of the crowd.

In 1999, our first year at CanWest Global Park, I was on the field in front of 6,500 fans and I drew the winning ticket for a television set. I was to look at the ticket and announce the winning section, row, and seat number over the portable microphone I was holding. Instead of drawing one of the seats, I picked a ticket in the overflow patio area where there were no assigned rows or seat numbers. I stood in front of 6,500 eager fans, trying to decipher what number from the ticket I should read that the fans would understand. It was a little embarrassing. While the situation was all above board, it looked, for a moment, like I had not drawn the number I was expecting. I finally read a stock number on the ticket that didn't sound like any seat in the park. It took our PA announcer several attempts to explain the number to the fans before we were able to ascertain the winner.

Jake – The Diamond Dog

Infamous snowmobile race

John – Psychedelic 60's night

Scout's sleepover

Goldie playing drums

Chapter 12: My Favourite Games

August 21, 1996 – Honour Olympic Athletes

I know the Goldeyes set two "world records", played the first game in franchise history at Winnipeg Stadium, and opened beautiful CanWest Global Park, but what I most remember is a game promoted as "Red Heat" on August 21st, 1996. We asked fans to wear red and come out to a game in honour of those Olympic athletes who were from Manitoba and who had competed at the Atlanta Summer Games. A fabulous crowd was in attendance, numbering 11,356, and mostly dressed in red.

We introduced each proud athlete, and it was a very impressive list. We had world champions, Olympic medalists, and a number of other great athletes from a variety of sports. A deep sense of pride filled the stadium as they came onto the field. I will never forget the singing of the Canadian national anthem. Michelle Sawatzky was a member of the Canadian Olympic women's volleyball team and she had a voice like an angel. While she was singing the anthem, a chill went down my spine. Never before had I heard so many people join in. It was a very gratifying feeling and I'm sure everyone in the stands was filled with excitement and emotion as they shared in the moment with the Olympic athletes. After the anthem, the athletes ran around the field with a huge Canadian flag to the tumultuous cheers of the crowd. It was an amazing start to the evening.

I met the athletes as they came off the field. They were so appreciative that the Goldeyes had chosen to honour them and give them an opportunity to thank the people of Manitoba for their support. It was a real love-in. That game ranks up there with the best highlights of my career. To top things off, the players went out and beat Duluth-Superior 3-1 as Jamie Ybarra notched his 11th win of the season. Ybarra told me afterwards that there was a lot of positive karma in the stadium.

August 29, 1995 – World Record

In the spring of 1995, Goldeyes' sales manager Val Overwater came to me and suggested that we attempt to set an all-time attendance record for a Northern League game. I was a little skeptical but believed in keeping an open mind to new ideas. We were averaging around 4,000 fans per game but Val thought we could sell 10,000 or more tickets. I wondered to myself why people would buy a ticket to a game just because we wanted to create a self-proclaimed record. Gradually, however, the idea caught fire within the office so I figured, why not. We had nothing to lose.

We contacted Guinness World Book of Records and were informed that there was no category defined as we wanted, so we had to create our own category. To market the campaign, we decided to call the game a "World Record". We determined it would be the largest ever attended game for a short-season professional baseball team.

I knew we could cheaply sell or give away thousands of tickets but that was not our goal. I have seen many completely bogus attendance numbers announced by other teams. You can distribute 100,000 tickets to a game to a bunch of people who likely will not attend. That doesn't make your attendance for the game 100,000. The Goldeyes concluded that we did not want to have a company buy thousands of tickets as a promotion and then give them away. We wanted this to be a real record where people would get caught up in the excitement and attend the game.

To generate large numbers of ticket sales, we created a package of 25 tickets for $100. Four dollars each seemed to be a realistic price for the tickets, which, as it turned out, were located everywhere throughout Winnipeg Stadium. Our first target was our corporate sponsors, who were already supporting us. If anyone would buy into the "World Record" concept, surely they would. Our success rate with them surprised everyone.

Our initial blitz sold 4000 tickets in one morning. With that number to bolster our morale, we tackled the challenge of setting an all-time record head on. We set aside three entire mornings where the only work allowed to be done throughout the office was selling "World Record" tickets. Any other caller was told the staff was tied up in a meeting and would return calls at noon. Every outbound call had to be related to selling tickets for the game.

The entire staff bought into the project and everyone was on the phone. We found an old cow bell and every time someone sold 25 tickets they would run over and ring the bell. After a while, it sounded like the fire alarm was going off! Everyone was a part of the operation and became more excited as the numbers grew. A wonderful side benefit occurred in the office. The entire process not only created an environment that helped sell tickets, but also dramatically increased morale. We were a team tackling a huge challenge together.

Everyone in the office participated, even Barb McTavish, who was not involved in sales. She contacted local charities to see if they could use tickets for the game. Every time she received an affirmative answer, I told her I considered that a sale. Several companies told us they could not use 25 tickets but would be happy to support the cause if the tickets would be used. Charitable organizations were a perfect fit for their tickets. I guess for these tickets, the bell rang twice – once when Barb contacted a charity that would use the tickets, and once when a company purchased tickets for the charity to use.

While we started the process by calling corporate sponsors, we ended up calling season ticket holders and many other companies that were not doing business with us at the time. Through the "World Record" game, we were able to develop new relationships with companies that continued into the future – a huge long-term benefit for the club.

Personally, I sold thousands of tickets for that game. Friends, family, and distant cousins were called. If someone owed me a favour, I called to collect. If they didn't owe me a favour, I asked them to buy 25 tickets anyway and I would owe them a favour. The whole project took on a life of its own and created a sort of frenzy in the office. It was a lot of fun and the concept worked.

The result was an amazing 20,749 tickets sold. The Goldeyes outdrew several Major League teams that night. There were people sitting everywhere. Some of the seats were not great for baseball but we received very few complaints. Goldeyes' fans made me feel proud many times during my eight years with the club and this was one of those times.

The outcome of the game unfortunately did not match the enthusiasm of the great crowd as the Goldeyes lost 6-2 to the St. Paul Saints. But it was still a night to remember. It was one of the first times at a Goldeyes' game that we saw the potential for packed stands and the energy that the fans create in that type of environment.

At the Minor League Baseball Seminar in the fall, I was asked to make a presentation to other attendees regarding the achievement because what we accomplished was truly amazing. How do you sell out a stadium that holds over 30,000 seats when you are averaging 4,000? As I learned with all major projects, you simply start at the beginning and believe.

How many times have you or someone you know come up with an idea, only to be shot down immediately with very little thought? Nothing is worse for office morale. I tried to maintain an atmosphere of open minds to new ideas because you never know when one will take on a life of its own. That is exactly what happened in the case of our "World Record" game.

August 28, 1997 – World Record

Two years later, we tried it again. Could we pull off another record? Talk was swirling around the Goldeyes' office that construction of a new ball park was imminent. I told everyone I contacted that the game would be their last chance to set a record that would never be broken. The Portland Beavers had run a similar promotion and had just surpassed the previous Goldeyes' record. We used the exact same format as we did in 1995 and received a similar response. The final tally was an attendance of 22,081, which did set a new record, and may have been a more remarkable achievement than our effort in 1995. There is usually more excitement the first time you try any promotion. The one thing we had going for us the second time, though, was that we knew it was possible. Unfortunately, the game results were a similar disappointment as the Goldeyes lost 6-1 to the Sioux Falls Canaries.

June 4, 1999 – Opening Day of CanWest Global Park

The opening of CanWest Global Park! Now that was a celebration worth having! The Goldeyes had survived since 1994 in a football stadium. Winnipeg Stadium had too many seats for baseball and not enough good seats. That's a pretty bad combination. The organization also had to deal with numerous people who worked for Winnipeg Enterprises, the city organization that controlled the facility. Combine that with the club's lack of control over concessions, parking, security, and building maintenance and you can understand the level of excitement that surrounded the opening of the new park. We were about to open a new state-of-the-art facility and everyone who worked there would be working for the Goldeyes. Since we would be responsible for everything in the facility, we would not be able to blame Winnipeg Enterprises for problems that arose. We would be completely responsible, good or bad. Even that was a beautiful feeling.

The plan on Opening Day, June 4th, 1999, was to open the doors a little early in case fans wanted to mill around. We agreed on a 5:30 p.m. gate opening, which was 30 minutes earlier than normal. A few workers were putting finishing touches on the facility throughout the day... okay, maybe it was more than a few workers and they were doing more than finishing touches. At times, it looked more like an army of workers still constructing the park.

At 5:15 p.m., I was standing on the field looking up at the suite level where welders were hard at work. Fiery slag was falling onto the grandstand seats below as they worked feverishly to have the suites ready for the much publicized opening. Paul Wiesek, the Winnipeg Free Press reporter who covered the Goldeyes in 1999, was standing beside me on the field, also looking up at the suite level. He shook his head and said, "You guys have a lot of balls!" I could only nod my head in agreement. I knew he wasn't talking about baseballs. It was insane that, right up to the last minute, so many people were working on the stadium.

Sam Katz walked by just then and I told him we would have to open the gates a few minutes later than planned because the welding waste material was literally falling onto some seats. He looked over and told me not to worry. It was a big park and no one would sit under the falling slag. Then he turned and walked away with a glazed look in his eyes. I just stared at him as he disappeared into the confines of the stadium. I presumed he was kidding but I didn't discuss anything else with him for the rest of the day. He was deep in thought about the "Opening Ceremonies" and what he was going to say to the fans.

The opening of CanWest Global Park was a big day for Katz. He had managed to build the park against tremendous odds and opposition. He was very proud on June 4th, 1999, and I was very proud of him for persevering.

Signs for the concession stands were also still being put in place. I kept radioing upstairs to see when the welding would be done. "Just a couple of more minutes" was the stock answer I received every time I called up all afternoon. The scheduled opening time of 5:30 p.m. arrived and still they were welding. I waited impatiently and, finally, word came down that the welding was complete. The concession signs were also cut and put in place. Quickly, we went into clean-up mode.

At 5:44, I announced over our two-way radios that we were ready. A portable table saw was wheeled into the uncompleted area on the concourse level where the merchandise store would eventually be located. As the entrance gates were opened, its blade was still spinning as the first fans walked through the gates of our beautiful new stadium.

The fans, of course, knew nothing of the drama. They walked into gorgeous CanWest Global Park with sparkles in their eyes. What a thrill it was for the staff to see the excitement on their faces as they set foot into their baseball stadium, which had been so long in coming.

Meanwhile, another drama had been playing out that day. League president Dan Moushon had flown in from Durham, North Carolina, for the opening. When he arrived in the afternoon, he took it upon himself to pitch in wherever needed. He even helped move picnic tables into the overflow patio area. All the while, he was waiting to meet with Katz.

The Goldeyes had not paid some league fees after repeated requests from the league office. Flow of money was a real problem in 1999. Moushon had a letter in his pocket that he was prepared to give Katz from league commissioner Miles Wolff, which stated that the umpires were not going to take the field if the league fees were not paid. He sat in Katz's office shortly before game time and patiently listened to a verbal barrage from Katz, who finally relented and wrote a cheque. The letter remained in Moushon's pocket. I can barely imagine the scenario if the game had been postponed because there were no umpires. When the game ceremonies commenced, I was disappointed to see that Moushon was not even acknowledged. It was a noticeable oversight.

The Sioux Falls Canaries were again the opposition in the first game at the new stadium. Unfortunately, the players, who were equally excited with the new park, did not get the job done on the field and were blown out 14-5.

Still, the day belonged to the new facility. All the hours of preparation, the thousands of decisions, the cramped office quarters over the winter, and the difficulty in working out of a construction site were all a distant memory. All of the frustration had been replaced by the beauty and wonder of the new park.

September, 1997 – Winnipeg/Fargo Playoff Series

While every playoff series against Fargo-Moorhead had its share of drama, it would seem impossible to top the 1997 series. For the second straight year since the team's inception, Fargo made the playoffs and met Winnipeg in the first round. Winnipeg was the first half champions so the Goldeyes hosted the first two games.

The two dramatic one-run games were both won by the Red Hawks, 6-5 and 4-3. They were exciting playoff baseball and it certainly looked like Fargo was going to beat Winnipeg for the second straight year. The remainder of the five-game series reverted to Newman Outdoor Field in Fargo.

I, along with most of our staff and hundreds of Goldeyes' fans, made the trek to Fargo for Game 3 of the series with only a faint hope that the Goldeyes could keep their season alive. When the games were in Winnipeg, there was work for me to do. I watched as much of the games as possible, but I always had one eye on every foul ball in case someone was hurt and I would be dealing with a multitude of issues as they arose.

In Fargo, all I had to do was sit in my chair and watch the game. The only problem was that I was too wound up to sit in my chair. The Red Hawks had a powerful batting line-up, anchored by ex-Major Leaguer, Darryl Motley. Every time they came to bat I could see them putting a big number on the scoreboard. The Goldeyes had beaten the Red Hawks seven out of 12 games during the regular season but none of that mattered now.

Game 3 was a classic and again the outcome was determined by one run. This time, however, the Goldeyes were triumphant, winning 4-3 behind the pitching of Jamie Ybarra. The series was going to Game 4. The Goldeyes' fourth starter, Rod Pedraza, had started the year well with a 6-0 record but had struggled thereafter and ended the season 8-5 with an ERA of 5.49. He was handed the ball and he pitched beautifully in Game 4 as the Goldeyes crushed the Red Hawks 8-1. A sudden-death Game 5 was going to have to be played.

Game 5 was another classic. By then, there was no point in my even having a seat. The pacing started during the pre-game ceremonies. Goldeyes' ace Rick Forney, who was the loser in Game 1, was the Game 5 starter. Forney was a tough competitor and I knew he would leave everything he had on the field. Game 5 turned out to be everything you could want in a playoff baseball game.

I was really keyed up. Sometime during the game, I literally bumped into Sam Katz as I was pacing back and forth in the concourse area behind the Goldeyes' dugout and he was pacing in the opposite direction. We laughed as we collided with each other but then quickly carried on with our pacing.

If I was in a certain location or position and something good happened in the game, I would try to stay there as long as good things were happening. Becoming that superstitious may sound a little pathetic, but we were completely wrapped up in the action. In fact, I don't remember being so caught up in the outcome of a sporting event before or since.

The Red Hawks jumped out to an early 2-0 lead but the Goldeyes responded with seven unanswered runs to take a 7-2 lead. But, there was no chance this game was going to be a runaway contest. The Red Hawks scored three runs in the seventh, then another run and loaded the bases in the ninth, with Darryl Motley coming to bat. My heart seemed to stop beating altogether. I'm sure I held my breath for his entire at-bat. Somehow we managed to keep the door shut and the Goldeyes won the contest 7-6.

The hometown fans were stunned but the ecstatic Goldeyes' fans celebrated in unison. From my perspective, the intensity of that series may never be exceeded. It seemed like only a dream that we could beat the mighty Red Hawks three straight games in their home park.

As a side note, the Goldeyes lost Game 5 of the championship series to the Duluth-Superior Dukes, a disappointing ending to the 1997 season. Years later, however, I can still feel the excitement that was flowing through my veins in Fargo during Game 5 of that magical series.

September 5th, 1995 – Sioux City Tie-Breaker

While the game itself was a dynamic contest, the best part of this story occurred prior to the start of the game. After winning the Northern League Championship in 1994, the Goldeyes found themselves in a close race during the 1995 campaign. They finished the first half of the season with a 25-17 record, which was good for a second-place tie with Sioux City. The St. Paul Saints held off the hard-charging Goldeyes to win the first half pennant by one game.

The second half of the season started badly for the Goldeyes. They lost eight of their first nine games. The playoffs looked a million miles away. A league rule in 1995 stated that if a team won both halves, its opposition In the Championship Series would be determined by the team that had the best record throughout the entire season. The Saints were fighting it out with the Thunder Bay Whiskey Jacks for the second half title.

Because the Goldeyes had such a terrible start to the second half, their only opportunity to make the playoffs was if St. Paul won both halves. That put the Goldeyes in the bizarre position in which losing to the Saints was in Winnipeg's best interests. St. Paul came to town with nine games left to play in the second half. The Goldeyes did manage to lose all three games of the series, but no one, to my knowledge, ever said out loud that it was good strategy to lose.

By sweeping Duluth in the last series of the season, Winnipeg ended up third in the second half behind St. Paul and Thunder Bay, with a won-lost record of 21-21 but an overall record of 46-38. Thunder Bay finished last in the first half and was well behind Winnipeg with its overall record.

The last game of the 1995 regular season for the Goldeyes was played on a Sunday in Duluth, where the game started at 2 p.m. Sioux City went into the last day of the season with an identical overall record as Winnipeg. The Explorers were playing at home but their game didn't start until 5 p.m. The Goldeyes were in limbo for several hours waiting for the outcome of that game to see if there would have to be a tie-breaker.

Sam Katz was in Duluth and he argued with league officials that if a tie-breaker was necessary, it should be played in Winnipeg where there would be a decent crowd. If agreed to, the Goldeyes could have headed home to await the outcome of the Sioux City game. Commissioner Miles Wolff did not agree. He determined that if a playoff was necessary, it would be played in Sioux City. His reasoning was that only one team would then have to travel – Winnipeg – since they were already on the road.

What were the Goldeyes to do? We didn't want to drive to Sioux City until we were sure a game was to be played. We decided to drive the short trip to St. Paul and wait there until we heard so the team bus was driven to the Mall of America where the players ate at Hooters Restaurant, which entertained them for a while.

The wait seemed like an eternity but finally word came that Sioux City had won. The bus headed back onto the highway for the four-plus-hour trek, arriving in Sioux City after midnight.

The tie-breaker game was a real jewel. It ended in the 10th inning when catcher Hank Manning led off with a solo home run to put the Goldeyes into the lead, 5-4. Mike Cather, who later went on to play for the Atlanta Braves, was the winning pitcher. The Goldeyes had earned the right to play in the Championship Series against St. Paul. While they lost that series three games to one, the unique events that led up to the tie-breaking game in Sioux City are what I remember most. The following season, the league office requested that all games on the last day of the season be scheduled as afternoon contests.

September 6th, 1998 – Game 3, Winnipeg/Fargo playoff game

I wrote previously about one of the finest pitched games in Northern League history between Jeff Bittiger and Oil Can Boyd. There was another game during the playoffs in 1998 that may have showcased the most dominating pitching performance I have ever witnessed.

Fargo had won the first two games in the series in their home park. The two teams boasted that they had two of the best closers in the league. Jeff Sparks for Winnipeg and George Schmidt for Fargo had completed dominant seasons for their respective teams. In Game 3 of the series they outdid themselves.

Schmidt came into the game in the seventh inning and pitched 6 1/3 innings, fanning eight batters. Sparks was even more dominant. He pitched the last 5 1/3 innings, striking out 12 Fargo hitters. Inning after inning, they matched pitching performances. Finally, in the 13th inning, the Goldeyes pushed a run across to prolong the series. It was spellbinding to watch these two warriors go at it. Jeff Sparks went on to pitch in the Major Leagues for Tampa Bay.

Two special games

Two other games were extremely important in Goldeyes' history and I certainly consider them two of my favourite games. Opening Day, June 7th, 1994, was the first game ever played by the new franchise. A new era of professional baseball was ushered into Winnipeg. This game is discussed in detail in an earlier chapter.

The all-star game and the all-star skills competition in 2001 were two of the biggest highlights of my career. An inside look at this major event is also included in a separate chapter.

Chapter 13: Against the Odds (CanWest Global Park)

Many times during the first few years of operation, I doubted a new baseball park would become a reality. Road block after road block was put in Sam Katz's way. His crowning achievement with the Goldeyes came with quite a struggle.

I was at the city council meeting when Katz said he would agree to the terms laid out by the city to build the park. I will never forget the look on Mayor Susan Thompson's face. She was shocked. She turned to City Chief Commissioner Rick Frost and said, "What did he say?" Frost answered that Katz had agreed to the terms laid out by the City. "Can he do that?" Mayor Thompson asked.

She had campaigned against building the baseball park at its downtown location. She apparently did not believe Katz would agree with the conditions the City had laid out for him to do so. I guess she underestimated Sam Katz.

Katz said Mayor Thompson had been given bad advice, which was why she was opposed to the location of the ball park. "Can you imagine getting the ball park built on city owned property in direct opposition to the mayor? That sort of thing just doesn't happen," said Katz.

Building a baseball park is not something that one does every day. We started using a local architect, as well as one from Denver who had built other baseball stadiums. Anyone who has built a home realizes the massive number of decisions that have to be made. A baseball stadium probably has 10 times as many.

As construction of CanWest Global Park was nearing completion, Katz asked me to finalize an agreement with the Manitoba Baseball Association that would allow amateur baseball to use the facility. The agreement was essential to the Goldeyes because government funding to help cover construction costs was conditional upon an amateur baseball access agreement.

Not everyone believed amateur baseball would be given reasonable access to the new facility and some of these concerned people were in the crowd at an association meeting I attended. The MBA previously had access to

Winnipeg Stadium but the daily cost of rental and staff was prohibitive so they seldom exercised that option. I believe my years of work in baseball and my understanding of their concerns helped calm everyone's fears and paved the way for an agreement. It's incumbent on the professional team to foster this kind of supportive relationship with amateur baseball.

Katz kept much of the park construction process to himself but Kevin Moore and I were at some meetings and made contributions. In fact, I was surprised when we would provide useful input at a meeting but then not be invited back to the next meeting. Moore and I took the whole process personally, of course, because we were going to have to live at this park once it was built. During one such meeting, Moore and I were adamant that the entrances to the new park be at one location so we could create some atmosphere on the promenade outside the gates. We had held this vision for many years, but it was only with the construction of the new facility that it could be realized.

But there could be no doubt that this was Katz's project and he had a multitude of tough decisions to make. How big should the offices be? What about the Goldeyes' clubhouse, trainer's room, coaches' offices, and weight-training room? Should there be a store on the concourse as well as at ground level? Should there be a children's playground and what type and price of equipment should go into it? What type of concessions, what size and type of seats to buy, should there be a video scoreboard and if so how big? The decisions seemed endless. We compiled a lot of research to help Katz make the best decisions possible. Some of those decisions were not easy and they were certainly not cheap.

The entire process started very tenuously. In early 1999, Goldeyes' accounts were tightly controlled during the building of CanWest Global Park. Money was at a premium. I was never sure of the exact details of the club's finances because Katz kept some of that information to himself. All I know is that as structuring of the finances to build the park was coming together, for several months getting a cheque out of him was like pulling teeth. My only choice was to start putting expenses on my personal credit cards. I'm not sure we would have had official Rawlings' game balls for Opening Day in 1999 if not for my willingness to charge the order to my card. I found myself in a position of having to explain to a lot of companies that they just needed to be patient until the money to build the park flowed in from all directions. Not everyone found that acceptable.

Our controller, Judy Jones, was the person on the front lines and she was afraid to answer her phone for a while because she was worried that someone who was owed money by the club would yell at her. I tried to calm her anxieties but it was difficult to be reassuring because I was not sure myself why there was such a problem. Fortunately, the dilemma was short-lived. Not only did funding sources for construction come through as promised but also, once the doors were opened and the fans responded to CanWest Global Park, money was flowing like honey. It was easy then to keep all creditors happy.

The excitement around the office was evident as the park was being built. Every week, Moore would trek over to the Richardson Building and take pictures of the site from high above to document construction progress. The pictures are a wonderful keepsake. We were finally going to be operating out of a baseball stadium.

CanWest Global Park is a wonderful place. While any new structure of its kind is exciting at the beginning, CanWest is standing the test of time because Katz made a myriad of good decisions when it was being built. To be sure, we were pushing him along the way but the final decisions were his to make. What most impressed me during the process was Katz's willingness, in the end, to pay the extra money and do it right. He wanted this facility to be one that everyone could be proud of. The Goldeyes' staff was happy with the facility, the players were impressed, and the fans and visitors have embraced the park with a passion.

I say the park is standing the test of time because 2006 is the eighth season the park has been open. It will be part of Sam Katz's legacy. At the very least, I believe it is his most significant achievement prior to becoming mayor of Winnipeg.

The year 1999 was tough on Goldeyes' employees. The job was all-consuming during normal times and 1999 was not normal. We were displaced for much of the year as the park was being completed and then we had to work in the middle of construction for the remainder of the year. We dealt with all of that while operating the organization out of a new facility during a hectic season. There was also much more corporate inventory to sell and the entire structure was a work in progress.

To make things even more interesting, baseball competition for the Pan-American Games in 1999 was to be held at CanWest Global Park. The Games would provide great exposure for the park and would put a lot of people in touch with the facility, but would also be an added stress on the staff. The park was busting at the seams during the Games. Many games drew 7,000 people, which was too many, back in 1999. Since then, expansion has increased facility and concourse space so 7,000 is now much more comfortable.

The Pan-American Games were very important. First and foremost, some of the dollars set aside for facility construction for the Games were used to help build the baseball stadium. Second, thousands of people were introduced to the park. No doubt that had a positive impact on them and they were more inclined to come back. The facility was great and the baseball was great. Canada won the bronze medal and actually beat both Cuba and the United States during the round robin – a first for Canadian baseball.

The impetus of the Games was significant to the construction of the park. The entire project was so tenuous at the beginning and Katz was fighting on so many fronts that an argument could be made that CanWest might never have been built without the support of the Pan-American Games.

During that trying year, the most difficult thing to deal with was that Katz had brought in new people to help with the building and operation of the facility. In particular, Al Golden, who was a City of Winnipeg councilor at the time, was overseeing construction. Golden had a domineering personality. No doubt, he felt he had to push the construction workers or the park would not be built on time. He may have been right, but that did not make him easy to deal with, especially when his attitude spilled over and was directed towards Goldeyes' staff, which did not appreciate the way they were treated. Their opinions were invalidated. Not a week passed when one or more of them did not come into my office and complain that they were frustrated and felt disrespected. At first, I tried to explain that these were stressful times and they should be patient. I soon realized, however, that patience was wearing thin.

Golden told me one afternoon that he was a part owner of the park, and that the staff better get used to having him around – a statement that Katz later told me was not true. The issue was so volatile that it was raised by a number of people at a year-end staff meeting. I believe Katz would have been facing a serious staff problem if Golden had been invited back to be involved after the 1999 season. He was not.

While I love CanWest Global Park, it is important to put everything in perspective. The new people who were involved in 1999 did not have the sense of history or a complete perspective on the organization. There might not have been a CanWest Global Park if the Goldeyes did not have a solid following in the previous five years. Without Winnipeg Stadium, there would have been no place to play initially and get the franchise up and running. Without the dedication of the staff, who had the unenviable job of selling tickets in a 33,000-seat football stadium for five years, none of what came later would have happened. This sort of perspective should not be forgotten.

Even the naming of the new stadium was not without some drama. Katz reached some kind of an agreement with Mind Computer Products and while different names were discussed, the name that Katz agreed to was Mind Field. My wife, Bev, and my mother were both upset with that name because it sounded like "mine field", which they felt was inappropriate for the Goldeyes' new home. They were not alone in their thinking, but when I informed Katz of their concerns, he told me he had made his decision. He directed me to create a splashy presentation to announce the new name during the last game of the 1998 season at Winnipeg Stadium. The culmination of that evening was a fireworks display, which ended with an expensive custom firework burning the words Mind Field. It was very colourful.

I am a big fan of Lloyd Axworthy, who was Canada's Minister of Foreign Affairs at the time. He was considered in 1998 for the Nobel Peace Prize after promoting a treaty to prohibit the use and production of anti-personnel mines. As the senior federal government politician from Manitoba, Mr. Axworthy's support was critical to guarantee government involvement and funding to help build the new park.

Providing government money for a facility named Mind Field must have posed a problem for him. Katz told me shortly after the 1998 season that all promotion of the name Mind Field was to stop immediately.

Suddenly, the name was dropped and CanWest Global Communications stepped forward to secure the naming rights. A potential problem became a significant benefit to the Goldeyes. Katz was very good at turning lemons into lemonade!

CanWest Global Park is gorgeous. It has already been the scene of many Goldeyes' baseball games, the Pan-American baseball games, and several concerts. The Guess Who concert may be the biggest concert held at the facility as of the writing of this book. Held in 2000, the concert was part of their reunion tour across Canada. It was a fabulous concert, even if the weather did not co-operate. The band actually had to leave the stage at one point because of lightning in the area but, through the delay and the pouring rain, the crowd would not go home. When band members re-appeared and continued the concert, they were greeted with a standing ovation. Burton Cummings sounded very genuine when he praised the faithful for staying through the rain as he commented that he must be back home in Winnipeg.

The concert was great but the steady downpour with thousands of people on the field did cause significant damage. The beautiful baseball field took a long time to get back to pristine condition. Economics dictates, however, that more concerts will be planned in the future. Let's hope they are not accompanied by rain and that better methods are found to protect the field.

CanWest Global Park was patterned after Newman Outdoor Field in Fargo. Winnipeg was fortunate in a way that Fargo built its park first. We were able to see the park first-hand in action and interview the people who were operating the facility. We were, therefore, able to correct any flaws the Red Hawks' organization saw with the design of their stadium. Not many things needed to be changed, but the knowledge gained from Fargo helped the Goldeyes build CanWest as one of the finest baseball facilities in the country.

The key to the design is the location of the concourse in relation to the field. You can walk on the concourse, visit the concession stands or the restrooms, and still be in touch with the action of the game. I am convinced that the design was important to the Goldeyes' success with attendance. So many people have said to me that a game is a social outing. If you walk the concourse, you are bound to meet someone you know. People can stand and visit as they watch the game. I would be surprised if stadiums built in the future did not use the same design.

It seems like a century ago that the Goldeyes were languishing at Winnipeg Stadium. When I compare the new facility to the old football stadium, it amazes me that we survived there at all. Attempts to create an environment in the press box area at the old stadium and call it a suite, for example, now seem comical compared to the luxury of the new sky suites at CanWest Global Park.

Many other changes were also dramatic. The seats at CanWest are comfortable and they all come equipped with backs and cup holders. There is ample leg room and the sections are restricted in size so that no more than 20 seats are placed between aisles. Compare that to the hard benches with no backs at Winnipeg Stadium. CanWest has a wide variety of quality and affordable concessions, a children's playground, a barbeque area, two merchandise stores instead of portable booths, a ticket office at the park instead of having to walk across to the arena to buy a ticket, and a promenade with activity prior to every game, which helps create a vibrant mood.

The staff thought they had landed in Shangri-La with the new facility and its offices that are the envy of every team in the league. The players also loved it, recognizing CanWest as a very classy facility. The clubhouse is spacious and there is a quality trainers' room, complete with whirlpool tubs, separate offices for the manager and coaches, and a weight-training room attached to the clubhouse. As well, a batting cage is under the third base grandstand for those rainy days or extra workouts.

Now, with the addition to the park that was completed in 2003, there is even more room. A great restaurant, Hu's On First, which is attached to the park, adds to the ambiance. Fans can enjoy a quality dinner, sit on the patio and watch the ball game.

I have been in a lot of stadiums and few can compare to CanWest. It's a true gem, but I would be remiss if I did not mention its few shortcomings. Nothing is perfect and some decisions were made that created problems. The most obvious problem at the beginning was the windows. During the first game played at the park, foul balls resulted in two windows being broken. I was appalled and Katz asked me to contact the window supplier. I was told the windows were fine and the two broken ones were merely an unbelievable coincidence. "You may not have another window broken all year," I was told. During the next game, three more windows were broken.

Needless to say, no amount of talk could solve the problem. Tests determined that the wrong windows had been installed; they did not meet the agreed-upon specifications. Thicker glass was required and every window facing the field had to be replaced. The fans thought it was funny for a while and held their breath for every foul ball. They would erupt in a loud cheer if a window was broken. The staff and the people in the suites did not think it was funny at all. By the time all the windows were replaced, everyone in the organization had seen enough broken glass to last them a life time. Taping up windows and cleaning up glass were daily occurrences during the first several games in 1999.

The baseball field itself was another problem. I don't believe we used the expertise that was available to us in Winnipeg through amateur baseball when it came to the field. The biggest problem was drainage. The field drained to the perimeter but the water had nowhere to go from there. During our first year, we actually hired pump trucks and ran hoses onto the field to pump water after a heavy rain. The following season, groundskeeper Don Ferguson dug trenches and placed drainage pipes all around the field. What a difference that made. Professional teams can ill afford to cancel games because of standing water on their field.

Other field issues included the pitcher's mound and the home plate area, which were too soft. Clay bricks had to be brought in and laid just under the surface to provide stability to these heavily trafficked areas. The field required constant vigilance but eventually was improved to everyone's satisfaction.

The scoreboard also created some problems. It was located too close to straightaway centre field. I have never been in a baseball park that has the scoreboard so close to the batter's eye. The batter's eye is the area directly behind the pitcher at the outfield fence and it is required to be a minimum of 50 feet wide. The scoreboard was located outside of the 50 foot area but every year hitters complained that the scoreboard distracted them while they were at the plate. Whenever a left-handed pitcher dropped down and threw from the side, from the batter's perspective, the ball appeared to be very close to the scoreboard.

The movement of rotating signs on the scoreboard could also be distracting. There was only so much that could be done, however, because advertisements had been sold on all of them. All signs on the north end of the scoreboard were eventually changed so that they did not have a white background. That was done to accommodate the hitters. The renovations and additions to the scoreboard in 2006 removed the rotating signs.

In comparison to what was done right, these flaws are minor. CanWest Global Park remains a wonderful facility. During construction, decisions were made at every turn to accommodate the fans. They are the real benefactors of this great ball park. CanWest Global Park is a gem that will sparkle in Winnipeg for a long time to come. My hat is off to Sam Katz for getting the job done with class.

L-R
–Groundbreaking ceremony
–CanWest Global Park
–1999 staff

Chapter 14: Rain, Umpires, and Some Strange Stories

Weather

A rain-out was far more complicated than I would ever have predicted. The rules of baseball specify that prior to the game, the general manager of the home team is responsible for determining if a game shall commence. Once the line-up cards are exchanged, the responsibility for playing, delaying, or calling the game reverts to the umpires. The umpires are sensitive to any input from the home team and the grounds crew, but the final decision is then in their hands.

It is worth pointing out that if it were raining anywhere in the surrounding area, the phone in the office would begin to ring around noon on a game day that had a scheduled 7 p.m. start time. People wanted to know if we were going to call off the game. If it were raining anywhere within a 200-mile radius later in the afternoon, the number of calls would be well beyond what we could handle.

Everyone who called wanted an immediate answer. They all had special circumstances that required a definitive yes or no to the question of whether we were going to play. Was the game going to be called off or not? When would we decide?

Professional baseball teams seldom call off games prior to a scheduled start time. In 1995, I cancelled a game around 5:30 p.m. The wind was so strong it blew over a large section of the right-field fence. The rain was so hard the dugouts filled with water and the weather office predicted a stretch of continual rain for several hours. In the newspaper the next day a picture that had been taken around 7 p.m. showed the field in brilliant sunshine. When I looked at it, even I wondered why we hadn't played. A better picture would have been our mascot, Goldie, swimming in the visitors' dugout.

The complexities of the decision prior to the start of a game are mind-boggling. Besides the fans, who are the most important people in the decision, many other factors are at play. The teams may or may not want to play, depending on their record, the condition of their pitching staff, or their travel arrangements. Players are usually happy to be told a game has been "banged" and they can go to the bar early, but managers want any advantage they can get. Team owners, of course, want every game to be played because a rain-out means lost revenue.

A lot of personalities were also in play when those tough decisions were made. Our manager, our players, the visiting team manager, the visiting players, the umpires, the owners, game-day workers, front office staff, the media, and the fans all had different perspectives on whether the game should be played. And all their opinions were usually strong and loud.

If a game was rained out and the same two teams were scheduled to play the next day, a double-header would be played. Both games would be seven-inning contests. That could be an advantage if a manager had a tired pitching staff because the team would need pitching for only 14 innings instead of 18.

A manager was also concerned that his starting pitcher might only pitch a short while and then, if the game were rained out, wouldn't be available for several days. Therefore, they only wanted to start the game if there was a realistic chance it would be played. Double headers are not easy to win, however, so teams desperate for wins do not like to play them.

The umpires were another factor during potential rain-outs because they represented the league and had a say as to whether the field was playable. A general manager could say he or she wanted the game to start, but the umpires could call the game off as soon as they received the line-up cards, if they thought the field was unplayable. A respected league like the Northern League tries to play every game. It does not have unnecessary rain-outs, which is good for credibility with scouts and fans alike. The umpires, as the league's representatives, are told to complete a game whenever possible.

The staff was on the front lines dealing directly with the fans. They wanted to know when a decision would be made because they were constantly being asked by fans, concessionaires, or other staff. I tried to keep everyone informed with any information at my disposal. Other big dilemmas were pre-game barbeques and suites. The food was already prepared so when fans showed up in the rain, we might feed them but then not even play the game. That caused a lot of confusion.

My best friends during those difficult times were the folks at the weather office. I learned to analyze the radar on my computer screen pretty well, but I always backed it up with confirmation from a real person at the weather office. I did that despite the fact they were wrong sometimes. I found they were pretty accurate if they were only predicting a short time into the future, but guessing ahead several hours dramatically decreased their level of accuracy. We were also concerned about the weather at a specific spot – right over the ball park – while they were usually more comfortable predicting weather somewhere in the vicinity.

Countless times over the years it would be raining five miles or eight kilometres away from the ball park but we would not get a drop. Nevertheless, I learned to interpret the information the weather office provided. Some weather patterns were easier to predict than others.

Once the Goldeyes moved into CanWest Global Park, the decision became even more complicated. With games selling out or coming close to selling out, there was nowhere to put people if a double header were to be played the next day because that regularly scheduled game would already be almost sold-out. That was another important reason we tried hard to play every game.

A lot of unforeseen logistics had to be looked after when a game was postponed. Because the start of the game the next day was moved forward an hour, a long list of participants was informed through all available media and the website. The list included all game-day staff, anthem singer(s), Baseball Buddies, 50/50 sellers, pre-game or during-game entertainers, ceremonial opening pitcher and the fans. It was so complicated that we created a rain-out checklist so no one would be forgotten.

Then we had to deal with the fans who had tickets for the rained-out game. Thousands of people had tickets they had to exchange for another game. They could almost never get the same seat they had purchased for the rained-out game and sometimes there were no equivalent-value seats available. In that case, we would give them the best seat available. Most people were understanding, but not everyone.

I have one good weather story to tell from my year in Sioux Falls. The summer of 2004 turned out to be one of the coldest and wettest ever recorded throughout the Midwest, including Sioux Falls, South Dakota. It could best be described as "the summer that wasn't." No doubt, Winnipeg was affected by that weather as well, but with a franchise like Sioux Falls, such adversities were much more noticeable because they had fewer pre-sold tickets. As previously mentioned, relying on game day walk-up tickets is very dangerous for a professional baseball team. In the summer of 2004, it was my worst nightmare.

On a Saturday night during the second weekend of the season, the Canaries were playing host to the Schaumburg Flyers. Rain had been forecast throughout the day but had never materialized so the game was started on time. During the bottom of the second inning, the sky began to blacken. I'm not talking grey; I mean black. I had never witnessed such cloud formations before. They seemed to reach from the sky and head straight for the ground.

Suddenly, sirens started blaring throughout the city. I had never heard sirens like that before, unless the police were in a parade down Portage Avenue in Winnipeg. While I was not sure exactly what they meant, I knew it could not be good! Sure enough, I turned around and the fans were all leaving the stadium seating area. The umpire immediately suspended play and the players ran to their clubhouses while everyone else headed underneath the grandstand. It was a tornado warning!

Justin Kutcher, our radio broadcaster, was from Connecticut. He called on his cell phone and asked, "What do I do now?" I told him I was appointing him our honourary captain and I expected him to go down with the ship. I thought he could keep broadcasting, kind of like the band on the Titanic. He didn't think I was very funny at the time. He went on the air and said, "I'm not from around here but when people get up out of their seats and begin to leave, I'm going to take that as a sign." And with that, he said, "We're going to send it back to the studio now, and I'm going to take cover."

A tornado did touch down five miles from the ball park. Then a violent prairie rain storm hit. Over five inches of rain fell in an hour. Not only was the field flooded, but many of the streets in Sioux Falls were impassable by car. The next two days we ended up playing back-to-back double headers because the game the previous night had also been rained out.

Another fun weather story occurred in 1999 during the playoffs. Winnipeg won the Central Conference that year and played the Albany-Colonie Diamond Dogs for the Northern League Championship. Albany won the first game at home 7-6. Game 2 was postponed early the next morning because the remnants of Hurricane Floyd were about to hit the New York area. I had never heard of canceling a game that far in advance. Of course, I had never experienced weather from the remnants of a hurricane either. It rained for 24 hours straight. All was not lost, however, because the Diamond Dogs arranged a trip for the entire team to go to Cooperstown and visit the Baseball Hall of Fame. It was a great way to spend a rainy day in New York and was my second visit to Cooperstown within a year.

To sum this all up, rain-outs were the bane of my existence. I do not miss the pressure of the decisions on rainy days. To this day, if I know the Goldeyes are playing at home and there is rain in the vicinity, I get anxious. I feel empathy for the staff, and general manager Andrew Collier in particular.

Umpires

Possibly the most bizarre incident I dealt with during my tenure in Winnipeg was the umpire strike in 1995. I was contacted by the league one morning and informed that umpires were refusing to work the games that same night. The local Manitoba Umpire Association, for some reason that escaped me at the time, decided to support the Northern League umpire's strike and refused to have their members umpire. A couple of our local umpires had to work with the Northern League umpires so I understood why they might not want to work. Why the Association as a whole felt the need to support a professional umpires' wildcat strike was beyond me. What was I to do?

After many calls, I found a senior league umpire, Ron Jeremy, from the Interlake Region of Manitoba who agreed to umpire the plate. I explained the situation and the events that had unfolded. He didn't agree with the position the Manitoba Umpire Association had taken. The other two umpires were Dave Underwood and Hank Lemoine. I knew these two guys from amateur baseball. Lemoine, to my knowledge, had never umpired a game in his life. He was a player. Underwood did umpire some youth baseball. They both did a credible job and performed a huge favour for the Goldeyes that night.

The managers also understood. They were very gentle when they questioned any call during the game. The game was played without incident and the issue was resolved the next day. An umpire strike was not on my regular checklist when preparing for a game.

Several other incidents involving umpires "brightened" my career. I was a big umpire supporter. Respect was big in my vocabulary and every part of the league was important to me. I guess all teams did not feel that way because umpires sure seemed to enjoy the way they were treated in Winnipeg. Butch Fisher, the Northern League Umpire-In-Chief for many years, never missed an opportunity to thank me for the way his boys were treated in our city.

The Northern League at that time had teams of two umpires who rotated throughout the various ball parks for the season. The third umpire was local and it was the responsibility of the home team to pay him. Winnipeg was lucky there were good umpires in Manitoba. Ron Shewchuk, Brian Hodgson, and Derek Dubell, along with Glen Johnson and Keith Johnson, all did themselves proud as umpires at Northern League games when I was with the Goldeyes. I knew them all and I was a little protective of them.

Some interesting characters umpired in the Northern League. Richard Katz (no relation to Sam Katz) was one of them. Katz was a good umpire but he had a volatile temper and reacted strongly to criticism from the players or managers. I liked him but one time I got into it with him because he was arguing with manager Hal Lanier. That was not so unusual, but Lanier was near home plate and Katz was behind first base. I was sitting in the stands and I could clearly hear Katz use language that we did not tolerate in the ball park. Because they were yelling at each other from such a distance, the fans could also hear the altercation. I needed to take some action. I made an immediate complaint to the league, which fined Katz, but he never seemed to be upset with me over making that call. I guess he realized he had crossed the line.

One of the more bizarre situations with an umpire occurred during the 2004 season when I was in Sioux Falls. Weather threatened prior to the game but was holding off. Finally, I received word from the weather office that we were certain to get hit hard within 10 minutes. Enough rain was coming to affect the field. I immediately ran onto the diamond and told the home plate umpire, Brad Hungerford, that we should pull the tarp over the field. That occurred as the starting pitcher was finishing his warm-up pitches just prior to the start of the game.

Sure enough, 15 minutes later it poured. The rain lasted for 20 minutes or so and I could see on the radar screen that it was clearing through the area. I told Hungerford we would soon be able to pull the tarp. He lashed out at me that he was in charge and he would tell me what we were going to do. I was taken aback by his brash manner because I was well aware that it was his decision to make as to when we could restart the game. I had thought we were on the same team in trying to get the game played.

The rain stopped and the fans were getting restless as brilliant sunshine flooded the field, yet the signal to remove the tarp never came. I confirmed with the weather office by telephone that rain had passed us and I went to find the umpire to ask about the delay. He was abrupt with me again and went in search of a television to check the weather. I told him I was on the phone with the National Weather Service and he could talk to them himself, which would be far better than expecting a television station to be up to date. He said he would not take the phone from me because I could have one of my friends on the line telling him what I wanted him to hear. Talk about an attack on one's character. How he could think I would do something like that is beyond me? I was outraged.

I guess he was under pressure, too, but when he then insinuated that I did not care about the safety of the players and the fans, that was too much. I contacted the league and informed Butch Fisher that this umpire had lost all perspective as to what his role should be. How an umpire could think that he cared more about the fans in the park than the general manager did, was beyond my comprehension.

I avoided Hungerford for the remainder of the series because I was still steamed at his attitude during the rain-delayed game. He asked me to come to the umpires' room after the last game of the series and apologized for his accusations and behavior.

Other times, I've had umpires who tried to take baseballs out of the park at the end of a game. I think one guy was trying to open his own sporting goods business. He had to go! Some of the umpires would complain about the food. Sometimes they would want a bunch of free tickets or free golf. Like players, there were some who were higher maintenance than others, but all in all, I liked the umpires and did whatever I could for them.

Other strange but true stories

No matter how much people prepare for a new challenge, inevitably, some unpredictable things are thrown at them. That was certainly the case in my position as a general manager of a professional baseball club. When dealing with 30 to 40 players per year, hundreds of thousands of fans, and some excitable staff in a high-pressure, high-energy environment, interesting things are bound to happen.

Juan de la Rosa

My most-unusual-player story occurred in 1995, the year that Juan de la Rosa came to play for the Goldeyes part-way through the season. He had been playing in the Toronto Blue Jays' organization and had recently been released. Juan was a citizen of the Dominican Republic but had been playing baseball in the United States for years.

One day around 11:30 p.m., shortly after Juan joined the Goldeyes, the team bus left Winnipeg for the U.S. after a home game. I was usually happy to see them leave town because when the team was on the road, I could find time to catch up on some work. This particular trip came at the conclusion of a six-game home stand and I was completely exhausted. Shortly after the bus was out of site, I jumped in my car and drove home.

I was fast asleep when the phone near my bed rang at 1 a.m. I answered sleepily and it took me a few seconds to recognize the voice on the other end of the line as field manager Doug Simunic. He was excitedly trying to explain that something was wrong with Juan de la Rosa's paperwork and the U.S. immigration officer at the border would not let him into the country. I told Doug to let me talk to the officer, hoping I could straighten out the confusion, but it became readily apparent that the officer's mind was made up. He was very officious and was determined that de la Rosa was not going to enter the country. He bluntly told me there was nothing to discuss and rudely hung up in my ear.

I was lying in bed half awake, wondering what to do when the phone rang again. It was Simunic and he said he had things all figured out. He was going to put de la Rosa in the luggage compartment under the bus and go back to the border and try to cross again! I bolted upright, wide awake. I screamed into the phone that he was not to do any such crazy thing. I had visions of the Goldeyes being banned from crossing the border for the rest of the season.

I told Simunic to take de la Rosa to the Emerson Hotel and leave him there and I would have someone go down and pick him up. I would sort out the paperwork mess the next day and try to get him to Sioux City in time for the game. Emerson, Manitoba, is a small quiet town located right at the border crossing. I phoned the hotel to tell them what was happening. They were very sympathetic and told me it would be no problem for our player to wait at the hotel for someone to pick him up. Then I sat and tried to figure out who I would call to go and get him. It was almost 2 a.m. I couldn't think of anyone so I put on some clothes and started driving. I arrived in Emerson just before 3 a.m.

I assumed Juan would be waiting in the lobby of the hotel when I arrived. As I pulled into Emerson, it was as quiet as our clubhouse after a tough loss. Not a creature was stirring. As I approached the front door of the hotel, I saw a yellow sticky note that read: "John, go to Room 12." I looked around in the still of the night and thought for a moment before deciding the note must be for me! I slowly walked down the dimly lit hall and knocked softly at Room 12. It was three o'clock in the morning and the knock sounded very loud to me. No response. I knocked again, a little louder, and heard movement behind the door, but still no response.

Finally, I said, "Juan is that you?" A voice from behind the door replied, "Si."

"Open the door Juan, it's John," I said.

The voice again could be heard from behind the door. "Si."

Slowly, the door opened just a small crack and I could see one eyeball staring into the hall. After he recognized me, Juan threw open the door and literally jumped into my arms. Here I was at 3 a.m. stumbling around the hall of the Emerson Hotel with a 6-foot, three-inch black man clutched in my arms. It would have made a great picture.

Did I mention that Juan did not speak very good English? I convinced him to get down and grab his bag. We walked back down the hallway and I got him into my car. As we drove back to Winnipeg, he was talking a mile a minute – mostly in Spanish. He was very hyper and very confused, but as he spoke I began to understand the depth of his concerns. I'm not sure where people are sent when they are in big trouble in the Dominican Republic, but Juan was convinced that when you were in big trouble in Canada, you were sent to the Emerson Hotel!

He finally calmed down and we drove to my home for a couple of hours sleep. Juan slept on the couch in the living room. At 6:30 in the morning, I was awakened by quite a commotion. I raced down the stairs to find Juan pinned in the corner of the living room by Shadow, our 100-pound bouvier. Shadow was a wonderful friendly dog but she had a deep frightening bark. She apparently believed for a moment that an unwelcome intruder had found his way into our house. Poor Juan was having quite a day. Once I reached the room, everyone relaxed and Juan and Shadow became friends. We had some breakfast and de la Rosa and I left for the airport.

After negotiating with U.S. immigration officials for some time, and finally convincing them that we did not have time to go to Calgary to file our paperwork before the season would be over, we came to an agreement that de la Rosa could use a multiple-entry document that would get us through to the end of the season. Juan, who had no idea what was going on, put his X on the documents and headed for the plane that was already boarding. As he walked through customs, he turned and gave me a huge smile and wave. The last words I heard him say were, "Don't worry. Juan hit the ball! Juan hit the ball!" Then he was gone. I stood there smiling for a few minutes, then headed into work to start a new day.

I was happy to see Juan make it through that ordeal. He found his way onto the flight and even managed to make the connection in Minneapolis, so he arrived in Sioux City in time to play that night. Simunic was very pleased with my efforts. And hit the ball, Juan did! He was one of our most productive hitters for the remainder of the year.

When Sam Katz asked me for a job description at the end of the season, I told him this story because it best described a day in my life as a general manager. How do you fit that into a job description? "Other duties as assigned" just doesn't seem to cover it adequately.

Speaking engagements were a significant part of my job as well. It was a great way to connect with people so I would accept virtually every offer I received. Anyway, I loved speaking to crowds. There was such a warm feeling about the baseball club in the community that I was always welcomed with open arms. Some people find public speaking draining but I found it could energize me, especially if the group was keen and asked questions.

I have spoken in front of small groups of 15-20 people and in front of hundreds. The most bizarre situation I found myself in was a speaking engagement in front of the Shriners in Winnipeg at a gentlemen's fundraising dinner. The price of the ticket included food, all you could drink, and a chance to win $1000 through an elimination draw. Prior to my speech, another speaker told some jokes. They were not jokes you would tell your mother but very off-colour, and they kept getting raunchier and raunchier as he progressed.

By the time I got up to speak, the crowd was getting a little loud. I started my speech and, while most people were listening, a little rumbling came from the back of the room. Suddenly, I realized there was a scuffle going on and, to my surprise, a couple of Goldeyes' staff members who were also attending the dinner, were right in the middle of it. They had told a particular gentleman to keep quiet because they wanted to hear my speech. I guess they felt it necessary to go over to this guy's table to emphasize the point. The Goldeyes' staff was always looking out for a member of the family. The loud-mouthed man got the message and the rest of the speech went off without incident. I did cut a couple of my stories short, however, to make sure we all got out of there in one piece.

Coordinating logistics, including team travel, was another part of the job. I decided early on that I would be very organized in that regard. At the beginning of every year, I created a spread sheet that noted all bus travel, the hotel to be slept in every night, and the date and time of every game. But even with all that ammunition, I received one of the worst calls of my career from Duluth one July night in 1996. The team had arrived in that city after an afternoon game in Thunder Bay, only to find their hotel didn't have any rooms. Dale Coulthard, our clubhouse manager, was very upset on the phone and I asked him if the sheet said the team was to sleep in Duluth. There was dead silence on the phone. No one had looked at the sheet.

On every other trip, if the team played an afternoon game, they would get on the bus and travel to the next city, but this was the 4th of July weekend so they were supposed to stay in Thunder Bay on Sunday night and travel to Duluth in the morning. Because it was the holiday weekend, rooms were almost impossible to come by. They tried a number of hotels, including a dive in Superior, Wisconsin. As the bus pulled up to the hotel, a man approached and started banging on the bus door, demanding to be let in. In unison, the players asked the bus driver to get out of there.

In the end, players slept all over the cities of Duluth and Superior. Some slept on couches while others slept on tables or the floor. What a nightmare! Scott Neiles thought he had lucked out when he and Hal Lanier found a room in a decent hotel that had a king sized bed. After checking in, Lanier tossed him a pillow and told him he could sleep on any part of the floor he wanted. While I didn't feel it was my fault the mix-up had happened, I still felt horrible. I can assure you, it never happened again because from that day onward, everyone checked and cross-checked the team travel sheet.

Communications director Jonathan Green was frequently trying to stir things up wherever he went. We were on our way to Sioux Falls one weekend to watch the Goldeyes play the Canaries. I crossed the border first in my car. When the U.S. border officer asked me for my occupation, I told him I was the general manager of the Winnipeg Goldeyes and that I was going to watch the team play in Sioux Falls. He quickly allowed me to proceed.

Ten minutes later, Green arrived at the border. When asked for his occupation, he also said he was the general manager of the Goldeyes. The officer told him someone in a previous car had said the same thing. Jonathan quickly retorted, "The staff are always trying to imitate me. They probably want my job!" They don't have a great sense of humour at the border, but this guy waved Green through. No wonder they checked my identification so closely and asked for a business card on subsequent crossings.

One of the funniest sights I have ever seen occurred at the Baseball Winter Meetings in New Orleans. One night, Hal Lanier, Andrew Collier, and I went down to Bourbon Street to partake in the festivities. We ended up in a club where blues music was blasting. It was very crowded and at some point later in the evening, Collier decided he wanted to dance. He started swaying to the music and the next thing I knew he was dancing with a gorgeous black woman. He had acquired a hat that he was wearing which was way too big for him and had ear flaps that hung down to his shoulders. He stood out like a sore thumb.

Most of the people in the bar were black and one very large gentleman seemed to take offence at Collier's dancing with his friend. Lanier and I were standing at the bar watching in amazement. Lanier looked over at me and said, "John, I'm too old to fight my way out of here!" I laughed and nodded, recognizing that he might not be kidding.

Collier was really into his moves on the dance floor and it seemed like he was oblivious to the large man approaching him. As the man confronted him and demanded to know what he was doing, Collier reached out and grabbed the huge cigar that was hanging from the guy's mouth and started smoking it. I was on my way to grab Andrew and get him out of there when the guy let out with a boisterous laugh.

"You've got a lot of jam, brother," he bellowed. Lanier and I will never forget the sight as Collier danced, wearing that crazy-looking hat and a big stogie hanging out of his mouth while the man and his friends clapped and laughed. We left soon thereafter. Lanier and I decided there was no point in pushing our luck or, more to the point, having Collier push it for us.

Another unique event changed the face of the 2001 playoffs. For the sixth consecutive year, the Goldeyes met the Fargo-Moorhead Red Hawks in the playoffs. For the second time in their history, the Goldeyes rallied from a 0-2 deficit and beat the Red Hawks three straight games to win the division series three games to two. The next series was to begin in Lincoln. The date of the first game was September 11th, 2001. Events occurred that day that changed our lives. The series was postponed for a week as the aftermath of 9/11 was felt throughout the world. Baseball was put into perspective.

The Northern League has had its share of firsts. Ila Borders was the first woman to play professional baseball. She pitched for three teams — Madison, Duluth, and St. Paul. Borders was a quality person. She loved baseball and wanted to play at the highest possible level. She was not always treated with respect because some people felt she should not be playing with men. In college, she was unbelievably hit at the plate 11 out of 11 times at bat. She received more than her share of abuse from fans, but also got a great deal of support from those who admired her courage and wanted to see her succeed.

The Northern League is not affiliated with Major League Baseball so teams do not fall under the same rules as the affiliated minor league clubs. The Northern League has, therefore, been invited to play touring teams. They have included the Russian National team, the German National team, a professional Japanese team, and the Colorado Silver Bullets. The Bullets were a touring women's professional team.

Being an independent league also allowed teams to bring in players that were suspended by Major League Baseball. Darryl Strawberry and Steve Howe were a couple of examples. They were suspended for violating the substance abuse policy. If the Northern League was built on the philosophy of "last chances", these two guys certainly fit the bill. Strawberry lasted less than half a season with the St. Paul Saints before his contract was purchased by the New York Yankees. Later that same year, he played in the World Series.

The Northern League experimented with a 20-second clock. The pitcher had 20 seconds to throw a pitch after receiving the ball back from the catcher. What a novel idea to try speeding the game up. Guess what – the 20-second rule is actually in the baseball rule book. The Northern League was merely trying to enforce it. Unfortunately, it caused problems at some stadiums. The clock was not used properly or the horn would go off as the pitcher was delivering the ball. The league did away with the clock after a few seasons but a 90-second time frame between innings, which the NL instituted, is still in use today.

A unique event occurred in 1996 on my way to a baseball seminar. The first leg of the flight took us to Chicago. I had just settled in my seat when the flight attendant came up to me and asked if I was John Hindle. I nodded my head and she informed me that the pilot wanted to see me. I said, "You're kidding, right."

"No sir," she responded. "Please follow me." I was taken to the front of the plane and there I was greeted by the friendly face of one of our player-host families; he was flying the plane. He asked me if I would like to sit up front in the cockpit with him so we could visit during the flight. I was thrilled to have that rare opportunity, which occurred in the days prior to September 11, 2001.

After the plane was in the air, we had a nice visit. As we passed over Madison, Wisconsin, I was asked if I would like to see the ball park of the new team that would be playing in the Northern League for the upcoming 1997 season. I thought that would be fun so the plane suddenly banked to the left and we flew over Madison and saw the field before the plane reverted back to its original course. Never before, or since, have I affected the flight path of a commercial aircraft.

While I worked with a lot of interesting people over the years, the most bizarre incident with a staff member occurred at a Christmas party. This young man had not been working very long for the Goldeyes. He was another person that Katz had hired without telling anyone. He appeared one day at the office and informed me that he was supposed to be a salesperson.

Unfortunately, he arrived at our Christmas party somewhat inebriated and it only got worse from there. Early in the evening, he approached me to talk about his skills as a baseball pitcher. I was polite as he proceeded to tell me he could strike me out on three pitches. We were having a pleasant chat about my favourite game so I smiled and said, "I'm sure you could. I'm a little out of shape."

But he kept repeating it over and over again. While I tried to remain polite, he was becoming increasingly more adamant that I could never touch his knuckleball or any of his other pitches. Other staff noticed my dilemma and tried to intervene by changing the subject with him, but he was relentless.

After some time, I turned away from him and walked clear across the room to talk with marketing manager Kevin Moore. As I approached Moore, I could see his eyes staring over my shoulder and I feared my pitching nemesis was following me. I was right. When he pulled my shoulder, spun me around, and started poking me in the chest – I had finally had enough.

I bluntly told him I had played a lot of baseball and represented Manitoba at many Canadian championships. I could hit his knuckleball or any other pitch he could throw and it would be best if he sat down and stopped drinking. He left shortly thereafter and never did return to the office. I guess he wasn't very happy with his job.

New employees hired after that event were given a version of this story by other staff as part of their initiation. They were warned not to challenge my hitting skills or they might be fired at any time. In reality, the employee in question was not fired. He simply never returned to work, but that part was left out of the staff version of the story. After the incident, I asked Katz if I could be a part of the hiring process for any new employees because I was the one who had to work with them and supervise them on a daily basis.

Chapter 15: Hosting the Stars

The Northern League played its first all-star game in 1997 in St. Paul. Thereafter, games followed in Sioux City, Fargo, and New Jersey, with Winnipeg's turn coming in 2001. I attended each and every game and in the back of my mind I knew we would eventually host the all-star game, so while I enjoyed the events, I was constantly looking for ideas we could use in Winnipeg.

The game in St. Paul was great. The night before the game there was a reception and Sioux City manager Ed Nottle sang songs and entertained everyone. The fireworks display at the conclusion of the game may have been the best I have ever seen. Even the players hung around to watch it.

The thing I most remember about the Sioux City all-star game was that George Brett was the honoured guest. Brett was one of my baseball idols growing up. Like myself, he batted from the left side and I still remember the excitement that was generated during his quest to bat .400 for the 1980 season.

By 1999, the Northern League had amalgamated with the Northeast League and the all-star game in Fargo was the first opportunity for competition between the two conferences. Fargo did a solid job with their all-star game but I started thinking the event could be so much more.

Then we went to the all-star game in New Jersey; it was somewhat of a disappointment. The luncheon was small and transportation was a problem. The highlight of the all-star festivities was the welcome party the night before the game. Attached to their stadium is the Yogi Berra Museum. When we arrived at the museum, Yogi himself was in attendance, which was an unexpected surprise.

Few people in baseball have had more stories attributed to them than Yogi. He is a living legend. Not many people are quoted more than he is. A few of the pearls of wisdom attributed to Yogi include: "It ain't over 'til it's over"; "When you come to a fork in the road.... take it"; and "You can observe a lot by watching." He is also well known for his work with youth, humanitarian, and charitable causes.

Fortunately, Hal Lanier knew Yogi from his playing days with the New York Yankees. Berra was excited to see Lanier and they hung out together most of the night. What an amazing experience for me to listen to them talk about stories of former great players! They knew the players personally so the stories seemed far more real than anything you might read in an article or see on television.

Hosting the all-star game in Winnipeg was very important to me. I felt a debt of gratitude to my colleagues throughout the league who had taught me so much and provided me with so many ideas that had helped make the Goldeyes a better organization and created a better experience at our ball park. Here was my chance to be the ultimate host and pay them back. I considered the 2001 all-star celebrations to be an opportunity to showcase our city, CanWest Global Park, and the entire Goldeyes' organization. If we turned a profit in the process, so much the better, but I knew the exposure would be beneficial to the Goldeyes, if we could pull off a classy affair.

While some of the planning for such an event starts a year in advance, a lot of the work occurs during the regular season. Anyone in the industry understands how difficult that is, with staff being very busy during the season – at times, overloaded. We could not have successfully held the all-star game in Winnipeg much earlier in our evolution as an organization but by 2001, we were a pretty smooth-operating machine and ready for the challenge.

Finding a quality hotel that could accommodate a luncheon of 600-plus people was the first priority. The Fairmont was located one block from CanWest Global Park and was the highest rated hotel in Winnipeg at the time. It was the perfect place to host the event if a deal could be arranged.

Fortunately, the hotel manager felt the same way. He believed that type of high-profile event in Winnipeg belonged at his hotel. We were able to quickly come to an arrangement that was good for both sides. The deal included all accommodations for the players and the luncheon. The hotel would receive extra room bookings from the visiting teams and players' families. Securing a great hotel was a perfect start to the planning of the event.

With accommodation taken care of, we were able to start planning all the other details. From the beginning, we wanted to raise the profile of the all-star game. Why not make the event a two-day celebration? Major League Baseball did, so I saw no reason why the Northern League couldn't. Boldly, we decided to go ahead. On the first day, we held a skills competition, which culminated with a home-run derby. On the second day, we held a luncheon and the all-star game. Each part of the event was broken down into specific responsibilities and one or two staff people were put in charge of coordinating it.

The break-down was as follows: accommodation, travel, transportation in Winnipeg, luncheon, entertainment, promenade at the ball park, Skills Competition, after Skills Competition party, radio and television broadcasts, VIPs, communication, player liaison, selling tickets to all events, youth clinic, All-Star Game and after All-Star Game party.

While I, as the general manager, was involved with much of the planning, it was impossible for one person to put together all the details for every event. What a great feeling it was to be working with a team of skilled and enthusiastic people that I trusted completely and who I knew would perform their jobs at the highest level. We were a powerful team and hosting the all-star game was a time when it really showed. We held regular meetings along with all our other obligations, and by the time the guests started to arrive, we were ready. We were so ready, in fact, that I, as part of being a good host, was able to go golfing in the morning of the Skills Competition with a few other general managers. I knew we were prepared.

I was glad I had gone golfing because I witnessed Tim Utrup, the general manager of the Lincoln Salt Dogs, ace a hole-in-one at the sixth hole at Kingswood Golf Course. Unbelievably, Utrup recorded three holes-in-one during that year. He is a pretty fair golfer but the chances of that happening must be astronomical.

Long before any work had been accomplished, I went to Sam Katz and asked him this question: "How much money do we have to make to consider the all-star game a financial success?" Initially, he was hesitant to answer – I presumed because he did not want to put a ceiling on profit. I was only asking the question so that I could get a handle in my own mind of where the definition of success would fall. I also wanted to spend money to make the event first class and did not want to be second-guessed as long as I met our profit target. He eventually gave me a number that I knew he had inflated since no other team had been able to meet such a profit in previous all-star games. I am pleased to report, however, that we easily surpassed his goal, generated revenue for the Field of Dreams Foundation, and still put on a fabulous show.

One of the first things that needed to be done was to finalize the VIP guests who would act as honourary captains for the two teams. These VIPs would throw out a ceremonial pitch prior to the start of the game and would speak at the luncheon. We came up with two great ambassadors of the game of baseball. Whitey Herzog was one of the greatest managers of all time. Hal Lanier had been one of his coaches at St. Louis and had won a World Series ring with Whitey in 1982. Lanier thought Herzog might come to Winnipeg for the all-star game because they were still close friends. I asked him to call Whitey and was thrilled to hear that Herzog was excited with the prospect of coming up to Winnipeg and spending some time with Hal. We quickly came to an agreement.

While that was taking place, I also contacted the Toronto Blue Jays to ask for their involvement. They agreed to send Ernie Whitt to Winnipeg. Ernie was a long-time Blue Jays' catcher and fan favourite. More recently, he had been a roving instructor with the organization and had managed the Canadian Pan-American Games baseball team in 1999 in Winnipeg.

Canada had had such success in baseball at the Games that Ernie Whitt had become a familiar name to baseball fans in Winnipeg. The Canadian baseball team became the "Darlings of the Games." Canada eventually lost to Cuba in the semi-finals and then beat Mexico to win bronze. I was very excited to have Herzog and Whitt both agree to come and help celebrate our all-star event.

The confirmation of Herzog and Whitt brought significant media exposure. That was very important in the Winnipeg market because we were trying to raise the profile of the event and having the media on board was critical to achieving that goal. The media seemed excited that these two high-profile baseball icons were coming to their city.

The Blue Jays were covering Whitt's expenses as part of their support so he was making his own travel arrangement, which was great for us. We were responsible for making arrangements for Herzog. As the deadline for booking the travel arrangements approached, I tried in vain to contact Whitey. I emailed his suggested itinerary but heard nothing in return. I was close to the panic stage when finally a response was received at the last minute.

But Herzog was upset that he was required to make a speech at the luncheon. Somehow he had forgotten that that was part of the original discussion we had had months before. We had already printed the luncheon literature and publicized that he was the feature speaker. I tried to reassure him by telling him we could interview him, so that he would not have to prepare a speech, but he was non-committal. Talk about stress. I was beside myself.

Fortunately, my friend and field manager, Hal Lanier, picked that exact time to walk into my office. He took one look at my face and asked me what was wrong. After telling him my dilemma, Lanier grabbed the phone and called Herzog himself. Shortly thereafter, Herzog called to inform me that everything was fine and he was looking forward to coming to Winnipeg for the all-star game. I slept a lot better that night.

I knew the significance of having Whitey at our event. Here was one of the most colourful figures in the game. His success as a manager was stellar and getting him was a real coup for us. He had agreed to come to Winnipeg for much less than his regular appearance fee as a favour to his friend, Hal Lanier. Lanier, in turn, had contacted and then convinced Herzog to come to Winnipeg because he knew how important it was to me. What a wonderful thing for a friend to do for me!

Whitey was just as much a character as I had imagined. He had a quick wit about him and was never short of stories to tell about his favourite game. To watch Herzog and Lanier interact was also a real treat. The respect and admiration they mutually shared for each other was evident to everyone who saw them together. For two days, I was immersed in the lore of baseball with two people whom I admire very much. That couple of days were as good as it gets. One of my most-prized possessions from my years with the Goldeyes is a picture taken of myself with Whitey Herzog and Hal Lanier.

One consequence of their relationship surprised me. In Winnipeg, when the team was asked to autograph a baseball, Hal Lanier signed his name horizontally across the ball between the two seams at the narrowest point, the premier location on the ball. Kangaroo court was in session if any rookie mistakenly signed in that area of the ball. I saw Lanier's signature there so many times that, in my mind, that was just the way it was supposed to be.

During the all-star game though, Lanier signed on the wider part of the ball and left the premier spot for his former manager, Whitey Herzog. It was a matter of respect to leave the premier spot on the ball for him. It made total sense after I thought about it because it was baseball tradition, but these balls would be the only ones signed by Hal Lanier in this fashion during his tenure in Winnipeg.

All-Star Kids Clinic

The all-star event was kicked-off with a player clinic at CanWest Global Park. Over 100 youngsters participated in drills on the field focusing on hitting, infield play, outfield play, base running, and pitching. Everyone was treated to lunch by the clinic sponsor, Salisbury House, and to a tour of the ball park, which was an interesting experience that included a visit the Goldeyes dressing room and the press box – not places you normally see when attending a game.

The clinic gave our event some added exposure since Salisbury House restaurants had been promoting it throughout the summer. Goldeyes' players were also involved, which was good for the organization. Ernie Whitt, who had agreed to be the head clinician, was great with the kids. It was a wonderful way to start our two-day event.

Prior to the Skills Competition, I had a meeting with the owner, the general manager and the president of the New Jersey Jackals. They wanted my input into how they could improve their organization. The 15-minute meeting they had requested turned into an hour, as I passionately discussed how the Goldeyes had arrived at the organization that they were currently watching in action in 2001. One of them commented, "We see the differences between your organization and ours. We just don't know what steps to take to get from where we are today to where you are." What an amazing compliment!

All-Star Skills Competition

In order to put on a first class all-star celebration during an already busy regular season, the entire staff had to contribute. Each event was treated like a separate show. Because it had not been done before in the Northern League, the Skills Competition was the most difficult event to coordinate. There were no blueprints. I had been to two Major League all-star games in Minneapolis in 1985 and Atlanta in 2000. At those events, the star status of Major League players made the home-run derby a separate extravaganza of its own. We didn't think a home-run derby in the Northern League would be enough by itself to capture the imagination of the fans. We believed we had to do more.

The fans would be in the park for about 2.5 hours. We wanted to entertain them throughout. While we touted the night as a skills competition, much more was going on. Sales manager Lorraine Maciboric, through a lot of effort and support from our corporate sponsors, created a fun environment on the promenade for fans to enjoy before they even entered the stadium. Various games were set up along with other interactive displays. A live band was also playing. Although it may have been a little less high-tech than the Major League Baseball Fan Fest, it accomplished the same goal. Fans were entertained on the promenade from the moment they approached the park. By the time they entered the gates, they were primed to have fun.

Allowing fans to be in close contact with the players was an important attribute of Northern League baseball. Prior to the competitions, everyone had an opportunity to get autographs from the players on both teams and we had Northern League players participate in four different skills competitions. Base running, catchers' throwing, outfielders' throwing, and the home-run derby featured many different players.

Each event required props and some set-up. Mingled throughout the events, we placed our radio broadcaster, Paul Edmonds, on the field with a remote microphone. He conducted interviews with our celebrities, the contestants, and other interested parties. He had a lot of fun with his interviews and eliminated the dead time on the field as a new event was being organized and thus, kept the fans entertained.

We asked other teams in the league to bring their mascots. Our plan was to have the mascots participate in various events similar to those of the players. Four teams responded to our request so it was a manageable number. Goldie, the Winnipeg mascot, not surprisingly, excelled in the mascot competition because he had been practising the events for weeks!

Our staff also interacted with the fans and threw products into the stands every 45 minutes, like we did at regular games, and we had a feature entertainer, The Piano Juggler, who played songs on a large keyboard by dropping balls on the keys. It was a unique act and we got a lot of mileage from our agreement with him because he performed at the skills competition, the luncheon, and the game.

We even had five fans come onto the field to participate in a home-run contest and a chance to win $25,000. It was a great promotion because many people thought they could hit a home run while in reality, few people are able to. The best promotions are the ones in which people think they actually have a good chance to win. We bought insurance for the contest in case someone actually did hit a home run but only one ball was hit out of the infield. That ball was hit by one of the last contestants and was hit hard, but foul. Nevertheless, the fan home-run derby added excitement to the evening, leading up to the main event.

The real home-run derby with the Northern League players was a little different. Not only did a lot of balls get hit out of the infield but an amazing number of home runs were also hit over the fence. My biggest concern became that we were going to run out of baseballs – that many home runs were hit. Because time was running long, we decided to complete the derby in two rounds. The final two hitters were two of the biggest power hitters in the league, Germaine Swinton from the Sioux Falls Canaries, and Ricky Freeman from the Fargo-Moorhead Red Hawks. What a show those two put on. In the final round, Swinton out slugged Freeman nine home runs to eight. The derby created tremendous excitement with the fans and brought the evening to a rousing climax. Everyone went home happy.

However, promotions director Barb McTavish, who was on the field, and assistant general manager Andrew Collier, who was in the press box, later told me what a nightmare the event was to coordinate because changes would occur at the last minute. The all-star managers, who were determining which players would perform in the events, took it upon themselves to change players without telling our staff. They had no comprehension of the fact that we had scripted each event and a new participant required the staff to scramble. At one point, McTavish told her team to throw their scripts away and listen to instructions over their radios.

But, instead of looking at it as a nightmare, I preferred to view it as the Goldeyes at our best. We were able to react quickly to fill-in time as necessary, or change the tempo on the field by slowing things down or speeding things up. We entertained our fans for a fun-filled 2.5 hours. The fans thought we had been putting on skills competitions all our lives. They were royally entertained and that is really all that matters.

During one of his interviews, Paul Edmonds spoke with former Major Leaguer Matt Nokes. Nokes, who had been selected to the American League all-star team in 1987, spoke highly of the Winnipeg event. Edmonds wrote in the Goldeyes' Fish Lines in issue No. 11 in 2001: "This had a Major League feel to it right from the start," said Nokes. "Winnipeg did a great job and I'm elated that I was able to be a part of it."

That type of comment, from a guy who had been around and played at the highest level possible, was a real testament to the job the Goldeyes' organization did during the all-star celebrations.

All-Star Luncheon

Many people might think there is nothing special about hosting a luncheon. I have attended hundreds of them over the years and they have all been similar. Some may have had better speeches than others and some may have had better food, but they were all basically the same. If you were at the Northern League all-star luncheon in 2001, you would have noticed a difference.

After participating in that luncheon, I have often wondered why organizers do not treat a luncheon like an event. That is exactly what the Goldeyes did. We approached the luncheon as if it were another game, with full production and planning. We were going to put on a show.

The luncheon was held at the Fairmont Hotel, which was excited to be hosting the prestigious event and went all out to showcase their establishment. The room was well appointed and the food was exceptional. The hotel did its job with class.

No other team at any other Northern League luncheon had sold so many tickets to the public. Some of the previous luncheons were arranged for only the players and team executives to attend. The Goldeyes wanted this one to be a public event. It was sold from the beginning as an opportunity our fans would not want to miss. The results were amazing. Close to 700 people attended.

We had a very tight itinerary. The event was scheduled to last two hours and we had activities spaced throughout to keep people entertained. The salads were on the table as the guests arrived to minimize commotion. We made the decision to have some of the activities occur while people were eating. The itinerary included grace, opening speeches, presentation of a commemorative watch to each player and coach, a comedian, our feature entertainer – the Piano Juggler – speeches from myself and Sam Katz, and interviews with Ernie Whitt and Whitey Herzog. We even found time to have short breaks for a silent auction to help raise money for our charity, the Field of Dreams Foundation.

Each all-star player sat at a different table, which added greatly to the experience for the fans. Because the event was in constant motion, it moved along quickly and I heard only positive comments from anyone who attended.

One of the many highlights was Dean Jenkinson, who was a great comedian from Winnipeg. The theme during his show was comparing the differences between Canadians and Americans. Most of the players and baseball executives were American because Quebec and Winnipeg were the only Canadian teams in the league. One of the jokes I most remember went something like this: Jenkinson had recently crossed the border into the U.S. and the customs officer had asked him if he had any firearms to declare. Jenkinson replied that he had none and the officer responded, "That will never do. Here, you better take mine!" There were many other jokes but this one struck the funny-bone of many of our American visitors. I enjoyed Jenkinson so much I hired him later to entertain at a family reunion.

Whitey Herzog and Ernie Whitt were also very entertaining. They were both interviewed by Paul Edmonds so they didn't have to prepare speeches. Whitt discussed his experience in Winnipeg with the Pan-American Games and his responsibilities with the Toronto Blue Jays. Everybody likes Ernie Whitt. He is somewhat soft spoken and a really nice man. He had genuinely enjoyed Winnipeg and it was easy to see that he loved his job. Whitt was a Major League catcher for many years and when Edmonds asked him who was the toughest out he had faced during his career, Whitt replied that it was George Brett.

Then came the interview with Whitey Herzog. What a treat! Whitey was charming and entertaining and Paul Edmonds did a great job of interviewing him. Few people can tell stories like Whitey. He talked about some of his experiences in Major League Baseball and managing the St. Louis Cardinals. The way he spoke about Hal Lanier, it was easy to see he held a great deal of respect for him.

Whitey directed many of his comments to the all-star players. He raised some eye-brows when he told the pitchers they should work mostly on their best pitch. Herzog believed that if you could make your best pitch better, that was the pitch that you would rely on to get hitters out. To the hitters, he said just the opposite. He told them to work on their weaknesses because Major League pitchers would expose those weaknesses in a hurry. It was very interesting inside baseball.

I believe the luncheon was one of the pivotal events that separated the Winnipeg all-star game from any other that had preceded it. It was interactive by including hundreds of fans and sponsors and it brought a great deal of class to the event.

All-Star Game

After the luncheon, all that was left was the all-star game itself, which, not to sound flippant, was a piece of cake. We knew how to run a baseball game, even if it was a special one. We had a few extra special guests but nothing we could not easily handle.

Once again, fans were greeted on the promenade with live music and games and, therefore, more atmosphere existed than for a normal game. Close to 7,000 fans jammed into

CanWest Global Park. You may find this strange, but I had to look up the score to be able to tell you that the east conference won the game 7 to 4. The results of the game were not important to me. Our job was to put on a first-rate show.

I do remember the weather, however. It was also very important to me. A storm was all around us, threatening to wash away one of the crowning moments in Goldeyes' history. We had purchased weather insurance in case it was rained out so there was limited financial risk, but we hadn't worked so hard just to have weather wipe-out our efforts.

Buying weather insurance was a unique experience. It wasn't linked to whether or not the game was actually played but paid off if the precipitation exceeded a specified amount over a specified time. The precipitation was measured at the closest Environment Canada weather station, which, in our case, was the Winnipeg Airport, some distance from the ball park. While rain fell all around us, fortunately, the baseball gods were on our side and the game was completed without delays.

However, since there had been so much rain in the vicinity, I decided to contact Environment Canada the next day. It was conceivable that we could have played the game in its entirety and still been paid the insurance money, if the rain at the airport had exceeded the insured amount. No such luck. There was rain at the airport but not enough for us to collect. Buying rain insurance seemed a lot like buying a lottery ticket or some other form of gambling, but it was necessary because the stakes were pretty high.

The Northern League 2001 all-star game was in the history books. At the game's conclusion, we held a party for players and team executives at Grapes Restaurant near the ball park. Player after player approached me and thanked me for treating them so well. I felt a deep sense of pride. In the morning, I picked up Herzog and Whitt and took them to the airport. They had both enjoyed themselves. Whitey told me to keep up the good work. He said I reminded him of Bill Veeck's kid. Being thought of in the same light as Mike Veeck, I took as a big compliment.

That was the pinnacle of my career with the Goldeyes. We had exceeded my highest expectations. We raised the bar for the league and for future all-star games. We also highlighted the organization, while at the same time exceeding financial expectations. What more could anyone ask?

Once it was over, I took it upon myself to write a short operational manual. It had been a tremendous learning experience and I felt that sharing my information with others could help benefit future all-star games. I attended the games in Quebec in 2002, Lincoln in 2003, and Joliet in 2004. All of them used that document as a reference. In fact, I personally helped my good friends at the Lincoln Saltdogs with their all-star game in 2003. Throughout the planning, one of their goals was to put on as good a show as Winnipeg had. That was quite a tribute.

Left – All-star game ticket
Below – Hal Lanier, Whitey Herzog, John Hindle

Ernie Whitt at kid's camp

Ceremonial first pitches
John, Ernie, (C)Ryan Robertson, Whitey

Chapter 16: Look Up, Pucker Up, and Kiss it Goodbye

Radio is a significant part of a professional baseball team's image in the community. It's a powerful medium and a baseball game is the perfect sport to listen to on the radio. A good announcer can help you visualize the play and bring you right into the ball park. Radio is also a powerful link between the fans and the players. A good announcer can dramatically increase interest throughout the community in the team and the players. The Goldeyes struck gold in this area when they acquired Paul Edmonds.

Continuity is critical to the success of any organization and Paul Edmonds has been on the air broadcasting games for the Goldeyes since 1995. During the inaugural season in 1994, Peter Young was the radio broadcaster. In 1995, Young was joined by a young Paul Edmonds who was his colour commentator. Since then, Edmonds has carried the load by himself.

The most memorable moment during the 1995 season came when the team was in Sioux Falls for a game against the Canaries. At a critical moment during the game, a ball hit by a Sioux Falls player was ruled a home run. To hear Peter Young describe the play, the ball was so far foul they almost caught it in the press box directly behind home plate. The batter had not even run to first base but had pivoted to return to the batter's box when he saw the umpire motion that the ball was a home run. Young was outraged. On-air, he would not let it go. Inning after inning he ridiculed the call and the umpires.

At the conclusion of the game, the umpiring crew was on the way to Winnipeg for their next series when Young went so far as to announce the licence plate number of their vehicle on the air. He asked fans to welcome the umpires to Winnipeg by dumping manure all over their car. The league was not impressed and fined both Young and the organization.

Witnessing the fans' response was one of the first times I realized the power of radio. I got several calls in the morning asking when the umpires would arrive at the park.

Most of the callers expressed anger at the Goldeyes being robbed in Sioux Falls and we had to provide extra security for the umpires for the series but, fortunately, no major incident occurred – and no manure was spotted. There was little doubt, however, that the umpires were considered the enemy more than usual while they were on the field. They were booed when they were introduced and harassed throughout the game.

Paul Edmonds took over solo broadcasts in 1996 and has been responsible for doing every broadcasted game since. The Goldeyes always wanted every game on the air, but during their first 11 years, they were only successful in doing so once – in 1995 on AM630, CKRC.

In 1996, the club reached an agreement with AM680, CJOB. The relationship lasted for nine years. CJOB was the most powerful station in the Winnipeg market so it seemed like the best one to broadcast the games. There was no possibility of broadcasting every game, however, so the Goldeyes took what was available to them. Over the course of the contracts with CJOB, the number of games broadcast each season was gradually increased to 67. When the Goldeyes played 96 regular season games in 2004, having only 67 of them on the air was frustrating for the club. Most teams in the Northern League were broadcasting every game.

Each year when the new agreement was signed, there was great optimism, but sometimes things didn't go as planned. One year, just prior to the season opening, I received a phone call on a Thursday from CJOB. The person was calling to inform me that the upcoming Sunday game could not be broadcast because CJOB had double-booked and had committed to a telethon for a children's charity.

When I expressed disappointment because we had already publicized that Goldeyes' games were on-air throughout the weekend, the person suggested that I contact the charity and tell them the Goldeyes would not allow CJOB to broadcast the telethon. The Goldeyes were huge supporters of children's charities in Manitoba. It was bad enough to be told we could not broadcast the third game of the season, but to turn around and try to make me feel like the bad guy seemed quite unreasonable. Professional organizations do not inform their fans and sponsors that something will happen, and then renege. It does not build confidence with the people who are supporting the organization. CJOB was always prepared to make the game up to our sponsors, but things like that created confusion for Goldeyes' supporters.

In addition, it appeared to me that the people at CJOB thought we had a lot of games taking up a lot of air time during the season, so missing one game would be unimportant when so many more were broadcast. But at the same time, the Goldeyes wanted all games on the air – thus the frustration.

In the early years, there were no concrete numbers to identify how many people were listening to Goldeyes' radio broadcasts. When the numbers became available in 2000, they surprised everyone because they were so high. Fans were listening in huge numbers – over 40,000 per game. The Goldeyes were thrilled.

CJOB was a powerful station with a large market-share and as one of their sports properties, the station promoted the team. The relationship was probably good for both sides over the years because the Goldeyes brought listeners to CJOB, which benefited the station, and CJOB listeners stayed tuned for Goldeyes' broadcasts. The relationship ended in 2005 when the Goldeyes moved their broadcasts to AM1290, where fans were then able to listen to every game.

Paul Edmonds was a young and volatile guy when he took the job in 1995. I have always been a big Edmonds supporter. I think it's his passion for the job, combined with his sense of humour, that appeals to me the most. Baseball had traditionally been broadcast in a calm, laid-back manner but Edmonds was more volatile than most baseball broadcasters. Most of his experience had been in hockey before he joined the Goldeyes, although in 1994 he had broadcast baseball games for the Lethbridge Mounties in the Frontier League. His hockey background came across loud and clear when he did baseball games. He quickly became the "voice of the Goldeyes" and secured his own enthusiastic fan base.

At the end of each season, Paul and I would have a meeting to discuss his work. My comment after the first year was that he needed to calm down just a little. I suggested that the exciting moments in a broadcast could be lost if everything was broadcast at a high intensity. He may have tempered his approach slightly after the first season, but he still had that edgy attitude that made him special.

How would you like to have a job where everyone can evaluate your every move, even when you're working out of town? That's the position Edmonds finds himself in every day. And evaluated he is. Sam Katz would listen to broadcasts and critique them, writing down all of his concerns. Sometimes he would have me call Edmonds and sometimes he would call himself. His criticisms ranged from mistakes in wording to Edmonds' being too unbiased, to a concern that he didn't promote upcoming games enough. I think those evaluations were pretty harsh. Paul was not perfect but I was convinced he did a great job.

Over the years, we got a lot of outside comments about Edmonds. Most of them were positive. One day, however, a gentleman was very upset on the phone because Paul had said during a broadcast that a pitch was "right down Portage and Main." This guy couldn't understand why he would say that. What did the pitch have to do with the two main streets in Winnipeg? Was the pitch on Portage Avenue or Main Street? How could the pitch be down both of them when the streets intersected? I told the caller that Edmonds was just trying to communicate that the pitch was right over the centre of the plate, just as Portage and Main was the centre of Winnipeg. The caller grumbled, "That's ridiculous", and hung up.

While I mentioned the comment to Paul, as I had all comments that related to his broadcasts, I did not suggest he refrain from using that particular metaphor. In fact, I smiled every time he said it, especially when I thought back to the phone call. As I have said, you can't please everyone all the time.

Other comments we received from fans included that Edmonds didn't say the score often enough, he made mistakes, using the wrong words, or he told stories that were too long. Everyone is entitled to their opinion. I can only imagine the critiquing I would get if thousands of people listened to every word I spoke while I was at work all day long. No doubt they would have a lot of suggestions for improvement. Talking live for three hours night after night is not easy. Paul is pretty good at taking suggestions from people and evaluating their validity. I guess that's how you improve your trade. Has Edmonds improved over the years?

You bet he has! He cares about his work and always comes to the park prepared and ready to go.

In Winnipeg, what people recognize most about Paul Edmonds' broadcasts are his signature calls. How about his famous home run call? "YOU CAN LOOK UP, PUCKER UP, AND KISS IT GOODBYE!" If we did a survey, I'm sure that would be the fan favourite.

And then there's, "FISH WIN! FISH WIN! FISH WIN!" When Edmonds first screamed those words over the air, people listening must have had chills go down their spines. He was very passionate on the air and Goldeyes' fans were tightly connected to him. When he was excited, his fans got excited with him.

After the conclusion of the game, when "FISH WIN" was first screamed over the air, I was sitting at our favourite haunt. When Edmonds entered the restaurant a few minutes later, a number of fans and staff greeted him with the "FISH WIN! FISH WIN!" chant. In the days following that game, everywhere I went people wanted to talk about "the call". It was that type of personal connection with the fans that convinced me Edmonds was an integral part of the success of the Goldeyes.

Following are a number of other sayings he has been known to throw out on his broadcasts over the years, with a brief explanation as to their meaning where necessary. They are a big part of the fun of listening to Paul Edmonds.

"Throw him a chair" – the batter has just struck out on a called third strike and is going back to sit in the dugout.

"Give him the golden sombrero" – the batter has struck out four times in the same game.

 "How YOU doin'?" – the Goldeyes have just done something really good.

 "He fell on his bumper" – a batter has been brushed back and landed on his derriere.

"The old automatic" – a called strike that the batter takes on a 3-0 count.

"GM John" – my nickname when on air with Paul.

"Here comes the local lad" – refers to pitcher Donnie Smith, a long-time pitcher with the club, who was from Winnipeg.

"Watch out you cabbies" – foul balls hit back onto Pioneer Avenue, the street behind the first base line at CanWest Global Park.

"A little home cooking" – a scoring decision may have favoured the Goldeyes.

"It's a cold night folks. You better cover those tomatoes."

"It's a great day to be alive."

"The grass is green, let's play ball."

"Thanks for listening folks and we'll talk to you tomorrow" (or day of next game) – the way Edmonds ends every broadcast.

Every now and then a new saying jumps into his broadcast and, no doubt, his fans have their own favourites. This list is by no means all-inclusive.

Edmonds was one of the staff members who literally grew up in front of my eyes during my career with the Goldeyes. Many of them were in their early to mid-20s while I was 42 the year I was hired. Interacting with these young and energetic people was a fun part of the job for me. We were friends, but some days I was more their boss and some days I was a surrogate parent. It all made for interesting relationships, which I still cherish today. I believe it kept me young-at-heart, which is a good thing. Edmonds was certainly one of the ones who kept me on my toes.

Anyone who has listened to Paul Edmonds, realizes he has a powerful voice and is very animated. It was inevitable that such an intense attitude would spill over into the office on occasion. He is loud and opinionated. On occasion, I needed to be loud and opinionated with him. It always worked to calm him down and now he makes fun of our discussions.

Paul is also a real funny guy. No one can imitate me the way he does. Whenever I was a little too stressed, it was very therapeutic to hang out with him and get his view on life. One of his best impersonations of me revolved around my attitude to rain-outs. Rain-outs were one of the most stressful parts of the job and I was known to discourage talk of precipitation during game days in the office. To hear Edmonds tell it in his animated fashion makes me laugh even now as I write about it. It went something like this:

"Rain! I don't want to hear the word rain. Even if Noah is marching the animals onto the ark two by two, I still don't want to hear about rain on game days."

At many staff functions, we would get to his impersonations at some point in the festivities. They were always done in fun and they were good for staff morale.

The Northern League All-Star Game in 2001 was one of the most significant events in my career and I made sure Edmonds was an integral part of the celebration. He was the roving interviewer during the night of the skills competition, the master of ceremonies at the luncheon, and he broadcasted the game. Sam Katz suggested we use a local television personality for the master of ceremonies at the luncheon but I was adamant that Edmonds was the only real fit. He wanted to do it and he had earned the right. He was dedicated to the Goldeyes and he was committed to making the all-star celebrations special. He knew how important the event was to me personally and he wanted to contribute to its success. He did a fantastic job and I was very proud of him throughout the two days.

To watch the radio broadcaster on a game day is a real eye-opener. Operating all the radio equipment would be enough of a job for most people, but that is just what he does to be able to perform the actual broadcast. I witnessed a funny episode in Sioux City prior to a game. The temperature was over 100F (34C) with high humidity. Most radio announcers were satisfied to have their crowd microphone hanging out of the radio booth but Edmonds was somewhat of a perfectionist. He knew he would get more realistic game noise if the microphone was located near the back stop. Then his listeners could hear the crack of the bat and the ball hitting the catcher's glove.

In order to accomplish that, he had to run the wire over top of the backstop netting so that it was out of the way of fans. The microphone was not heavy enough to throw that far by itself so he attached it to a bat and tried to throw the bat over the backstop netting. He was standing among the seats, trying to throw this bat over the net, and several times it hit near the top of the net without going over and fell to the ground. Edmonds was standing there drenched in perspiration, getting more than a little frustrated. The sight was comical, although I don't think he thought it was funny at the time.

Finally, he succeeded in throwing the bat over the netting and the expression on his face was one of a "job well done." His expression reminded me of a player's when he is standing on second base after just hitting a double that cleared the bases. There was a sense of pride in the accomplishment. He was then ready to start the show.

Every night Edmonds put on a live performance. It was a pressure job and I knew how much of himself he threw into each broadcast. I recognized the effort because I knew how much of myself I put into my public speaking engagements. Some nights, by the time he would sign off the air at the conclusion of a game, he would be exhausted. During those marathon games, which happened on occasion, I would try to go on the air with him later in the broadcast so he would have someone to talk to and create a change of pace on the broadcast.

I loved being on the air with him and while I was, my staff radio was turned off because I was talking to our fans and watching the ball game. The radio booth was like a small sanctuary for me. We always had fun together, too. Edmonds frequently had inside information from talking to players or coaches prior to the game, so I was interested in what he had to say. Every game I was on air with him, he would ask me if I knew the answer to his trivia question. Usually I would guess but would frequently be wrong, so it became a bit of a joke that the general manager was somewhat clueless. It would have helped if I had my record book to look up stats.

One of my favourite recollections of being on air with Paul was the night he asked me a question and while I was answering, the batter tipped a foul ball just over the backstop netting and right into the radio booth. Instinctively, my hand shot out and caught the spinning ball. I didn't miss a beat and, without hesitation, I continued talking. Paul interrupted me, blurting into the microphone, "What a catch folks! A bare, one-handed catch! Goldeyes general manager John Hindle is known for being a good baseball player, and he sure has convinced me. I'll get out from under my chair now!"

That was a fun moment on the air. My reaction was mostly instinct and I was a bit lucky to catch the ball one-handed. I never told Paul, but it had really stung when I caught it. I guess now is time for the truth. My hand hurt for a week!

As I walked around the ball park, it always made me smile to see fans listening to their radios during a game. Many people had an ear piece in one ear listening to Edmonds while their other ear was listening to the PA announcer. Many times I heard fans discussing what had been said on air. "Did Paul call that play an error?" one might ask another listener. Sometimes there was just a murmur of laughter throughout the crowd if he had said something amusing.

Edmonds is also a good interviewer. He can ask the tough questions but he is fair and gives his guest a good opportunity to answer. While he has never wanted a colour commentator with him on every broadcast, he always lights up and has a lot of fun when an interesting guest joins him. I asked him who some of his favourite guests have been. He said Pete Rose, Pat Gillick, Rob Lowe, Whitey Herzog, Ernie Whitt, Brian Duva, and Chris Kokinda came to mind. He was sure that there were others so the list is by no means exhaustive.

In 1995, Edmonds tried to work full-time in the office but after Christmas we mutually agreed it was a bad idea. In 2002, however, he again joined the staff on a full-time basis, selling in the off-season and broadcasting the games during the season. He has done very well this time, enjoying it more and having a great deal of success.

Each year at the end of the season, Edmonds negotiated a new one-year contract just as all the other staff did. Usually, the contract included broadcasting the games on the radio and doing some writing for the newsletter. He was an easy person to negotiate with because his requests were seldom unreasonable. He was not the type to ask for a huge raise, expecting to negotiate down. He frequently came with an initial offer that he was hoping to have accepted, which was also my style, so we often had an easy time negotiating a new deal.

In fact, one year he asked for a raise of $1,750. I'm not sure how he came up with that amount but I felt it was reasonable so I agreed. When it came time to sign a new contract, I had rounded it off to a $2,000-raise. He never forgot the gesture. I valued Paul and it was a very small way of showing it. I can imagine Sam Katz shaking his head as he reads this because he would think I was crazy for giving someone more money than he had asked for.

Edmonds has become a celebrity in the Goldeyes' organization. Many people like to talk to him and share their experiences on how he has touched their lives through his broadcasts. The amazing success of the Goldeyes can be attributed in part to the quality of the radio broadcasts. I hope Paul broadcasts Goldeyes' games for many years to come. I feel a great deal of comfort when I turn on the radio and hear him on the air.

Paul Edmonds

L - Hal Lanier giving clinic during spring caravan
R - Max Poulin – Library reading program

Chapter 17: In the Community

One of the greatest things about being involved with a professional sport's franchise was the ability to touch so many lives. The thousands of fans who came to watch the team play were immediately affected by their experience at the park. If they had a good experience, they took a positive message out to other people. It was the best form of advertising. But to reach people outside of the park, professional teams must also be active in the community. The Goldeyes implemented many programs over the years for that purpose.

Speaking to groups was also an important way to meet people. The owner, general manager, manager, mascot, and radio broadcaster were all available for appearances. Requests from service clubs, schools, and sports associations were most common. I've driven 150 miles to talk to 10 people and across the street to talk to 500. I've judged motorcycles at a Shine and Show at a Harley Davidson dealership and floats at the Festival of Lights Parade. I toured to various Scout meetings to promote awareness of the "Scouts Sleepover" and appeared on numerous television and radio shows to wave the flag. I don't remember ever turning down a speaking engagement unless there was a scheduling conflict.

Possibly the most important public service step taken by the Goldeyes was the formation of the Winnipeg Goldeyes Field of Dreams Foundation. The registered charity used the strength of the organization and the celebrity status of the players to raise money for children's charities throughout Manitoba. In turn, the process provided the organization with a great deal of good will throughout the community.

Much of the money was raised at the park with the fans who attended the games. For example, fans were given an opportunity to participate with the charity by pledging an amount of money for every strikeout the Goldeyes' pitchers registered throughout the season. The fans could cheer for the home team and make a charitable donation at the same time. This was not a new concept. Other sports organizations had accomplished the same goal by having their fans donate every time the home team scored a goal in hockey, a touchdown in football, or a home run in baseball.

It can work with any statistic that is measurable. If the fans choose to participate, the fundraiser can be very effective.

In addition, many unique items were auctioned off during games. People would pay for game-worn or autographed memorabilia, generating funds for the charity both at the park and at many other events.

Other money for the charity was raised away from the ball park. Events such as annual golf tournaments, memorabilia auctions at different fundraisers, dinners, and speaking engagements were a few of the possibilities. Sam Katz and I spoke many times per year at different functions on behalf of the Goldeyes. While no fee was charged for the majority of the engagements, a donation to the charitable foundation was gladly accepted. The Field of Dreams Foundation has raised hundreds of thousands of dollars since its inception.

A professional baseball team can also liaise with other charities in the community. Many times we helped charities generate awareness and funds for their organization. The Breast Cancer Pledge Ride, for example, had 60 Harleys parade around the field prior to a game and then set up a display on the concourse. Goldie rode on the back of one of the Harleys. The bikes created a lot of noise and made an amazing visual presentation.

Other programs were designed to increase awareness for the baseball club and to benefit the community at the same time. The baseball caravan was one such program. The Goldeyes would travel to various sites around Manitoba to talk baseball and connect with people. The entourage would make stops at schools and talk to the students and put on mini-player clinics. The itinerary would usually be determined by the interest in the community.

I attended a function in Altona, Manitoba, a small town with a population of about 3,500, as part of the caravan. Hundreds of people, mostly kids, showed up to listen to, and talk to our players and staff. Other towns with larger populations might have had only a few people show up for autographs. Most of this depended on the organizers in the various locations. Inevitably, something good came of every event. You can never have too much good will in the community.

Another program I started in Winnipeg was the library reading program. I first heard of the idea at a seminar and molded it to work for the Goldeyes. Players were asked to volunteer to go to a library and read a baseball story to young children. The library used the players as an incentive to encourage children to read and to sign up for their summer reading program. The number of children who registered dramatically increased after the partnership was formed. It was a win for both organizations. The media found it to be a feel-good story and put pictures in the paper showing players talking and reading to groups of young children. What great exposure for the ball club.

I read several times to young children during "reading month" promotions at various schools. Usually, I was handed a baseball book to read, which was followed by a question-and-answer session. I always enjoyed interacting with the kids. They are so direct. "How much money do you make?" was the most common question I was asked.

When they arrived in Winnipeg, all players were informed that the Goldeyes' organization would treat them professionally and in return they would be required to sign autographs on request and perform charitable work as needed. But only once while I was with for the Goldeyes did a player come to me and ask if I could coordinate some charitable work for him. Chad Thornhill, who played and coached for the Goldeyes, asked to work with the Diabetes Foundation. We were able to accommodate his request and Thornhill became a big benefit to the local chapter.

The Holiday Baseball Camp around the Christmas season was another event that continued year after year. Far removed from the baseball season, the Goldeyes held a camp for approximately 100 young baseball and softball players. A marquee player or past player was usually flown in for the event to increase interest. Wonderful media exposure often accompanied the camp at a time of year when baseball was not front and centre.

For a number of years around the holiday season, the Goldeyes participated in the Festival of Lights parade in Winnipeg. Held annually, the parade was a celebration of the coming Christmas season and highlighted the spirit of lighting up the city. Winnipeg can be cold in the winter months but the spirit of Winnipeg people is very warm indeed. Numerous Goldeyes' staff members, initially spearheaded by sales director Lorraine Maciboric, would help decorate a truck and sing and dance throughout the length of the parade. Thousands of hearty Winnipeggers would line the streets downtown and cheer the floats and participants as they passed. Twice, I was a judge in the parade but I abstained from voting when the time came to evaluate the Goldeyes' participation. The organization did, however, win a spirit award and Goldie won an award for humour.

Other, more imaginative programs also brought the Goldeyes into the community. "You've been ticketed" was one such program. In conjunction with the Winnipeg Police Department and the RCMP (Royal Canadian Mounted Police), the Goldeyes would provide free ticket vouchers to be given to citizens who were found by the police to be complying with various laws, to recognize citizens for doing a good deed, or to simply allow police officers the opportunity to connect with youth.

In 2000, the Goldeyes participated in a fundraiser that made me a little uncomfortable. Dates with six players were auctioned off at a local night club to the highest bidder. Each lucky bidder got lunch for two with their "date" at Red Lobster Restaurant and a pair of tickets to a home game during the Northern League season. I was unsure how this would be perceived by everyone but the funds raised were all to be donated to charity, and lunch sounded pretty safe, so I begrudgingly agreed to allow the promotion to proceed. A certain amount of pressure was placed upon me, especially when the sponsor announced that it had already advertised the event before I was even aware of it.

I went to the club to watch the proceedings and to monitor the players' behavior. It was bordering on the wild side as they were put on a stage to strut their stuff. To increase the bids, some of the players did a bit of a striptease. Shirts came off and even a couple of pairs of pants (underwear remained – at least in the bar). The crowd certainly got into it and was getting pretty loud. One after another, the players were auctioned to the highest bidders. The size of the bids surprised me. Well over $1000 was raised from the bidding alone, which was to be added to a portion of the door cover charge to make a nice donation to our charity. I left as the bidding was concluding, hopeful that we had survived a potentially embarrassing situation. That hope was short-lived.

Early the next morning, I arrived at the office and inquired as to the final outcome of the event. I was assured by the staff that had organized the auction that everything was kept professional and the evening had been a success. In fact, the night club was so pleased that it wanted to host another auction. I was relieved that things had turned out but told the staff that this type of event had too many potential problems so I did not want a recurrence.

Minutes later, I received a call from a frantic mother who told me her daughter had not returned home the previous night. She had contacted her daughter's friend who informed her that her daughter had won a date with a Goldeyes' player. The woman was livid that the Goldeyes would be involved with such a promotion. I told her the promotion was for lunch with the player but that I would immediately attempt to find her daughter. Some quick investigation determined the player involved and after many rings, he answered the phone and informed me that the missing girl was indeed with him. I guess I was naïve to believe that someone would bid just to have the priviledge of going for lunch. The mother and daughter were quickly united but never again during my tenure were the players involved with a promotion even remotely similar.

I also participated in a couple of unique community events when I was in Sioux Falls. Public figures volunteered to cook their favourite dishes and provide samples to anyone who had paid $25 to enter the event. People roamed from booth to booth sampling a wide array of delicacies. Assistant general manager Larry McKenney and I cooked up bratwurst and provided three different types of sauces for people to try: mild, tangy, and hot. Everyone laughed when they saw Canaries' staff cooking brats in the middle of winter.

One other event in Sioux Falls was the annual Easter egg hunt. Children up to 10 years of age were invited to the ball park to search for Easter eggs that were spread out all over the outfield. Inside the plastic eggs were pieces of candy. Kids were divided into various age groups. I was told we could expect 100 kids or so – 500 showed up! It reminded me of the story told elsewhere in this book of "Disco Demolition Night" in Comiskey Park.

Public address announcer Dan Christopherson was trying to entertain the children by having them sing a song as we got everyone organized on the field. He primed the music and then he yelled over the PA system, "Okay kids, now everyone sing a song on the count of three – one, two, three, go!" Hundreds of kids immediately stormed the field almost trampling me in the process as they grabbed Easter eggs while many others started singing and waiting patiently for instructions. What a zoo! Some kids ended up with no eggs. We had carefully put aside a bunch to ensure no one went away empty handed but the hunt was a big part of the excitement for most of them. A newspaper article the next day slammed the organization for the mix-up. Even when you're trying to be a good corporate citizen, a promotion can backfire so easily.

Community events remained, however, a fun part of the business for me. I loved being able to connect with so many people. Even when something didn't work out as planned, it just encouraged me to do it better the next time. I believe that's called learning.

Chapter 18: Saying Goodbye

The 2001 season was over. Once again, the Goldeyes had reached the playoffs and had even advanced to the Championship Series, only to come up a little short in losing to the New Jersey Jackals. It was a difficult loss because it was the third time in four years that the Goldeyes had been denied in the Championship Series.

Nevertheless, the season had been a huge success. We set the all-time Northern League attendance record, averaging 6,445 fans per game, beating the St. Paul Saints for the second year in a row. These numbers included 34 sell-outs out of the 42 games played. In addition, we ran the most successful all-star game in Northern League history. The Goldeyes were at a pinnacle.

The end of the season signaled the time to begin my yearly deliberation about my future. At the end of every season, in a state of exhaustion, many staff members would determine if they wanted to go through the grind again. Over the years, as the season concluded, I had learned not to ask anyone, including players, if they were coming back because their answer meant almost nothing. I'm sure just as many players told me they would be returning and didn't come back, as said they were packing it in, only to return on Opening Day the next season.

Previously, there had always been a great deal more to look forward to in upcoming years. For several years, the new park had been on the horizon. But 2001 was different. I had accomplished many of my goals. I had set out to operate the greatest all-star game ever and I felt we had succeeded. We set attendance records, played the Russian National Team, and entrenched ourselves in a love affair with our fans at our beautiful new ball park. What was there left to do?

Things were also changing at Home Run Sports. For eight years, my modest sporting goods business had survived without me in full-time attendance. My husband and wife management team, Scott and Carla Neiles, had their first child in June 2001. Megan Jayne was a beauty and Carla was staying home with the baby. I had a great deal of respect for Scott and his sales ability but I was not sure how he would feel about dealing with all of the administrative issues involved in running the company. After all, Home Run Sports was my company. I had started it in my garage and while I had not been there too much in the past eight years, I still had significant equity in the business. It was important to me that it continued to survive, or even flourished.

Then, there were issues at the Goldeyes. I was a little perturbed at Sam Katz for not wanting me to go to Lincoln for the playoff games. I was a professional baseball general manager. I believed my place was with the team during the playoffs. I had not missed a playoff game in the first seven years and did not feel right about missing one in 2001. Eventually, he changed his mind and told me if I really thought I should go to Lincoln, he would not stand in my way.

As it turned out, on September 11th, 2001, all air transportation was shut down after the terrorist attacks. That tragedy occurred on the day the series was to begin in Lincoln, so I was unable to fly. The series ended up being postponed for a week as the aftermath of 9/11 was felt and I never did make it to Lincoln. It was still frustrating to think that I needed his permission to watch our own team in the playoffs. I felt that I had earned the right to make that decision.

And then there was the issue that had been bothering me for a long time. Sam Katz had not fulfilled his promise to sell me a small portion of the Goldeyes. The promise dated back to the night he was going into a meeting with Winnipeg Enterprises Corporation (WEC) in 1997. Just prior to the meeting, he told me it looked like he was going to be selling his 50 percent share of the Goldeyes to WEC. The relationship between the two had deteriorated to the point that the "shotgun" clause of their agreement had been triggered by WEC. Katz had to accept the offer to buy his shares, or pay WEC the exact amount it wanted for its shares.

I told him if it turned out he was buying instead of selling, I would be prepared to buy 10 percent of the team that night. WEC was offering to buy or sell 50 percent of the team for $325,000 so I could easily figure what 10 percent was worth. The seller netted a nice profit since the original cost in 1994 to purchase the entire franchise was $100,000.

Katz told me that if it turned out he was buying instead of selling, he would accept my offer upon which I smiled and pulled out my cheque book. He laughed and said he appreciated a man who put his money where his mouth was but we should wait and see what happened. During the meeting that night, he did decide to buy the club.

Once he bought the Goldeyes, there was always some reason why we could not deal with the issue of my purchasing shares. Whenever I brought it up, he was waiting for more information to be put together. Soon thereafter, the new park began to look like a reality. The issue lay dormant for months because we were so caught up in the construction of the new facility and there was precious little time to meet to address ownership.

As late as January, 2001, Katz came to me and said he was working on a proposal that would sell me seven percent of the team. Where he came up with that number, I have no idea but I waited the entire year for the offer to materialize. At the end of the season, I cornered him and told him I wanted a firm answer on the cost of shares. I wouldn't leave his office without an answer and he finally admitted he was not going to sell me any shares. I asked him if he thought that was right after all the promises he had made and he said he felt bad about it, but there was nothing he could do because he now had partners. I was extremely disappointed. That broken promise was an additional factor in my decision to leave the organization.

I had taken great pride in managing the Goldeyes, and I was not alone in feeling that pride. Many of the staff looked at their time with the team as more than just a job. It was personal. Leaving the Goldeyes had not been an option for me before because I had worried that my leaving would negatively impact the organization. But things were different now.

My assistant general manager, Andrew Collier, had developed significantly in the previous couple of years. The Goldeyes were selling-out most games and I knew they would sell well over 200,000 tickets before a single pitch was thrown for the 2002 season. If ever there was a time my leaving would create the least amount of stress in the organization, that time had come.

I decided to bounce the idea off of Katz to get his reaction. I asked him to have lunch with me at the local deli, Ira's, where he and I would go on occasion. There, I asked him if he would consider Andrew Collier as the new general manager if I left the Goldeyes. He responded that Collier had earned the right to have a shot at the job. I was very pleased with that answer and told him I was considering moving on.

One of the reasons I gave him was that I was disappointed he had not followed through on his promise to sell me a percentage of the team. I also mentioned that Home Run Sports could use my help. I asked if anything had changed with the ownership issue and he replied in the negative.

We then proceeded to talk about the upcoming World Series and life in general. There was no further talk about my leaving, at all. I went home that night and informed my wife that I had had lunch with Katz and was pretty sure I had told him I was considering leaving, but that his reaction so shocked me I was not sure he even heard me. Moments later, Katz called and asked me jokingly if we had had lunch that day. I expressed my surprise at his reaction to my news and he said he had been a little shocked and not sure what to say. That didn't happen to Sam Katz very often.

At no time during that day or in the weeks to follow did he ever try to talk me out of my decision, which was also disappointing to me. I had committed my heart and soul to his baseball team for eight years and I thought he should at least try to salvage the situation. Maybe that was just being naïve on my part. I guess his reaction spelled out the reality of our relationship to me. It did not feel very good.

We set a date for my departure and I asked that I be able to tell the staff in person at an upcoming meeting. Together, we brought Collier into Katz's office beforehand and told him what I was going to do. At no time during the process was I sure that I was doing the right thing. I still loved the job and I still loved the Goldeyes.

As the staff meeting approached, I prepared a speech. These people had been so close to me I knew it would be a difficult task, and it was. The night before the meeting, I called Hal Lanier to tell him what I was going to do. He spent an hour on the phone trying to talk me out of it. That was the hardest time for me because I felt so close to Hal and I knew I would really miss him and the baseball side of the business.

Here is the speech that I delivered at the end of the staff meeting the following day.

November 6, 2001

"Eight years ago, I accepted a job with the Goldeyes. Sometimes it seems like 80 years ago, while other times it seems like mere months. As I listen to staff concerns recently, I almost want to laugh about some of them. Even five years ago, we were a bare bones operation, but now our expectations are so much higher. What is still valid today and has existed since Day 1 is the organization's desire to get better. That attitude, in large part, defines the success of the Goldeyes.

I've done my best work here. At times I have been accused of being too harsh or strict and sometimes too soft – and frequently this happened regarding the same event from different people's perspectives. I have very few moments that I regret. Not that I was perfect – far from it. But I always had my heart in the right place and did my best to represent this organization with class.

That brings me to you people. The reason I survived here eight years was because of the people. I've spoken of teamwork often to you and it was never rhetoric to me. I meant it and I felt a part of it. I gained strength from it. I always cherished your best moments and shared them with you, and I tried to stand beside you during your tough times.

But the best days were this summer. Barb (McTavish) and Andrew (Collier) have spoken of one day as the worst – the All-Star Skills Competition. Barb, this was us at our best! We were able to take a night of chaos and present a great entertainment package that people rave about everywhere I go. It wasn't easy, but if it were easy, anyone could do it. The all-star festivities were the greatest. I could never thank all of you enough for selling the tickets, planning and operating the events, promoting them, and treating our guests with such class. You did yourselves proud and I was so honoured this summer to be a part of this team.

What I am about to say is one of the toughest decisions of my life. I have decided to leave the Goldeyes effective November 30th. I feel like there is a hole in my heart and that is because of the people in this room.

The Goldeyes are in the best shape they have ever been. We are a jewel in the City of Winnipeg and I know that you can keep this going, and indeed grow, for a long time to come. Sam has accepted my resignation and, fortunately, he has agreed that Andrew will be the next general manager. So Andrew, I was there when this baby was born. I now consider her an adolescent. Take good care of her!"

Your friend and colleague,

John

I do not clearly remember all that happened during those few minutes but I do remember marketing director Dan Chase muttering, "Oh no!" as he realized what I was about to announce. When I did look up, I saw tears streaming down the cheeks of Barb McTavish and Lorraine Maciboric. I lost it totally then and could not finish speaking.

There was silence for what seemed like hours but was probably only a few seconds. I believe I stammered that the meeting was over and Katz, who had been speechless until that point, said, "No, just wait for a moment." He slowly began to speak. I recall he said that it was obvious how hard this was on me and everyone else in the room. (Later, he told me he thought he had been at a funeral.) He said we should not leave the meeting sad, but rather rejoice in all that had been accomplished on my watch. We sat for a few minutes and slowly people started to leave. There were hugs all around and then several of us went to a local restaurant.

Going to the restaurant was really good for me. I was able to compose myself a little bit. I remember more about what went on at the restaurant than about the end of the meeting. In particular, I remember the moist eyes Dennis McLean flashed at me as he hugged me goodbye. Dennis had always been grateful for being given the opportunity to work for the Goldeyes. It was I who was grateful for his humour, positive attitude, and uncanny sales ability. I could always count on Dennis when I needed that final ticket push. I was able to share fun stories with many other staff members and let the significance of my decision sink in a little bit further.

So the deed was done. I stayed for another month to ensure Collier was up to speed and to make sure the transition was as painless as possible. I was able to say my goodbyes one on one and I left feeling loved and loving those I was leaving behind. I was leaving the company I had watched over from its birth in Andrew's capable hands.

During the last few weeks, I received some interesting email. Many of my fellow general managers were sorry to see me go. We also heard from Goldeyes' fans. One colourful gentleman emailed Katz to tell him to open his wallet and find the money needed to keep me. I think Katz was surprised by the reaction, but he never did make any attempt to keep me.

The goodbye party was really something with plenty of food and several presentations. Sam gave me a new set of Jazz golf clubs. Another gift was an enlarged picture of all the staff. Barb McTavish knew that present would be hard on me because of my strong feelings about the team. The picture was the essence of my years with the Goldeyes.

Still another endearing present was a glass jar crammed full of notes. Each staff member had written his or her favourite memories on pieces of paper. The notes were a long-lasting present because I could read them at my leisure in the days, weeks, months, and even years that followed. They were packed with years of stories, feelings, and observations. They were personal and filled with emotion and I will cherish them forever. Even now, I can pull out a note and read it and a wave of emotion floods over me. I will quote a few here.

"It's been my pleasure working for you, although you always made me feel like I was working with you."

"After being the father figure to the most screwed up, diverse, complex, sometimes crazy bunch of people ever, you can do anything."

"This will not be goodbye, rather good luck and see you later. I will miss seeing you every day."

"You should be proud of what we have accomplished. We've come so far since the beginning."

"I'll do my best not to screw it up." (This one must have been from Andrew.)

"I will really, really miss working with the very best."

"I remember seeing my first Saints' game and wondering if we could ever be as good as them."

"Thanks for encouraging me to do the best possible job and to not sweat the small stuff."

"Not only are you my friend, but also a great teacher and the best boss."

Some of my nicknames were also listed in the jar, including "GM John, Papa Bear, and Sweet Swinger."

Eight glorious years of my life came to a conclusion on November 30th, 2001. I knew then and I know now, it had been my dream job. I never treated it like a job but rather as a critical part of my life. I lived and breathed the Goldeyes. They will forever remain entrenched in my soul.

Chapter 19: The Sioux Falls Experience

Moving On

Leaving the Goldeyes was one of the toughest things I have ever done. For eight years, I woke up in the morning eager to get to work. Now my focus was going to change to my baseball business, Home Run Sports. While I still had a lot of work to fill my days, it was very different work.

Home Run Sports had survived all the years while I was working for the Goldeyes because the company had a solid base of customers, the rights to sell some exclusive products in Canada, and because great people worked there.

The year 2002 marked the first year I worked at Home Run Sports full-time. It turned out to be a great year for the business, which I don't believe was a mere coincidence. The company recorded its biggest profit ever and expanded its reach across Canada.

Scott Neiles must have enjoyed his job at the store better when I was not around, however. He came to me in late 2002 and asked if he, Carla, and a couple of partners could buy the business. I was shocked. Here, I had left the Goldeyes and, more recently, had turned down a possible job at the Northern League office because of the business. If I sold it, what was I going to do?

I was placed in the position of having to make a fairly quick decision and after weighing the options, I decided to proceed with the transaction. We came to an agreement and the business was sold in January, 2003. For the first time in my adult life, I had to figure out what people without baseball in their lives did during the summer.

I spent much of the year catching up on projects in my private life that had been set aside for many years. I also had a desire to play a lot of golf during the summer instead of the three or four games I could usually squeeze into my busy life while I was involved with baseball. I played over 70 rounds of golf in 2003 and thoroughly enjoyed it. That did, however, create a different dilemma for me. I had always assumed that if I found the time to play a significant amount

◆ golf, my game would dramatically improve. This theory ▸rned out to be flawed!

◆ other thing I did in the summer of 2003 was to help my ◆ friends at the Lincoln Saltdogs with their Northern League all-star game. I really liked Lincoln and the people that worked for the Saltdogs. I provided them with a procedural manual that described how we operated the event in Winnipeg in 2001 and I was a consultant whenever they needed me. I drove to Lincoln a couple of days before the game to help with the final stages.

As it turned out, my biggest contribution was to act as a cheerleader for the Saltdogs' staff. They were very worried about the execution of the skills competition, which I could readily relate to because the Goldeyes' staff was equally concerned in 2001. I kept assuring them that they were in good shape and actually ahead in their planning compared to where the Winnipeg organization had been prior to the 2001 skills competition. The event in Winnipeg had been a great success so I was sure that Lincoln would also produce good results. I was right and their worries, although natural, were unfounded. The 2002 all-star game was a fun time, and it sure felt good to contribute again.

While at the all-star game in Lincoln, I visited with Northern League owners and general managers. I guess it was obvious that I was keen to get involved with baseball again but there was no opportunity in Winnipeg. I had talked to Sam Katz on occasion so he knew I was looking, but he had no suggestions for me to pursue. Andrew Collier was doing a good job and the Goldeyes were enjoying continued success. If I was to get a job in baseball, it was going to have to be away from home.

One of the people I talked to in Lincoln was Mike Veeck, president of the St. Paul Saints and part owner of the Goldklang group of baseball teams. He wanted to know how I was doing and what my plans were for the future. Veeck is quite a character and a very funny man.

The next time I talked to Veeck was when he called to ask me if I might be interested in a job with one of his teams. He had a new franchise in the Can-Am League in New Haven, Connecticut, and he still had a small ownership stake in the Sioux Falls Canaries. I told him I was interested. At the same time, I also discussed an offer from the New

Jersey Jackals' organization, whose owners were looking into the possibility of adding another team in the Can-Am League.

An opening did become available in Sioux Falls. After calling the league office to make sure that no positions were available there, and weighing all of my other options, I accepted the job as general manager of the Canaries. I left home without my wife, Bev, at least for the first season. With Sioux Falls being much closer to Winnipeg, it was comforting to know that I could jump in my car and be home in seven hours, if necessary (six if I was in a hurry).

Sioux Falls

My experience in Sioux Falls was intense. I still loved baseball, the Northern League, and being a general manager. I looked forward to the challenge of working with one of the original members of the league. It was an adventure to be working in another country in a baseball job I was excited about, and I realized not many Canadians would be in that position. As I drove down Interstate 29, I was pleased that so many people were confident in my abilities.

Geographically, Sioux Falls was centrally located and I believed it was an important team for the Northern League. I had been there a couple of times to watch the Goldeyes play the Canaries and I liked the city. I knew the Canaries stadium would not have some of the luxuries I had been accustomed to at CanWest Global Park but that was not very relevant to me.

The ball park in Sioux Falls had been renovated in 2000 in a joint effort by the City of Sioux Falls and the Canaries. The 5.6-million-dollar renovation was christened on June 2, 2000, at the home opener, which I had attended. The new "Birdcage" drew national attention when USA Today writer Mel Antonen wrote a feature story on the unique retrofit. The project received praise for the integration of an older existing facility with more modern elements, including a new state-of-the-art video scoreboard. The stadium was a charming place to watch a ball game.

The renovation also included seating for 4,029, a new spacious clubhouse, a merchandise store, new concession areas, luxury suites, and group barbeque areas. The offices for the staff, however, were completely ignored. Only the general manager had an office and it was very small. All other staff members had work cubicles.

The first order of business was to get a visa to work in the U.S., an expensive and time-consuming process. I had to provide so many letters of reference, you would have thought I was applying for the job of President of the United States, not the general manager of a baseball team.

The Canaries hired a local immigration lawyer, Henry Evans, to expedite the application. Evans was a wonderful guy – young and energetic and he found my case particularly interesting. He loved baseball and told me stories about his father taking him to Municipal Stadium in Cleveland to watch the Indians play. The opportunity to help me and the Canaries was very appealing to him. The proudest person the day the visa approval came through was Henry Evans. That day, Henry was at home jumping for joy when his young son started jumping with him.

"Now the baseball man can work here, right daddy!" said his son. "He sure can," said Henry, "but don't tell your friends at day care until the Canaries send out a press release!"

In the mountain of paperwork that was sent to the United States Immigration Office to support my visa application was a great supporting letter from Miles Wolff, founder of the Northern League and long-time commissioner. Another was from Marv Goldklang, owner of the St. Paul Saints and several other minor league baseball clubs. Other letters of reference were provided by Sam Katz, Hal Lanier, and Andrew Collier from the Goldeyes. It was a strange experience to have such successful people, whom I respected so much, write letters on my behalf, particularly the individuals from outside the Goldeyes' organization with whom I had not worked directly. I suspect their kind words helped expedite the visa.

Now that I was legal, we planned a press conference so I could introduce myself to the people of Sioux Falls. At my request, Mike Veeck flew in from Charleston, South Carolina, to add some pizzazz to the event. Mike was well-loved in Sioux Falls and was widely welcomed whenever he appeared. The coverage of the press conference was fantastic. I was very pleased with the media and the Canaries' faithful who turned out to meet me. It was a very exciting day. I considered it a re-birth of sorts and the press conference reminded me of the day in 1994 when I was introduced as the first general manager of the Winnipeg Goldeyes.

The Canaries were an established franchise. I arrived in time for their 12th season and the organization had traditional ways of operating. I decided there were two things I would need to be careful of when I arrived. First, I did not want to repeat too many times, "This is the way we did things in Winnipeg." Second, I did not want to change too many things. Change is difficult for people and I already knew there was going to be significant change. I decided to change something only if it would have a noticeable positive impact on the organization. Smaller issues would be saved for a later time.

The Canaries had not shown an operating profit for several years. While I was driving to Sioux Falls, I had visions of turning things around and operating in the black. Shortly after arriving, I realized the challenge was far greater than I had anticipated.

A number of problems existed in the Canaries' operation. Many things that I took for granted with the Goldeyes needed to be addressed, the most important being a lack of excitement around selling tickets. Ticket sales, which are the life blood of any sports franchise, were almost an afterthought. Worse yet, the staff didn't seem to see a value in the tickets. And if the staff didn't see a value, how could the organization expect the fans to see one?

Tickets were offered for free as throw-ins in corporate contracts and were traded as though they were blades of grass in the outfield. If you bought a loaf of bread or any other product at the local supermarket, you could get two free tickets to a Canaries' game. If you bought $20 worth of product from another food supplier, you received four free tickets. And there was no cost to the companies involved. The Canaries didn't see any dollars for those tickets. They were free in the hope that people would show up at the games.

At the same time, 40 percent of season ticket holders had not renewed their tickets for the upcoming season. Losing 40 percent of the season ticket base would have put the franchise in jeopardy. My very first decision upon arriving in

Sioux Falls was to hold all season ticket holders' seats from the past season so they could renew them if they chose to, instead of releasing them for re-sale. I did that even though the deadline had passed for renewals. Then I started calling the ticket holders to ask if they would give me a chance to win their confidence. Many of them decided to renew.

It became readily apparent that my goal in Sioux Falls needed to be to patch the dike. My contract included a bonus based upon the profit that was achieved, but I quickly realized that profit was not realistically attainable in the short term. Survival was the main focus.

I learned a lot about the attitude of the Sioux Falls' fans in a hurry during those initial calls to the season ticket holders. Two responses were particularly common. Many fans were tired of a losing team and wanted to support a winner, and free tickets were so prevalent in the market that buying tickets seemed pointless. I decided to bring things to a head at a staff meeting.

I told everyone that we were going to establish new ticket prices and whatever we agreed to, would be the set price for the upcoming season. The agreed upon price was then not to be discounted. I told them I didn't care if they all agreed the best ticket in the stadium should sell for one dollar. That would become the new price but no one would be able to buy the ticket for 50 cents or to get one for free unless approved as part of a promotion.

An interesting thing happened in the meeting. As the staff looked at the prices, their attitudes began to change. They compared prices of Canaries' tickets to other sports teams' tickets in Sioux Falls. They compared them to other teams in the Northern League and finally to other events or activities that people could spend their money on in the community. Suddenly, one staff member commented to the group as if he had come to a revelation, "Hey, our ticket prices are really low!"

From that moment on, tickets were valued in the office. We would still trade tickets or include them in corporate packages, but there was an expectation that the value of the tickets would be considered as part of the entire deal. Free tickets to the public were eliminated. I felt the organization had turned a corner.

Another issue I examined was the distribution of half-priced beer at the concession stands. Half-priced beer was sold for an hour prior to game time; whenever the designated visitor's batter struck-out during the game, no matter how many times that occurred; every time the Canaries turned a double play; and during special game-night promotions. Also, one-dollar beer was sold throughout the entire game on Thursday nights. When a salesperson came to me and said she wanted to sell a promotion where fans in an entire section of the stadium would receive half-priced beer throughout every game, I decided to address this issue as well.

I asked the previous year's concession manager, Julie Malmberg, if anyone paid regular price for beer. Her answer was, "Not many." It made no sense to me. I determined that cutting back on the half-price beer had to be done. We canceled the double-play promotion and reduced the strikeout batter promotion so that only their first strikeout of the game triggered the half-priced beer.

You would have thought I had declared beer and baseball to be a bad combination. That was far from the truth. Few people enjoy a beer and a baseball game more than I do. I was simply attempting to run the Canaries in a prudent business-like manner. There was an outright revolt from a number of Canaries' faithful. I talked with a few upset fans and decided to reinstate the half-priced beer after every strikeout by the designated visitor's batter. That small change helped appease the situation somewhat – mostly because a dialogue had been initiated.

The backlash was part of the initial price to be paid for making changes to deal with excessive discounting. It is the primary reason why I do not believe in discounting in the first place. It's easy to start but very hard to stop. People who are used to getting free tickets are not inclined to pay for them later, even if the cost is only five dollars. Unless free or discounted tickets are supporting charities or some other promotional venture, they create far larger problems than they solve. I found as that season progressed, however, that fans started arriving more and paying for their seats. It takes time for new ideas to be accepted.

An event that changed my experience in Sioux Falls was my attendance at a "meeting" of the "A-Pole Gang". It was a group of fans that seemed to be constantly growing in numbers, who attended a lot of games, and who congregated before and after every game under the sign that designated Section A in the parking lot. I learned a lot about the Sioux Falls' fans by attending a couple of their sessions. They also learned more about me. If I could start over in Sioux Falls, I would attend one of their sessions as soon as I arrived. The A-Pole Gang even started its own website, where members could communicate with each other and keep abreast of team developments.

The staff members who worked for the Canaries were good people. They desperately wanted the franchise to succeed. I really enjoyed their company and, in fact, they were particularly important to me because I was living in Sioux Falls by myself and had not yet developed friendships outside of work. In fact, I worked so much there was very little life outside of work.

A fun consequence of working in the United States was recognizing the differences in language between American and Canadian English. Everyone knows the most noticeable difference is that Canadians say "eh" while Americans say "huh", but I discovered many more. Americans say "bathroom" even if there is no bath or shower in the room – Canadians say "washroom" – both say "restroom". Americans ask for "the check" – Canadians ask for "the bill". Canadians, when writing, have kept the "u" in many words, like neighbour, flavour, odour, humour, and cheque, while Americans have dropped it.

Perhaps the difference that made people in the United States laugh at me the most was my comment, "I'll phone you later." Canadians, at least where I came from, use the word "phone" both as a verb and a noun. Americans only used it as a noun.

But the most fun I had was playing trivia with my American friends. A sure-fire question if you wanted to win a trivia contest with a South Dakota resident was to ask what a "chesterfield" was. I never found a person who knew. Most Canadians would know it is another word for a couch or sofa.

Cultural differences are interesting and still a constant source of entertainment when I am in the United States. Of course, not all Canadians talk the same as I do, nor do all Americans talk the same as South Dakotans. Regional differences significantly affect language. We had a lot of fun in the office with our differences.

The City of Sioux Falls is really wonderful. There is a lot of new construction, the city is very clean, easy to get around, and there are more restaurants per capita than anywhere else in the world – or at least it seemed that way to me. The people are rock solid Midwest folks.

An interesting collection of people made up the Sioux Falls Canaries' family. Principal owner Ben Zuraw, the man who hired me, was a soft spoken giant of a man. Standing six feet, seven inches, Zuraw was an avid baseball fan and he loved the idea of owning a professional baseball club. He did not love the idea, however, of losing money on his investment or of his team losing on the field. During a game, it was almost impossible to talk to him about any significant issue because he was so wrapped up in the action on the field. He became agitated when the Canaries did not play well. Every now and then during a particularly poor effort on the field, you could see Zuraw sitting out behind the outfield fence all by himself, languishing over the woes of the club, and there were significant woes in 2004!

One of my funniest recollections of Zuraw occurred in his house. He owned a beautiful home overlooking a golf course. When I arrived in Sioux Falls, he offered it to me until it was sold or until I found my own accommodation. While I was away on a short vacation, the house did sell and his wife, Ann, came to Sioux Falls and removed virtually everything except a couple of beds and sent it all back to their home in North Carolina.

I returned to a huge empty house where I stayed for another few weeks. During that time, Ben came to visit. Late one night, we were having a heart-to-heart talk, passionately discussing the state of the Canaries. He was pacing back and forth through this huge empty living room, which could have passed for a gymnasium. He was quite a sight as he waved his arms in all directions and emphasized his points as he strode from one end of the room to the other. I often got a kick out of dealing with Ben Zuraw.

Another owner who had lived in Sioux Falls for a few years and was president of the Canaries was Jeff Loebl. Loebl had moved to California prior to my arrival and I did not expect to have much contact with him. I soon realized, however, that he was still active. Many of the things I was changing were things he had either instituted or approved. Unknown to me, as I critiqued the operation, I was perceived by Loebl as critiquing him.

I had been hired to turn the fortunes of the Canaries around. That required some changes. If people who instituted things I was changing were offended, there wasn't much I could do about it. The conflict between Loebl and me was a huge drain on my enjoyment of the job. He kept asking me for reports, which included revenue and expense projections, which were difficult for me to complete since I had not been in Sioux Falls for a complete fiscal year. I recognized an owner's need for that information but with the operation on life support, I felt I needed to concentrate my efforts on maximizing sales while minimizing expenses, rather than completing more reports.

Another character who was unique to the Sioux Falls' scene was minority owner Terry Prendergast. He was a local lawyer who, along with his law partner, Vance Goldammer, was very visible in the community and at the park. Prendergast looked somewhat like a mad scientist. His hair was frequently disheveled, he had large glasses, and he moved and talked quickly. He was a very smart man and oh so passionate about the Canaries. He was active with the club in surfing websites looking for player information or statistics. He would maintain charts on our salary cap records and work actively with manager Doc Edwards to help provide him with information about available players. Many times I wondered when Prendergast ever found time to get his legal work done.

He sat in the same seat behind home plate every game, keeping score and listening to the radio. If the radio broadcaster made a mistake in scoring or in any other fact, Prendergast would wave his arms trying to signal that a mistake had been made. In 2004, that drove radio broadcaster Justin Kutcher crazy because it distracted him from the action on the field, so I had to ask Prendergast to hold some of his concerns until the end of the game. Terry Prendergast was a kind and decent man and one of the interesting cast of characters who made up the Sioux Falls Canaries' family.

Another cast member was Larry McKenney, for whom the Canaries had created the most unique job description I had ever heard of for any employee. McKenney, who had worked for the Canaries since the inaugural season in 1993, was the assistant general manager and the groundskeeper. How's that for diversity! He was one of the most beloved people I have ever met. Everyone in Sioux Falls knew him and thought he was wonderful. He is a smart guy and opens a lot of doors in the community for the baseball club.

McKenney had been a farmer for much of his life so he would humour the organization during the winter months by wearing a tie and going on sales calls, but he was happier when April rolled around and he could put on his overalls and take care of the field and the stadium. He planted over 4,000 flowers each season throughout the stadium. The ball park was his pride and joy. He touched a lot of lives in the community and was an anchor in the Canaries' operation. A year after I left Sioux Falls, he was the only employee still remaining in the organization from the time I was there. That continual change-over in staff was not beneficial to the club.

One of my interesting experiences in Sioux Falls was in hiring staff. Justin Kutcher had some baseball broadcasting experience and he had helped provide background information to Joe Buck and Tim McCarver during many television broadcasts, including the World Series. One night, I was listening to CDs that had been sent to me for the vacant radio position in Sioux Falls. I listened to disc after disc to find an on-air voice that appealed to me.

Suddenly, one CD nearly knocked me off of my chair. The voice was magical and familiar to me. It was Joe Buck! Buck is one of the best in the sport's broadcasting business and he had agreed to introduce Kutcher on the CD. What a great way to make your CD stand out from the rest. I also liked Kutcher's voice and after checking out some references, I convinced him to come to Sioux Falls.

While many staff members were sensitive about hearing what they were doing wrong, Kutcher welcomed any constructive criticism. One night he asked me how I enjoyed his previous night's broadcast so I told him. I suggested he was not animated enough (Maybe Edmonds had spoiled me) and that he kept repeating himself in one of the stories he had told. I didn't want to say any more because I thought he was doing fine and I didn't want to discourage him.

He asked me if there was anything else and when I said that was enough for one day, he replied, "I value your opinion and I'm not going to get better unless you give me all of your suggestions. Don't worry about my feelings. This is how I learn and improve." What a refreshing attitude! Maybe it's a common characteristic of radio broadcasters because Paul Edmonds was the same way.

The other staff members in Sioux Falls in 2004 were young and each of them had only one year of experience, except for the three new people I hired, who had no experience. There was some talent, however. Julie Malmberg, for example, left the Canaries after the 2004 season and was accepted into the prestigious MBA program at the University of Oregon. Part of the focus of her studies was in Sports Business from the Warsaw Sports Marketing Center, along with only 10 other students. She recently received her Master's degree from this program and no doubt, she will make her mark in the world.

But even though they had limited experience, the staff had learned some bad habits. New ideas were treated with doubt and anxiety. A stock answer to a new idea was, "This has been tried before and it didn't work." I was surprised that these relative newcomers to sports marketing had such negative feelings towards new ideas. I had to tell them the "fleas in the jar" anecdote on occasion. It took a long time for the staff to loosen up and have fun with our promotions. One day, I tried to encourage them to be open-minded by announcing that the next person to trash a new idea without giving it fair consideration could look for alternate employment. This was my attempt at jolting them into a new outlook.

When I was hired, the Sioux Falls' owners hoped I would be able to turn the fortunes of their team around. I felt the organization had been mediocre for a long time, and I was only interested in being exceptional. I tried to change the experience at the games so fans would enjoy themselves more and come back. We changed the name of game-day staff from ushers to fan services representatives and had them toss product into the crowd during the games and interact with the fans. We created some new promotions and tried to create a new energy in the park. It took a while, but it started to percolate as the season progressed.

Unfortunately, in 2004 we were fighting the weather, which is the one thing a club has no control over. Precipitation affected well over 50 percent of Sioux Falls' home games. Simply put, it was brutal. Some in the Midwest called it the "summer that wasn't." Cool temperatures and high precipitation set records throughout South Dakota. We had one game postponed by tornado warnings. I was not crazy about Sunday games starting at 5 p.m. because I was a big believer in Sunday afternoon games. I was told, however, that in Sioux Falls, the weather was so hot in the summer that no one would attend an afternoon game. That was definitely not the case in 2004. If anything, afternoon games would have been a blessing because it was usually getting too cool for our fans by the end of the evening games.

The schedule was also terrible. The Canaries went six weeks during the prime part of the season in June and July without a weekend game. That was a disaster for a team that didn't sell a lot of advanced tickets and relied on good sales on weekends. When a Saturday night game was finally played at home in late July, the Canaries drew over 4,000 fans when the average attendance was below 2,500. Many people left because they could not buy a seat and were not prepared to accept standing room or grass berm tickets.

The people of Sioux Falls were looking for a winner because during the pre-season, the team looked dominant. We won most of our exhibition games in 2004. In a game we played in Yankton, South Dakota, against the Sioux City Explorers, Juan Thomas, "The Large Human", one of our veteran hitters, hit a ball so far over the centre-field fence I think it landed in the Missouri River. There was a great deal of excitement surrounding the team heading into the season.

However, just as it was getting started, two players were sold to Major League organizations. One veteran, Ron Wright, arrived in town injured and never did fully recover, and Juan Thomas left for Mexico before the season even started. A good-looking team was decimated. The Canaries in 2004 never recovered and ended-up last in the standings in both halves.

Bad weather, an unfair schedule and a poor team record – all were challenges to attendance numbers. The job of the organization was to keep going and to sell as many tickets as possible, no matter what the adversity but, looking back, those factors had a big impact. Hence, I didn't achieve all the success I was looking for in Sioux Falls. The job was obviously more than a one-year restoration project.

I offered to work half-time for 2005 but the organization decided a new incoming general manager needed to have complete autonomy. Disappointed, I returned home at the end of the 2004 season. I had mixed emotions to be sure. The job in Sioux Falls was not done by any means. A few good things had happened but so much work was left undone. It's not my nature to leave unfinished work. I decided, though, that I needed to be home more. I found living away from my family and friends to be more difficult than I had anticipated. My parents were not getting any younger and Bev was not yet comfortable leaving Winnipeg.

I was surprised that the incoming general manager was not interested in discussing the status of the operation with me upon his arrival. He was intent on doing things his own way from scratch. I understand the concept of wanting to start fresh, but I felt that he carried this to the extreme. He held a meeting with the staff 10 days before the 2004 season was over while I was still the general manager. I considered that disrespectful and it hastened my departure from Sioux Falls after the season had concluded.

As I left Sioux Falls, however, I felt positive about the overall experience. I met some wonderful people and helped the franchise as much as I could in one year. I'm glad I went and I left feeling convinced that the Canaries' organization could be successful.

As this book was in its final stages, block buster news was reported. Four teams, including the Sioux Falls Canaries, were leaving the Northern League to form a new league. I doubted that it would affect the people of Sioux Falls very much because they would decide to go to the ball park based on the quality and value of the entertainment, the weather, and the opportunity to watch good baseball.

Chapter 20: Houston (Fort Worth) — We Have a Problem

On September 29th, 2005, a major bomb exploded in the Northern League (NL). The St. Paul Saints, the Sioux Falls Canaries, and the Lincoln Saltdogs all announced they were terminating membership in the league. The announcement came as a shock to almost everyone. The revelation was so dramatic I was moved to write a new chapter for this book.

I believed I was in a unique position to comment on the split, having worked in the league both in Canada and the United States. In Sioux Falls, the club was closely aligned with the Goldklang Group, which owned the St. Paul Saints and I knew the people involved in the decision.

First, let me say that as the story evolved, I was fascinated by the attempts of the parties to put a positive face on the situation. I understand it's the job of a good manager to disseminate information in favour of his or her investment, especially during a crisis. And I think it's also human nature for most people to want to believe that everything is okay.

There are limits, however. My Mother told me that during World War II, when she was stationed in England with the Red Cross in 1944, the British government initially told its citizens that the V2 bombs Germany was sending over into England were actually exploding gas mains and not bombs at all. Eventually, the government had to give up the charade because the British people had nicknamed the bombs the "flying gas mains."

Maybe, I'm just a skeptic, and I question things more than most people. I need to see documentation and logic before I am apt to accept someone's conclusion. In the case of the Northern League split, fans in any one city usually heard only what their team had to report. I looked at the issue from both sides. In particular, though, I tried to determine why the four teams had left.

Following is a brief synopsis of information disseminated by the teams affected by the league split starting with the teams who left.

In the words of Saints' President Mike Veeck on the St. Paul website: "We have enjoyed a wonderful ride in the Northern League, but as time goes on, you realize that you crave the energy and excitement of building something new and fresh. We look forward to that opportunity and that challenge."

An excerpt from a letter written to Saints' fans by St. Paul general manager Derek Sharrer states: "It is difficult to express in words just how excited we are about this venture. Please understand that while this new league will be impressive in 2006, it is 2007 and beyond that we are truly excited about. This vision is one that extends well into the foreseeable future and one that we think will eventually reshape and strengthen independent baseball as a whole."

From the headquarters of another of the departing teams, the Lincoln Saltdogs, came this: "This is a wonderful opportunity for the Lincoln Saltdogs to be involved with the creation of a new independent league. The Saltdogs will have fun being part of the new league's development," said Lincoln president Charlie Meyer.

According to Canaries' majority owner Ben Zuraw, "As the original Northern League franchise we have enjoyed our long-time association with the league's members. However, we feel that our new league will provide the right atmosphere for the Canaries to continue to thrive in the world of professional baseball."

Sioux Falls president John Kuhn was a little more specific. "As happens in relationships, both personal and business, sometimes goals and visions change, and a change has to be made. Our decision resulted from the realization that the vision of the Sioux Falls Canaries was shared by a minority of the league members, rather than a majority. The response to the news has been overwhelmingly positive."

At the same time, the NL also tried to make the split look like a positive move – a tougher challenge for the league and Commissioner Mike Stone since he was in the position of having to explain why teams would leave the most "preeminent independent baseball league", which the Northern League was apt to call itself. A review of the websites of the remaining eight clubs revealed that they either did not mention the split or they simply placed on their websites the press releases issued by the league. Following is an excerpt from one of those releases, which was titled, "A Message to Fans of the Northern League". It was posted on September 30th, 2005, and quoted Stone.

"The owners of Northern League clubs are genuine in extending the departing members best wishes as they pursue their next endeavors. At the same time, the Northern League will continue its tradition of providing fans with the highest quality independent professional baseball as a family-oriented, fun, and affordable experience. The member clubs of the Northern League are united in their optimism regarding the league's future and they look forward to the continued growth and prosperity of the league. We have already begun the process of dealing with the issues that have resulted from the departure of these teams. I am confident that the Northern League will emerge as a stronger and more cohesive league as we move forward."

Did anyone actually extend best wishes to the departing owners? I doubt it. A few may have said "good riddance" but it is unlikely that anyone said "good luck." While tensions at league meetings might have been reduced by the split, it is hard to fathom how anyone could really perceive this as a positive move for the Northern League.

The league's most famous franchise (St. Paul), two of the original founding members (Sioux Falls and St. Paul), and one of the most successful newer franchises (Lincoln) were leaving the league. St. Paul is a major American city and Veeck and Goldklang are notable and connected people in the baseball world. The St. Paul Saints brought more high profile names to the Northern League than any other team. Leon "Bull" Durham, Jack Morris, Darryl Strawberry, J.D. Drew, and Matt Nokes have all worn a Saints' uniform. The Saints have had a television documentary, a couple of books, and numerous national stories told about their exploits. Actor Bill Murray was also part owner of the Saints. He attended games in St. Paul and sometimes in other Northern League cities. All of this brought exposure to the Northern League, particularly during the first few years. Whenever I was at a baseball seminar or meetings in the United States and I would tell someone we played in the Northern League, their response would inevitably be – "Is that the league that the St. Paul Saints play in?"

There was also uncertainty about the future. Would other teams follow suit? Within a couple of days, the Sioux City

Explorers also announced they were leaving the league. Their decision made sense because it was important for them to remain in the same league as Sioux Falls and Lincoln due to the close proximity to those two cities. That left the Northern League with eight remaining franchises – three Canadian teams, three teams in the Chicago area, Fargo-Moorhead, and Kansas City.

It seemed apparent that the departing teams were not being offered best wishes. Less than a week after the league press release expounding such niceties, the Northern League claimed that it had an obligation to fulfill the leases to the stadiums in Sioux Falls and Sioux City. If the Northern League placed its own team in Sioux Falls, it would have completely undermined the Canaries' franchise. Mike Stone's position was that he was simply protecting the NL to ensure that it would not be held accountable to make payments on the leases.

That was an unnecessary worry. The lease he was referring to in Sioux City had expired and the lease in Sioux Falls had been changed. The City of Sioux Falls who had the ultimate authority to determine who played in the Sioux Falls stadium announced that its agreement was with the current owners of the Canaries and it would not allow the Northern League to use the stadium or hold it responsible for any payments. This did not surprise me because I knew the current owners had spent hundreds of thousands of dollars of their own money during the ball park renovations in 2000 and had been diligently making the lease payments ever since. It did not make sense to me that the City of Sioux Falls would abandon that relationship.

The league quickly changed focus and, in an attempt to show a positive front, issued the following statement: "On October 17th, 2005, the Northern League of Professional Baseball announced that the 2006 structure of the league will consist of eight teams in two divisions. It was also announced that the owners of the league's eight teams have unanimously agreed to a historic solidarity designed to strengthen the present and future of the league. In a forceful show of confidence in the league and in each other, the owners of the eight clubs have voted to subject any team desiring to defect from the Northern League to substantial monetary penalties. This will apply to any of the existing eight teams and any expansion teams that may enter the Northern League in the future."

The Northern League was moving on and dealing with the 2006 season. It needed people to start thinking about the future rather than the past.

But, who were the departing teams going to play against? I assumed they must have already had a new league in place but that was not the case. The departing owners were operating with a lot of faith that something would work out. When they announced they were leaving, no firm plans had been established. Only three teams had left initially so they knew they didn't have enough to form a league on their own. All sorts of different scenarios went through their minds: an interlocking schedule with teams from the Northern League; finding new cities to join them and form a new league; and playing games throughout the country against many independent teams, including those in the Central League.

Any hope of playing against Northern League teams vanished when, shortly after the split, the league voted to ban inter-league play, including exhibition games, against any of the departing teams. Some bitter feelings remained among Northern League owners.

At the same time this was happening, a new league in the southern United States, the United League, was exerting enormous pressure on the Central League. Some of the Central League teams had already decided to join this new league when the club in Jackson, Mississippi, announced it was going to cease operating because the Mississippi Braves, an AA affiliate of the Atlanta Braves, had begun operations in 2005 in the nearby city of Pearl. The United League was then able to secure the lease to the stadium in Edinburg, Texas, and convince the owner in St. Angelo, Texas, to join them.

All of these events left the Central League with only five remaining teams looking for a solution to their own problems. The four departing Northern League teams were the answer. An announcement was made outlining the formation of a new league, the American Association of Independent Baseball League. The name "American Association" held a lot of tradition, especially since the original Saint Paul Saints had played in the old American

Association. The new league was going to consist of a south division with the remaining teams from the Central League, and a north division with the former Northern League teams and the addition of St. Joes, Missouri.

But the big question on everyone's mind was "Why?" The most successful independent baseball league in North America was being split apart at the seams. How could anyone think this was a good idea? What factors had led to this decision?

I was aware that tension had mounted at league meetings. I suspected the announcement that the three teams were terminating membership in the league was really the result of the frustration the departing owners felt towards the direction the league was taking. I was not sure if this answered the question as to why the teams had left. At the very least, I was not satisfied that I had the full story.

Marv Goldklang and Mike Veeck entered the world of independent baseball in 1993 at the urging of their friend, Miles Wolff. In the beginning, I am told, there was a great deal of camaraderie between owners. Everyone looked at the big picture and how decisions would affect the league as a whole. League meetings were filled with excitement and wonder. I know for sure that the general managers' meetings could accurately be described in that fashion. Now Wolff was gone and a rift between owners had developed.

That must have become a drain on the fun and excitement that some felt in owning a Northern League baseball club. In virtually every interview after the split, Mike Veeck commented that he wanted to go back to having fun at the ball park. I believe those statements came from his heart. "Fun is Good" is the name of his book, published in 2004, and "fun is good" is an accurate assessment of the way Veeck likes to live his life. He was no longer having fun in the Northern League. I would hear almost the identical words from Lincoln owner Jim Abel.

The beginning of the current crisis, in my opinion, occurred in October, 2001, when Miles Wolff walked into the owners' meeting and announced he was tendering his resignation as Commissioner. The owners then proceeded to hire Mike Stone, former president of the Texas Rangers, who lived in Fort Worth, Texas. The ties to the past were severed further when the owners also decided to move the league offices, including baseball administration, to Fort Worth after the 2002 season. It was not a unanimous vote.

Bruce Thom, the owner of the Fargo-Moorhead Red Hawks, was philosophical when he discussed the rift between owners. "St. Paul acted like they had more knowledge and experience than the rest of us," he said. "That created some resentment among the other owners."

Marv Goldklang is a successful attorney. His company, the Goldklang Group, owns several minor league baseball clubs, including the St. Paul Saints, and he is a minority owner of the mighty New York Yankees. He has a good reputation in the baseball community. Goldklang told me he was discouraged with some of the attitudes within the Northern League. He found league meetings had become tense. Every issue seemed contentious and accusations of wrong-doing were plentiful. He looked around the table at his last meeting in September of 2005 and realized how far things had slid off the track from the days when the league was getting started. He cited some examples.

The owners in Kansas City and Schaumburg tried to run the infamous X-Box promotion during a scheduled Northern League game in 2005. The plan was to have two fans face-off at home plate and play a computer baseball game, the result of which would count for the score for the first two innings of the actual league game.

What if the score after the second inning was 10-0? What if this game affected the playoff chances of one of the teams involved? Goldklang felt the promotion was not professional and put the league in a bad light. He received numerous calls from people in the baseball community who all condemned the idea. Mike Stone told me he initially authorized the promotion as an exhibition but would never have sanctioned it to count as part of the real game.

At the September league meeting in Chicago in 2005, Goldklang was disappointed that the owners spent no time discussing how they could help the struggling franchises in Edmonton, Calgary, or Sioux City. Instead, they spent time discussing an idea to move all league playoff games to Las Vegas. "Bizarre" doesn't even begin to describe what he thought of that idea.

Then, there was the issue of the investigation that was conducted into alleged salary cap violations against the

Saints. The system of launching these investigations in the Northern League required an owner to file a complaint accompanied by a $5,000-cheque. The money was returned if the allegations were substantiated.

The league hired a private investigator to probe into the charges against the Saints and Goldklang was convinced that the Commissioner's office had not been forthright with him regarding the investigation. Goldklang informed me that the private investigation company filed its report in October of 2004 concluding that there was no salary cap violation in St. Paul. When Goldklang asked what the status of the investigation was in March of 2005, he was informed that the investigator's report had been received but had not yet been evaluated. When it was uncovered that the report had indeed been filed in October, Goldklang was upset that the league had not accepted the conclusions in the report but had continued to investigate.

According to Stone, the reason for the delay was that new information had been presented to the league that required further investigation.

Reports leaked from several sources that the St. Paul Saints were going to be found guilty of salary cap violations. St. Paul was furious. The Saints contacted Commissioner Stone and asked him to dispel the rumors and end the investigation. Stone's response was to send an email to all Northern League teams informing them that matters such as the alleged salary cap violation and resulting investigation were confidential. No team was to publicly discuss the issue, and would be subject to penalties if it did.

Finally, a letter from Stone to Goldklang in May of 2005 confirmed that the investigation had been completed. The Saints were never charged with a salary cap violation. Other Northern League owners told me they still had suspicions and did not understand the Commissioner's decision not to act. It never appeared to me that Stone was hesitant to act in such matters and he told me that in his opinion there was simply not enough substantiated information to warrant a violation.

Once the investigation was concluded, the Saints were somewhat rebellious. Bryan Gaal was one of the Saints' players interviewed about the allegations. During an exhibition game against Winnipeg in the spring of 2005, St.

Paul made a PA announcement making fun of the investigation. The announcement went something like this: "Will Bryan Gaal please report to the fan services booth to collect his appearance fee!" Winnipeg complained and the league fined the Saints $2,500 for violating the directive not to talk about the investigation. The irony of the situation was that it was the Saints who asked for the league office to take action in the first place to quell the rumors and protect their reputation. Goldklang was not impressed. He felt that the league was determined to take its pound of flesh from St. Paul.

Commissioner Stone did not see it that way. "St. Paul violated my directive to not talk about the investigation," he said. "I could not understand how they thought the PA announcement was appropriate when they were so concerned that other teams were challenging their reputation."

All of this, no matter how annoying, was not the most important reason why St. Paul decided to leave the league. Goldklang was concerned that some teams were unduly influencing Commissioner Stone. This was the same concern that some Northern League owners voiced regarding Goldklang and Veeck when Miles Wolff was the Commissioner. It was this level of distrust that seemed to be at the root of the problems between Northern League owners.

Goldklang had wanted to discuss his concerns at a league meeting in July during the 2005 all-star game in Gary but his request had been refused by the league executive committee.

He then arrived at the meeting in Chicago in September eager to have an open discussion. "We had a limited opportunity in Chicago to discuss our concerns in connection with a performance review of Stone, but received little support from most of the other owners," said Goldklang. "The issue on the table at the time was whether to continue with Stone as the Commissioner through the 2006 season, which we opposed, but which was agreed to by a majority of the owners." It should be noted that the league eventually hired a new commissioner in February of 2006.

Goldklang was told in Chicago that a special meeting of the league executive could be arranged with him in two weeks but when he asked what would be on the agenda, he was told it would be a "tough love session" directed at the St. Paul owners. That was the final straw. He left the Chicago meetings and contacted his partner, Mike Veeck. He informed Veeck that he could no longer deal with the current Northern League owners. He felt that the spirit of partnership was missing and it was time for St. Paul to look at other options.

I asked Mike Veeck to explain why he supported the decision to leave the Northern League. He was very candid with his response and gave me a lengthy list of reasons.

Veeck was a big supporter of independent baseball. He felt that the Northern League owners had become far too insular. They were not interested in forming relationships with other independent leagues. Only with a closer affiliation with other independent leagues, did Veeck feel there might be a chance to build a stronger relationship with organized baseball. He was also looking for a larger marketing presence, which affiliation with other independent leagues could bring.

He, too, was upset by some of the ideas coming out of league meetings. The X-Box promotion and the neutral site for playoff games were two examples. He believed the league needed a renewed attention to leadership – one that Miles Wolff could bring to the table. Starting a new league with new partners sounded like a lot of fun to him. "The new league will be fun for the fans and for the owners," he said.

Veeck considered himself and Goldklang "founding fathers" so to speak, but he felt that their input was no longer valued in the Northern League. To him, it was a question of respect. Veeck and Goldklang continually found themselves in the minority over issues at league meetings. This was the same league they had helped create and to which they had brought a great deal of attention and prestige.

Possibly, Veeck's most telling issue came during the 2005 season. He was asked by Commissioner Stone and the owner of the Cracker Cats to help the Edmonton franchise. Veeck flew to Edmonton with Saints' general manager Derek Sharrer to talk with the Edmonton staff. He spent two days there working with them before returning to his home in

South Carolina. "No one called to say thanks for the help," Veeck told me, "I was very disappointed."

He said he also believed certain teams in the Northern League continually violated the salary cap and were not being held accountable. Instead, his St. Paul Saints had been the subject of a long investigation that he felt was vindictive. Veeck didn't believe partners were supposed to act that way. He yearned for an environment where trust was a key ingredient in the relationships. For all of these reasons, he seemed convinced they were doing the right thing.

The story was similar when I discussed the league break-up with Saltdogs' owner Jim Abel. He told me he still liked some of the owners in the Northern League but he felt very much in the minority at league meetings. "Our opinion did not seem to matter," he said. "Baseball should be fun for everyone, including the owners. Northern League meetings were not fun!"

These two reasons seemed to be at the heart of his decision but there were other factors as well. For example, despite the fact their new league included a team in Florida, one in Louisiana, and three in Texas, Lincoln's travel was reduced by 2,000 miles for the 2006 season. Abel was also a big Miles Wolff fan. He felt the league had destabilized after Wolff left. It was Miles who fired him up in the first place to get involved in owning a baseball team and it appealed to him to get involved in a league where Wolff would again play a role.

He enjoyed his initial meetings in the new league and he felt there was give and take from all sides and a consensus seemed much easier to reach. Abel felt that Lincoln could be very happy with its new partners.

Mike Stone's stint as Commissioner of the Northern League came to an end prior to the 2006 season. There was much he had to deal with during his tenure. I asked him if he missed the Northern League. "I miss the baseball end and the successes we realized," he reflected. "I don't miss the conflict that was so prevalent near the end."

Commissioner Stone suggested that the four teams may have split because discussions had taken place to institute the buy-out clause if any team were to leave the league. Goldklang disagreed with this analysis because he believed unanimous consent would have been required to implement such a clause in the shareholder's agreement. After the four teams left, the remaining owners unanimously agreed to institute the buy-out clause.

It is apparent that Northern League owner's meetings had become somewhat of an ordeal. There was no shortage of egos in the room. I believe these egos clashed once too often.

When I got right down to the core issue, it became simple to me why the teams had left. Veeck and Goldklang from St. Paul, Zuraw from Sioux Falls, and Abel from Lincoln, decided the Northern League environment wasn't right for their businesses. It would have been much easier for them to stay but their discomfort with the situation outweighed the benefits. I understood their decisions but as an ambassador of the Northern League for 10 years, the news still saddened me.

As this book went to print, the story was still unfolding. Marv Goldklang told me, "The first-year meetings of our new league were filled with such positive energy it was a real treat to participate. That is the way it is supposed to be," Goldklang declared. Goldklang, Veeck, Zuraw and Abel all told me during the 2006 season that they believed they had made the right decision.

I asked Bruce Thom what Northern League meetings were like after the split. He said," The eight remaining teams acted like equals. Everyone's opinion was validated and no one ownership group was trying to impose its will on the group." Everyone seemed to be happy.

In the Northern League camp, there was some relief among the remaining owners when the split was announced. The expansion trend to larger centres had placed Sioux City and Sioux Falls among the small markets. These two teams were now gone. St. Paul was certainly not a small market but the tension between St. Paul and some of the other franchises was now eliminated. The remaining NL owners maintained a positive front. There were still eight franchises and the future could still be positive. After all, the resurrected league had started in 1993 with only six teams, although those teams had been much closer together geographically.

I did question the decision to create the opt-out penalty. I understood the desire to show solidarity but new cities that wished to enter a professional baseball league in the central part of the continent now had two choices. Would a new interested owner be influenced negatively by this opt-out payment requirement? "That is a two-edged sword," said Bruce Thom. "New owners may indeed feel a sense of security and commitment because of this requirement in the Northern League." Time will tell if he is correct.

Another danger, as both leagues move forward, is the competition on the field. There are only so many good players to go around. Northern League managers have recently complained that finding players is getting harder and harder. It is likely that the formation of the American Association of Independent Professional Baseball League and other independent leagues will make everyone's job just a little more difficult to recruit quality players.

The transition period is important for all concerned. Doug Simunic echoed those sentiments: "2006 is a critical year for the Northern League. We need all remaining teams to show that they can be successful financially, especially Calgary and Edmonton. The Northern League can ill afford to lose any more teams," he concluded.

While this may well be true, the American Association also had some teams in 2006 that struggled with attendance. Northern League teams, as a whole, drew significantly higher attendance numbers in 2006 on average than did the American Association. Both leagues appeared, though, to have work to do.

While this chapter of the Northern League may be over, the story is most certainly not finished. The success of both leagues now rests in the hands of the owners and league executives. Can the current teams all be successful? Can the owners work together in unison, making decisions that benefit the entire league? As new cities from the region show an interest in the ranks of professional baseball, which league will they be inclined to join? These unanswered questions will keep this story alive for years to come.

Epilogue: Lost in the Black Hills

When I think of the number of hours that were spent writing this book, the story I am about to tell still sends shivers down my spine. It begins in Rapid City, South Dakota. My wife, Bev, and I were taking a summer vacation during July of 2005. I wanted to go to Sioux Falls and watch the Canaries play. I felt there was much unfinished business there and I was unsure how I would feel when I attended a ball game.

Prior to arriving in Sioux Falls, we decided to go to one of our favourite vacation spots, the Black Hills of South Dakota. We toured the area for a couple of days and decided to fill the tank with gas in Rapid City before heading in the direction of Sioux Falls.

I went inside to the store while Bev filled the gas tank. Upon returning, I opened the trunk and grabbed a drink from the cooler. I remember closing the trunk lid but I know now that the latch did not catch. As we pulled out of the Exxon station and up to the traffic light, a car behind us honked its horn. I noticed the trunk had come open so I jumped out of the car and closed it. As I got back in, Bev said the laptop had been right at the top of things in the trunk. I glanced in the rear view mirror just as the light turned green and thought I saw something black lying on the road about 100 feet back.

I took off on the green light and made an illegal U-turn and returned to the area where I thought I saw the computer. Nothing was on the road – absolutely nothing! We glared at the pavement in disbelief. I pulled the car back into the Exxon lot and started walking about looking for a sign of the computer bag. After searching the trunk three separate times, we determined that the computer had fallen out when the trunk popped open. I felt sick to my stomach. Months and months of work were in that bag. I had backed up my book on a flash drive but had foolishly also left it in the computer bag.

Two days earlier, the air-conditioner in the car had completely failed. Now, with this sudden turn of events and the temperature outside soaring to 90°F (28°C), our composure level was next to nil. I was in a state of shock thinking that all of my work might have been lost.

During the next few hours, we completed a police report, put a lost-and-found ad in the Rapid City Journal, and visited the businesses close to the intersection several times, hoping someone would return the computer. We decided to stay in Rapid City overnight at a hotel right at the infamous corner.

We were losing hope that the laptop would be found. I considered it stolen because it had disappeared in less than a minute. Bev, being an eternal optimist, still hoped some Good Samaritan would contact us through the ad in the paper. The next day we checked the businesses in the area one last time and then decided to move on.

We were trying to forget our dilemma as we traveled through the Badlands and stopped for a little picnic. Bev convinced me we should stay at a nice little resort in Chamberlain, South Dakota, on the Missouri River because the hot car was very uncomfortable. I agreed, realizing in the back of my mind that we would be closer to Rapid City if we did get a call that the computer had been found.

Most of our conversations throughout the day eventually reverted to the lost computer. Who would have taken it in those few seconds? Would someone respond to the newspaper ad? We talked about what we would have done if we had found something that valuable. My cell phone was kept charged and with us at all times.

We traveled on to Sioux Falls the next day to see a ball game and Sioux Falls first baseman Juan Thomas asked me to golf with him the next morning. I was glad to do so because I really liked Juan and thought it would make me feel a little better. Somehow, I could turn the story about the trip with no air conditioner and the lost computer into an amusing anecdote.

At nine o'clock the next morning, my cell phone rang. A man stated that he had my computer! He asked me to describe it and the location where I had lost it, which I did without thinking. The caller said he was in Chicago and had purchased the computer from a guy in Rapid City. He was a trucker and would not be returning to South Dakota for weeks.

I told him we had filed a police report and I talked with him at length to determine if it was actually my computer. He told me his name was James Carr. From the beginning, I was a little skeptical because his answers didn't seem quite right, but I was so desperate to get my computer back that I wanted to believe his story.

He told me he would be glad to send me the computer, but he wanted to recover the $400 he had paid for it. All I had to do was send him the money by Western Union and he would FedEx the computer to me immediately. When I asked if I could drive to Chicago and meet him, he said he was too busy moving around. My suspicions increased and I began to wonder if he was conning us with our own property!

When the lengthy conversation finally ended, I was visibly upset. The guy had given a return phone number beginning with 219, which was a Chicago area code. I called him back as he had requested but again the call lasted far too long. James Carr had an answer for everything. We didn't know what to think. I decided to call the police for advice. No one was available at the time of my call but I was told a detective would contact me shortly.

We were just debating whether to send the money when the cell phone rang again. The voice on the line said, "Is this John Hindle?" to which I replied in the affirmative. The person then said, "I found your computer."

"Oh really," I replied. I was very careful not to give this person any information but to have him describe the computer to me. It only took him a minute to convince me he was telling the truth. He lived in Hill City, South Dakota, not far from Rapid City. He gave me his name, address, phone number, and instructions on how to get to his place to pick up the computer. I was relieved and excited. The timing of the second man's call was incredible!

Within minutes, the police called and after hearing my story, the detective told me the man in Hill City was legitimate because he was able to verify the information he had given to me, but James Carr, on the other hand, was probably an alias who was running a scam. The officer told me he was likely calling every person who offered a reward in an ad in every American newspaper.

We packed a few things in our hot car and traveled the five-hour trip back to the Rapid City area. We drove with hot 96° F air blowing in the windows so we could hardly hear each other speak. During the trip, we received two more calls from area code 219 but we didn't answer the phone, as per police recommendations, even though Bev wanted to tell James Carr that the police had a bead on him.

We found the house in Hill City with little difficulty. A very nice man greeted us and we soon recovered the laptop in good condition. Apparently, he had pulled out of the hospital in Rapid City and saw a bag on the street so he opened the door of his car as he drove by and grabbed it. He never did stop, which is why we didn't witness it.

We made the long drive back to Sioux Falls in the blazing heat and through a severe thunder storm. James Carr called again a few days later, only this time his name had been changed to Bill Smith. I told him to stop bothering me. I had recovered my computer so obviously he was lying and did not have it. That was the last we heard from him.

Never again did I keep my back-up copy of the manuscript anywhere near the computer. In fact, I frequently made multiple copies just for my own piece of mind.